Modern European and Chinese Contract Law

Modern European and Chinese Contract Law

A Comparative Study of Party Autonomy

Junwei Fu

Wolters Kluwer
Law & Business

Published by:
Kluwer Law International
PO Box 316
2400 AH Alphen aan den Rijn
The Netherlands
Website: www.kluwerlaw.com

Sold and distributed in North, Central and South America by:
Aspen Publishers, Inc.
7201 McKinney Circle
Frederick, MD 21704
United States of America
Email: customer.service@aspenpublishers.com

Sold and distributed in all other countries by:
Turpin Distribution Services Ltd.
Stratton Business Park
Pegasus Drive, Biggleswade
Bedfordshire SG18 8TQ
United Kingdom
Email: kluwerlaw@turpin-distribution.com

Printed on acid-free paper.

ISBN 978-90-411-3459-2

Printed in Great Britain.

About the Author

Dr Junwei Fu is currently teaching at Beijing Institute of Technology School of Law.From 2002 until 2006, Junwei Fu obtained his Bachelor of Laws from China. In June 2007, he graduated from his Master in International Economic and Business Law at University of Groningen Law School, the Netherlands. Throughout his academic career, Junwei Fu received a number of scholarships and honours. From September 2007 to August 2010, he worked as a Ph.D. researcher in Tilburg University Law School. During the period from August 2008 until August 2009, Junwei Fu was a visiting scholar at Washington University School of Law in St. Louis, United States. Since August 2010, he has been promoted as an Assistant Professor in Tilburg University Law School. In addition, he has been working for the China desk of the law firm of VMW in Amsterdam.

Table of Contents

List of Abbreviations

Acquis Group	Research Group on the Existing EC Private Law
AIC	Administration of Industry and Commerce of China
CAOs	Collective Employment Contracts
CFR	Common Frame of Reference
CISG	1980 United Nations Convention on Contracts for the International Sale of Goods
CLC	The Contract Law of the People's Republic of China
DCFR	Draft Common Frame of Reference
ECJ	European Court of Justice
EU	European Union
GPCL	The General Principles of the Civil Law of the People's Republic of China
NPC	National People's Congress of China
PECL	Principles of European Contract Law
Resolution	Resolution of the Strengthening of the Work of Interpretation of Law (1981)
SCNPC	Standing Committee of the National People's Congress
SMEs	Small- and Medium-Sized Enterprises
SPC	Supreme People's Court of China
SPP	Supreme People's Procuratorate of China
Study Group	Study Group on a European Civil Code
Unidroit Principles	Unidroit Principle of International Commercial Contracts
WTO	World Trade Organization

Foreword

This book represents the first extensive comparative study of party autonomy in contract law in the European Union (EU) and China. It emphasizes fundamental contrasting notions and approaches to party autonomy, both on a theoretical level and in various concrete doctrines, such as interpretation, contract validity, adaptation of contract, termination, mandatory rules and the constitutionalization of contract law. The book is well timed: both in the EU and in China the society efforts to effect contract law reforms are currently underway.

It is to be expected that these reforms will not be put through in isolation from each other, since China is now the EU's second biggest, and the EU, China's biggest trading partner, and because of exposing Chinese contract law to global and European development, has been part of a process of accommodation that started in the 1980s. The study offers a meaningful and outspoken contribution to this process, for example, by pointing out that the influence is mutual rather than unidirectional and that certain Chinese doctrines, such as the adaptation of contracts in case of fraud and threat, are more sophisticated than their EU counterparts.

The book is also a foundation for future research and elaboration in the ongoing debate in the EU and China on improving contract law. At this point differences arise. Should these improvements aim at promoting welfare, remedying market failures, serving state interests, protecting the weaker party, establishing an area of freedom, security and justice in which persons, goods, capital and services move freely, or some sort of prioritized mix of these goals?

Junwei Fu, was educated in China at Hu'nan Agricultural University. He has published several articles on EU contract law and on the comparison with Chinese contract law in, for example, the Oxford University Comparative Law Forum, the Civil and Commercial Law Review (Beijing), the Journal of the Party School of the Central Committee of the Communist party of China (Beijing)and, most recently, in a book with Prof. Liang Huixing (eds.) published by Martinus Nijhoff, *Draft Civil Code of* People's Republic of China.

Jan B.M. Vranken
Professor of Methodology of Private Law
Tilburg Law School
Tilburg University, The Netherlands

Preface

The law of contracts in fact, is to make the individuals exercise their freedom without any damage to others. Freedom of contract can be regarded as one of the most fundamental principles in the law of contracts, which ultimately serves the private autonomy of individuals. However, the exercise of freedom cannot impair others' interests and the welfare of the state. So the law of contracts has to set out parameters of good faith and fair dealing, social justice, and human rights among others, which have a mandatory nature, as binding rules to ensure that freedom is well exercised. In brief, contract law consists of the rules that recognize freedom and set out some limitations to restrict it. The default rules provide the freedom, which guides the parties to conclude the contract while also filling in the gaps in the contract, whereas the mandatory rules restrict the individuals' freedom since the parties can only be bound by them without any other choice. It is reasonable to say that the law of contracts is constructed around the principle of the freedom of contract.

In ancient China, Confucianism had been the dominant thought ruling society since the *Han* dynasty to maintain the hierarchy of the state, and it continues to influence the Chinese methods of living and thinking today. The key value of Confucianism is self-cultivation, which can be seen as a remarkable limitation to party autonomy since it lays down a great deal of rules for people to behave obediently. Among those values, morality (*li*), which is to instil in the individual, an inner sense of awareness of the acts that are shameful, or propriety, has a significant impact on civil society. Civil issues were, then, considered minor matters, whose resolution was suggested through extra-legal mechanisms, such as mediation. The transplantation of modern civil law into China began in the early 1900s, and the first draft of the Chinese civil code, which is mainly based on the German and the Japanese civil codes, was completed in 1911. In the later decades, several draft civil codes had been completed. However, Chinese legal history mentions that a draft civil code was only implemented for a short time between 1928 and 1930, though it is still in force in Taiwan today. After the establishment of the People's Republic of China, until the 1980s, it is true to say that policy assumed the role of law in society. The primary development of modern Chinese civil law began from the 1980s when the open-door policy was implemented. It is thus true to conclude that in ancient China, the system and the concepts of modern civil law were absent, and the dominant thought was to restrict party autonomy and promote the hierarchy of the state.

In the 1980s, three contract laws namely, the Economic Contract Law, the Technology Contract Law, and the Foreign Economic Contract Law were implemented. However, after the 1990s with the advent of the market economy, The Contract Law of the People's Republic of China (CLC) was drafted to replace the three contract laws of the 1980s. But The General Principles of the Civil Law of the People's Republic of China (GPCL), which was adopted in 1986, is still being implemented and serves as the basic principle for Chinese civil law, and even the future civil code.

On the contrary, in Europe, Roman private law and its centuries-long scholarly interpretations have contributed to a solid foundation for the development of modern European private law. The principle of freedom of contract, in particular, a reflection of party autonomy, had become a fundamental rule since the 1800s. However, in recent years, especially since the 1980s, the Europeanization of private law has become a hotly discussed issue, and it would be correct to say that consumer protection since then has embarked upon this process of Europeanization. In the past several decades, the directives have played an important role in the converging of European private law, which consists of the primary part of *acquis communautaire*. However, the convergence was not satisfactory, and in academia, it is argued that the diversity of private law constituted obstacles to the development of a single-market economy, and the value of social justice needs to be promoted. A uniform civil code has since then been advocated.

However, the idea of a uniform civil code presents numerous problems for the EU society such as: (1) whether the EU has the power to adopt a civil code; (2) is it feasible to adopt a civil code for the EU; and (3) how to construct this civil code. As is widely known, the law of contracts constitutes the main part of the private law. The Lando Commission completed the drafting of the Principles of European Contract Law (PECL) in 2003 to enable development of a single-market economy. This Commission's work has been subsequently continued by the Study Group of von Bar. The Draft Common Frame of Reference (DCFR) is the result of the efforts of the Study Group together with the *Acquis* Group. As the PECL and the *acquis communautaire* have been integrated into the DCFR, which is a possible model for the political Common Frame of Reference (CFR) advocated by the European Commission, it is true to say (a part of) the DCFR can most probably be endowed with some legal effects by the official organs, or at least it can assist development of the future European private law as it has provided some concrete issues for discussion. Also, the purpose of the DCFR drafting committee, consisting of about 250 scholars and lawyers, is to find the common core of European private law.

So until now, the DCFR/PECL is one of the most appropriate places to look for the current and future European contract law, though its ability to represent the common rules of Europe is still being discussed.

In modern contract law, party autonomy as expressed in the idea of the freedom of contract is a fundamental principle in most countries, and people have struggled for centuries for it. Both the CLC and the DCFR/PECL follow this tendency. Under the DCFR/PECL, the parties are endowed with the freedom to enter into the contract, choose the other party, and determine the contents of the contracts. It does the function of serving the free market within the EU. However, the freedom is not arbitrary. It has to be restricted by good faith and fair dealing, social justice, and fundamental rights. But on the contrary, in China, the concept of the freedom of contract has not been clearly stated, and only the notion of contract voluntariness is used instead. To some extent, the reluctance to use the term 'freedom of contract' reveals the obstacles in recognizing party autonomy in China, mainly due to the influence of Confucianism and Socialism. However, although the freedom is not clearly stated in the CLC, voluntariness still has to be restricted to the socio-economic valuation, which consists of traditional social ethics and the current economic situation. In the case of traditional social ethics, the CLC is influenced by good faith, fairness and public interest, which are consistent with the values of Confucianism. As to the current economic situation, the principle of equal status and the promotion of business transactions, which are aimed at fostering the development of market economy, are observed as the fundamental principles mentioned in the CLC and directed at restricting the individual's freedom. Since party autonomy, a more philosophical concept, serves as the basis of the freedom of contract, it is reasonable to conclude that party autonomy in Europe has a wider scope than in China, since the freedom of contract has been obviously recognized in Europe and is limited to good faith and fair dealing, social justice and fundamental rights, whereas in China the contract voluntariness is used instead of 'freedom of contract', and this is limited to good faith, fairness, public interest, equal status, and the promotion of business transactions. This difference can be reasonably explained using the different roles and functions of party autonomy, which are rooted in the historical and cultural backgrounds. Although modern Chinese contract law is a transplant from the Western countries, each term possibly has different meanings after it is combined with the national characteristics. The concept of 'freedom of contract' is the obvious example. When it was transplanted into China, the concept was changed to mean a voluntariness of entering into a contract, and the reason of this change was attributed to the deeply influential thoughts of Confucianism and the ideology of Socialism, both of which are reluctant to accept the ideology of party autonomy. Also, public interest is a fundamental principle in the CLC, which is absent under the DCFR/PECL. Although it can be observed in all the national private laws that the individual's freedom cannot be violated, in China this concept is understood broadly to include collective interests and interests of the state and parties. This difference is due to the Socialist background of China and the fact that collective interests are certainly superior to personal interests, the assumption of which is also consistent with Confucianism, which advocates that personal interests are subject to public interest. It is thus true to say that, the differences in contract law between Europe and China can be reasonably concluded as, party autonomy which is influenced by both, historical and cultural backgrounds.

The conclusion can be tested by a detailed doctrinal comparison. It is worth mentioning that in Chapter 3, there is no in depth analysis of each doctrine as this may lead to each doctrine being written as a separate book. However, this dissertation attempts to make a hypothesis and test whether the same can be falsified, which makes it more interesting as this attempt may lead to an in depth comparison in the future. Therefore, from the general description of the comparison of each of the doctrines, it may be satisfactory that if there are differences then they can be used to test whether the hypothesis can be falsified.

For the interpretation of the contract, both the DCFR/PECL and the CLC set out the common intention as the standard for the judges to dig out for their interpretation. However, in the CLC, the concept of true meaning is used although it is argued to be equivalent to the Western concept of common intention. This difference is also attributed to Chinese history, for in traditional China, the judges were encouraged to discern the truth between the parties, based on which modern Chinese contract law could adopt the concept of true meaning. Also, in the DCFR/PECL, the preliminary negotiation and subsequent conduct are relevant circumstances, which the judges have to consider, whereas in the CLC they are not stated as relevant situations. As the preliminary negotiation and subsequent conduct refer to the communication between the parties, it is from these relevant circumstances that mutual intentions can be better observed. It is thus correct to say for the purposes of interpretation that the DCFR/PECL is more respectful towards subjective minds of the individuals, which is an expression of party autonomy. However, in both the DCFR/PECL, party autonomy has to be limited to good faith and fair dealing, social justice and the protection of human rights. *Contra proferentem* is an obvious rule flowing from justice, which is an exception to subjective interpretation, as the rule is to maintain the substantive fairness between the parties and to give an interpretation against the party, which provides the standard contract. However, after the comparison, it is easy to see that in the CLC, the *contra proferentem* rule is only limited to the standard contract, whereas under the DCFR, it is extended to the party which can dominantly influence the contract although the terms have even been negotiated. So it is reasonable to say that in the DCFR, fairness is interpreted more broadly to protect the weaker party than in the CLC.

The same can be observed in the pre-contractual liability, which focuses on maintaining the value of good faith and fair dealing between the parties. Individuals are free to decide on whether to enter into a contract. However, good faith and fair dealing is the primary limitation to the exercise of this freedom, and both the DCFR/PECL and the CLC set out several rules to penalize the party, which negotiates in bad faith. A difference in pre-contractual liability between the DCFR and the CLC is seen in the DCFR, where the information duty required in the Consumer Contract Law has a lower standard than in the CLC. Under the DCFR, the parties have to disclose information, which can be reasonably expected by the other party, whereas in the CLC, a deliberate intention to conceal is the standard to measure such duty. So it is true to say that in the DCFR, the concept of (substantive) fairness covers a wider scope than in the CLC.

The validity of contract is subsequently compared, and includes the traditional defective of wills covering 'mistake', fraud and threat, and the recent development on unfair bargaining power. To address mistakes, the CLC uses the concept of significant misunderstanding, which has a broader scope than the concept of mistake explained in the DCFR/PECL, as the former refers to any misconception about the law, the facts and the contract itself, whereas the latter concerns itself with the misconceptions about the law and the facts only. Both, significant misunderstanding and mistake require the misconception to be material. However, in the CLC, the material is determined by the objective method that demands the consequences of serious loss. On the contrary, in the DCFR/PECL, this is judged by the subjective way which entails that the party should know or expect to have known that the other party would not enter into the contract if he knew the truth. As to the fraud and threats, the constitutional elements are similar in both, the DCFR and the CLC. However, as to the effects of these in the DCFR/PECL, the contract can only be void if it was concluded under fraud or threats, whereas in the CLC, three types of effects such as, adaptation, avoidance and invalidity are outlined. Under the CLC, if the defect does not harm the interests of the state, then, the contract can be adapted or avoided, otherwise it can only be invalid. It is difficult to give a reasonable explanation to all these differences in meaning between contract laws in Europe and China. However, it is obvious in the CLC, from the aspects of fraud and threat, that unless the public interest is set at a high level, which no contract can touch; otherwise the contract will certainly be invalid.

The recent movements on unfair bargaining power are ultimately to maintain substantive fairness between the parties, which restrict individual autonomy. The rules on unfair exploitation and unfair terms have been regulated in both the DCFR and the CLC. However, it is obvious that the provisions with regard to unfair terms in the DCFR are more concrete and detailed than in the CLC, which can be easy for the parties to predict the consequence of their conducts. Except for this, the non-individually negotiated terms are within the scope of (substantive) unfairness in the DCFR. It is therefore true to conclude that (substantive) fairness has a broader scope in the DCFR and aims at protecting the weaker party.

With regard to recognition of party autonomy, both the DCFR and the CLC acknowledge that the contract can be adapted or terminated mutually by the parties. However, with regard to the mutual intention to adapt the contract, the CLC sets an additional rule, which requires that the content of modification will be definite, and the registration or approval required by the law or regulations shall be followed for any change. The registration and approval system in China makes it easy for the state to control the contract, which has a close interest in the state or the collective organization. In some contracts, such as the Chinese-foreign joint venture contracts, any modification is effective only upon approval. This difference is obviously derived from the Chinese characteristic of maintaining the welfare of the state. Except for the mutual intention to modify or terminate the contract, both the DCFR and the CLC set numerous conditions for the party to claim for the adaptation. In the DCFR, there are three conditions under which modifications can be claimed. These are mistakes, excessive benefits or unfair advantages, and change of circumstances, whereas in the CLC, there are two additional conditions, which are fraud and threats which enable modification. This difference can be explained through the traditional theory in European contract law where modification was not widely recognized. Due to this limitation, it is difficult for the current European contract law to broadly accept all types of modifications. However, in China, it is possible to modify contracts concluded under fraud or threat for the promotion of business. With regard to the unilateral termination, both, the DCFR and the CLC set force majeure, frustration, anticipatory repudiation, and unreasonable delay as the basis for termination of contracts. However, in the CLC, an additional provision provides for other laws or regulations, which could be the reasons for the termination of these contracts. This provision is very vague and only an administrative regulation, which may constitute the foundation for the termination of a contract. This difference is derived from the Chinese characteristics, which state that the administrative department has to have a wide power to intervene in private contracts.

The mandatory rules in the contract law itself, under the DCFR state the implementation of good faith and fair dealing into more concrete situations. In the CLC, however, except for good faith and fairness, the public interest is also a primary function of the mandatory rules, which can be demonstrated through the validity of the contract. Last but not the least, differences can be observed from the constitutionalization of the contract law process. In Europe, the protection of human rights has been absorbed into the development of private law since the early twentieth century, and some cases demonstrate that the constitutional rights have been directly applied to private law issues and this has been found at both the national and EU levels. It is true to say that the protection of fundamental rights has become a tendency of modern European private law development. On the contrary, in China, the direct application of fundamental rights to private law cases still meets with many problems, and the recession of the official reply to the *Qi Yuling* case somehow reveals that the direct application of Constitutional Law is not allowed. The same can be observed from the protection of social justice, which is another perspective of looking at the constitutionalization of private law. In recent years, the value of social justice has been strongly advocated in Europe and the DCFR has integrated the social solidity as its overriding principle. The provisions for protection of the weaker party and the consumers under the DCFR are obvious examples to reflect the integration of this value. In contrast, although social justice has been rooted in Chinese society for a long time, it has not been widely conveyed for the protection of the weaker party in the modern contract law.

It is therefore reasonable to conclude party autonomy has been recognized in both, the DCFR/PECL and the CLC. However, in Europe, it is more restricted to good faith and fair dealing, the protection of human rights and social justice, whereas in China, it is more restricted to the collective interests and the welfare of the state. Although the CLC was drafted at the end of the twentieth century after the market economy was implemented, and though it is largely transplanted from the Western countries, it is now clear that the Chinese characteristics mainly in the expression of the fact that personal interest and freedom are subject to the public interest, and which are derived from the country's own culture and history, are deeply rooted.

Introduction

> China is the single most important challenge for EU trade policy. China has re-emerged as the world's third economy and the biggest exporter in the global economy, but also an increasingly important political power. EU-China trade has increased dramatically in recent years. China is now the EU's second biggest trading partner after the USA, and the biggest source of imports. The EU is China's biggest trading partner.[1]

In view of the close economic relationship between China and the European Union (EU), particularly in recent years, a comparative legal study is an obvious approach to identifying and understanding the differences between both societies, and may help promote their future economic cooperation. In this business relationship, private law provides the fundamental rules governing market transactions, real rights, compensation for wrongful acts and other types of civil relationships between citizens.[2] It serves as the principal legal mechanism for the market to produce and distribute the wealth of society. At the heart of private law are the rules governing contracts.[3] Given that contracts are a significant economic institution that allows the exchange of goods and services, which in turn leads to an efficient allocation of these goods and services, these rules have a profound impact on market transactions.[4] Ultimately, the law of contract is about the practices of entering transactions and exchanges, and of making the commitments binding

---

1. <http://ec.europa.eu/trade/creating-opportunities/bilateral-relations/countries/china/> (last accessed in November 2010).
2. Study Group on Social Justice in European Private Law, Social Justice in European Contract Law: A Manifesto, *European Law Journal*, vol. 10, 2004, 654.
3. *Ibid.*
4. Martijn W. Hesselink & Gerard J.P. de Vries, *Principles of European Contract Law*, Kluwer, 2001, 80.

for future economic activities.[5] It is arguably the most dynamic area of private law.[6]

The Contract Law of the People's Republic of China (CLC), which had been drafted mainly by Chinese academic jurists between 1993 and 1999, was adopted in 1999 by the National Congress of the People's Republic of China to replace the previous three contract laws: the Economic Contract Law, the Technology Contract Law and the Foreign Economic Contract Law.[7] The CLC is designed to reflect contemporary Chinese social and economic life.[8] While it mirrors the current economic and globalizing developments, it reveals the limited freedom or autonomy in Chinese social life. In other words, the CLC reflects the tensions between the imperatives of state control and individual freedom.

In litigation, when the CLC does not cover a particular issue, a Chinese court will also consider the General Principles of the Civil Law of the People's Republic of China (GPCL), which were adopted at the Fourth Session of the Sixth National Congress of the People's Republic of China on 12 April 1986, and it became effective on 1 January 1987. The GPCL serves as a basic code for the civil law in China,[9] and the courts use them to decide the case.[10] Moreover, the judicial interpretation made by the Supreme People's Court of China (SPC) in the form of notice (*gui ding*),[11] reply (*pi fu*)[12] or opinion (*yi jian*)[13] is another important source of Chinese contract law.[14] Some scholars describe these judgments as quasi-legislation.[15] In 1988, 1999 and 2009 the SPC delivered opinions on certain issues concerning the implementation of the GPCL[16] and the CLC respectively.[17] It has the implied power to give an interpretation of specific issues when there is

5. Hugh Collins, *The Law of Contract*, Cambridge University Press, 2008a, 1–3.
6. Stefan Grundmann (ed.), *An Academic Green Paper on European Contract Law*, Kluwer Law International, 2002, 1–15.
7. Liming Wang, Fundamental Principles of China's Contract Law, *Columbia Journal of Asian Law*, Spring 1999, 2.
8. Huixing Liang, zhong guo he tong fa qi cao guo cheng zhong zheng lun de jiao dian [The Debates in the Drafting Process of the Contract Law of China], 1996d, 13–14.
9. John Shijian Mo, The General Principles of Civil Law, in Wang Guiguo & John Mo (ed.), *Chinese Law*, Kluwer Law International, 1999, 95–100.
10. Bing Ling, *Contract Law in China*, Sweet & Maxwell, 2002, 36.
11. *Notice* refers to the norm and guideline on judicial administration.
12. *Reply* refers to the response to requests for instruction from high people's courts and military courts on questions of specific judicial application of law.
13. *Opinion* refers to rules on how the law should be applied regarding a specific issue or category of issues.
14. Zhao Yuhong, Law of Contract, in Wang & Jone (1999), *supra* n. 9, 221.
15. Ling (2002), *supra* n. 10, 32.
16. Opinions of the Supreme People's Court on Several Issues Concerning the Implementation of the General Principles of the Civil Law of the People's Republic of China (For Trial Implementation) deliberated and adopted by the Judicial Committee of the Supreme People's Court on 26 Jan. 1988.
17. Interpretations by the Supreme People's Court of Certain Issues Concerning the Application of the Contract Law of the People's Republic of China (Part One), 29 Dec. 1999; Interpretations by the Supreme People's Court of Certain Issues Concerning the Application of the Contract Law of the People's Republic of China (Part Two), 9 Feb. 2009.

ambiguity in the law.[18] Not only can these opinions serve as guidelines for lower courts, they can also clarify the law.[19] Furthermore, although judicial decisions in concrete cases do not have any binding effect on other cases in China, an increasing number of case decisions are now extensively reported at various levels nationwide for making the law application consistent. And the requirement of consistency in the application of law in the lower courts to avoid appellate reversals enhances the status of those judicial decisions.[20] With regard to Chinese contract law, the focus of this dissertation will therefore mainly be on the CLC, supplemented by the GPCL and judicial interpretations (opinions, notices and replies), as well as some judicial cases.

In Europe, convergence in private law has in recent years shaped a new legal culture. EU directives and the case law from the European Court of Justice (ECJ) serve as the legal basis for the Europeanization of contract law. A variety of scholarly groups, such as the Lando Commission, the Gandolfi Academy, the Trento Common Core project, and the *Ius Commune* Research School have stressed this convergence process.[21] Their scholarly output, although some of it is critical of the existence and feasibility of European contract law, includes the Principles of European Contract Law (PECL). As a 'product of work carried out by the [Lando] Commission' attempting to reflect the 'common core of solutions to problems of contract law' and trying to 'assist the European courts and legislatures concerned to ensure the fruitful development of contract law on a Union-wide basis',[22] the PECL has received 'a favorable reception in (at least) academic circles'.[23]

The work of the Lando Commission has been continued and improved on by the *Study Group on a European Civil Code* and the *Research Group on the Existing EC Private Law* through the Draft Common Frame of Reference (DCFR).[24] Originally, the DCFR, 'represent[ing] a body of general principles that underpin modern contracts',[25] was expected to be a pre-code or even a code of contract law devised by scholars.[26] However, the DCFR extends the coverage of contract

18. Zhao Yuhong, Law of Contract, in Wang & Jone (1999), *supra* n. 9, 221.
19. *Ibid.*
20. Ling (2002), *supra* n. 10, 33–35.
21. Jan Smits, The Future of European Contract Law: On Diversity and the Temptation of Elegance, Paper presented at the Conference towards a European *Ius Commune* in Legal Education and Research, Maastricht Faculty of Law, 25–26 Oct. 2001, 3–4.
22. Ole Lando & Hugh Beale (ed.), *Principles of European Contract Law: Parts I and II*, Kluwer Law International, 2000b, xxi.
23. Smits (2001), *supra* n. 21, 4.
24. Christian von Bar & Eric Clive (eds), Principles, Definitions and Model Rules of European Private Law: Draft Common Frame of Reference, Full Edition, Vol. 1, European Law Publishers, 2009, 10–12.
25. Martin J. Doris, *Dispute Avoidance and European Contract Law Dealing with Divergence*, European Law Publishing, 2008, 37–38.
26. Martijn W. Hesselink, A Technical 'CFR' or a Political Code? An Introduction, in Martijn W. Hesselink (ed.), *The Politics of a European Civil Code*, Kluwer Law International, 2006, 4.

law. Not only does it include general contract law, it also deals with some areas of non-contractual obligations, such as unjustified enrichment and property law. The first DCFR manuscript was presented to the European Commission on 28 December 2007 and its complete drafting covering most of the PECL at the end of 2008.[27] The concept of European contract law can be found in the EU treaties, in such secondary treaty law as directives, in case law, and in general principles of private law. The DCFR, however, aims to combine the existing community law in the area of general contract law with the remaining material of private law.[28] Although both the DCFR and the PECL are still under discussion regarding their legitimacy to be presented as a common core of European contract law, in this dissertation the DCFR and the PECL are considered as a prime perspective for a study of European contract law (for reasons that will be elaborated in the first chapter). The main focus will be thus on the DCFR, with the PECL completing the picture regarding contractual obligations.

'If we leave what remains of the socialist systems, the primitive and the religious laws out of consideration, the contract laws of the world all have a West European origin', as Ole Lando says.[29] It is widely accepted that Chinese contract law has been deeply influenced by Western norms and that globalization evens out the differences between China and the West.[30] Even so, Chinese contract law still differs considerably from its counterpart in European contract law. As expressed by Pitman B. Potter, despite the influences exerted by foreign legal norms, Chinese law remains dominated by its local legal culture, and the development of its legal system over the past twenty years, the process of which reflects a discourse of selective adaptation of foreign norms about law.[31] When compared with Western law, the main features of Chinese legal culture mostly concern limitations on party autonomy, individual freedom and personal interests.[32] The hypothesis of this dissertation is that contract law in China differs considerably from Europe due to historical and cultural differences in roles and functions as well as in the substance of party autonomy.

Crucial to this approach is the relationship between personal or party autonomy and freedom of contract: '. . . personal autonomy is an ideal of self-creation, of people exerting control over their destinies. An autonomous life consists in the

27. Christian von Bar & Eric Clive (eds), *Principles, Definitions and Model Rules of European Private Law: Draft Common Frame of Reference,* Interim Outline Edition, European Law Publishers, 2008, 41.
28. Von Bar & Clive (2009), *supra* n. 24, 1.
29. Ole Lando, The Structure and the Legal Values of the Common Frame of Reference (CFR), *European Review of Contract Law*, vol. 3, 2007a, 246.
30. Haflidi K. Larusson & David J. Sharp, West Meets East: The New Chinese Contract Law, *Ivey Business Journal*, November 1999, 65.
31. Pitman B Potter, *The Chinese Legal System: Globalization and Local Legal Culture*, Routledge, 2001, 2.
32. Herbert H. P. Ma, The Chinese Concept of the Individual and the Reception of Foreign Law, *Journal of Chinese Law*, Fall 1995, 208–212.

pursuit of freely chosen activities, goals and relationships'.[33] Party autonomy, then, reflects self-determination: individuals can freely decide how to organize their lives. Party autonomy and the concept of freedom of contract are closely connected. Both are fundamentally based on the concept of liberty or complete (or minimally restricted) individual freedom of choice. It allows people to use their general abilities and necessary institutional facilities as well as considerable freedom to enter into contracts. Generally speaking, there are two approaches to the relationship between party autonomy and freedom of contract: horizontal and vertical convergence.

1.1. THE HORIZONTAL CONVERGENCE APPROACH

As expressed by Kimel, liberty has always provided particularly powerful arguments concerning the importance of people's ability to voluntarily undertake obligations towards others.[34] It respects the will and consent of individuals. Both party autonomy and freedom of contract are closely connected with liberty, the only difference being that party autonomy concerns private law as a whole.

In fact, the principle of party autonomy is recognized by most Western legal systems in international contacts to allow contracting parties to choose the law to which their agreement is subject.[35] It can also be referred to in such areas as arbitration law, business law, property law, private international law, and sometimes even in family law. However, party autonomy has different interpretations in these fields. For example, in private international law, it refers to the choice of law and permits parties to choose the law of a particular sovereignty to govern their contract,[36] whereas in property law, it often points to the individual's freedom to deal with property. In contract law, freedom of contract is usually referred to as a concrete expression of party autonomy. Both in fact, horizontally reflect the idea of liberty as entailing unrestricted or minimally restricted freedom, and they often converge. In the horizontal approach, 'the expression of party autonomy will be used synonymously with freedom of contract'.[37] The DCFR seems to adopt this approach, as the title of Article II.-1:102 is 'Party autonomy' whereas its substantive content concerns freedom of contract.

33. Dori Kimel, Neutrality, Autonomy, and Freedom of Contract, *Oxford Journal of Legal Studies*, vol. 21, 2001, 482.
34. *Ibid.*
35. Gerhard Wagner, The Virtues of Diversity in European Private Law, in Jan Smits, *The Need for a European Contract Law Empirical and Legal Perspective*, European Law Publishing, 2005, 4.
36. Mo Zhang, Party Autonomy and Beyond: An International Perspective of Contractual Choice of Law, *Emory International Law Review*, vol. 20, 2008a, 511.
37. Dagmar Coester-Waljten, Constitutional Aspects of Party Autonomy and Its Limits – The Prospective of Law, in Stephan Grundmann, Wolfgang Kerber & Stephen Weatherill, *Party Autonomy and the Role of Information in the Internal Market*, Walter de Gruyter, 2001, 41.

1.2. VERTICAL CONVERGENCE APPROACH

In the vertical convergence approach, two strategies can be distinguished.

In the first strategy, as analysed by earlier scholars such as John Stuart Mill, and contemporary scholars such as Friedrich Hayek in *The Road to Serfdom* (1945), Friedman in *Capitalism and Freedom* (1962), Robert Nozick in *Anarchy, State and Utopia* (1974), and Charles Fried in *Contract as Promise* (1981), individual autonomy is seen as a paramount social value and a central precondition to individual freedom of contract; so party autonomy arguably precedes freedom of contract. The value of party autonomy concerns the conditions that are necessary for people to live autonomous lives and that respect their freely chosen pursuits.[38] It allows people to voluntarily undertake obligations and to acknowledge the binding force of such obligations, which in turn respects people's autonomy.[39] It is a social value mechanism for people exercising their freedom. Freedom of contract is therefore considered to derive from the value of party autonomy and autonomy is thus interpreted as 'freedom *to*'. Without autonomy, there is no freedom of contract.

The other strategy advocates that freedom of contract predominates in party autonomy. Freedom is a fundamental human right that includes, for example, the freedom of expression, the freedom to work and the freedom to enter into obligations.[40] To lead a valuable and autonomous life, a sufficient range of options needs to be available.[41] Derived from the fundamental right to freedom, the principle of autonomy was acknowledged.

In the same way, the individual's right to engage in civil activities that contract law is the foundation of private law, freedom of contract serves as a fundamental basis for party autonomy. Freedom of contract precedes party autonomy and autonomy is interpreted as 'freedom *from*'.

At first glance, both approaches seem reasonable. The vertical approach considers party autonomy and freedom of contract to constitute a top-down relationship, while in the horizontal approach the meaning of the two concepts is fundamentally linked to the notion of liberty. This dissertation supports the view that autonomy precedes freedom, as 'personal autonomy entails respect for freedom of contract'.[42] The value of personal autonomy entails respect for people's choices and for their freely chosen pursuits. Also, from a philosophical viewpoint, contract law theories determine to what extent contract doctrines are consistent with autonomy.[43] In Chinese legal history, freedom of contract was not recognized, as the concept of individual autonomy was meaningless. But the DCFR does not distinguish between party autonomy and freedom of contract – the title of

38. Kimel (2001), *supra* n. 33, 482.
39. *Ibid.*
40. Article 16, Charter of Fundamental Rights of the European Union (2000/C 364/01).
41. *Ibid.*, 487.
42. *Ibid.*, 483.
43. Jody S. Kraus, Reconciling Autonomy and Efficiency in Contract Law: The Vertical Integration Strategy, *Social, Political, and Legal Philosophy*, 2001, 420.

Article II.-1:102 is 'party autonomy' but it in fact deals with freedom of contract. When, as is done in this dissertation, party autonomy is taken to serve as a basis for freedom of contract.

The aim of this dissertation is to test the hypothesis – contract law in China differs considerably from Europe due to historical and cultural differences in roles and functions as well as in the substance of party autonomy – by comparing the fundamental principles and several main doctrines of both systems of contract law. It consists of four chapters. Where the first one is a brief introduction to the history of private law in China and Europe, the second chapter contains an analysis of the fundamental principles of both contract law systems. To test the hypothesis, the third chapter offers a comparison of several of doctrines underlying the DCFR/PECL and the CLC: interpretation of contracts, pre-contractual liability, contract validity, adaptation and termination of contracts, mandatory rules and constitutionalization of contract law. The final chapter aims to conclude whether the hypothesis can be falsified and if so, to what extent.

Chapter 1
A Brief History of Private Law in China and Europe

As Gordley points out, 'one could not compare legal rules without seeing their place within a "system" ', which employs a certain vocabulary corresponding to a distinct of legal concepts.[44] Not only is a particular vocabulary used, certain methods are also usually adopted to interpret these concepts, and specific conceptions of social order are frequently employed to determine the means of application and the function of law.[45] Since the external history is a significant vehicle to get to know how certain concepts and legal methods have evolved in a society, this chapter will briefly introduce the external history of civil law development in China and Europe. The Chinese philosophy of Confucianism and its influence on the law will be described in section 1.1, which will also review the concept of contract in ancient China and the main stages of civil law development in Chinese legal history. Section 1.2 will give a historical introduction to European contract law, explore the recent convergence of European private law and describe the values of the DCFR/PECL.

1.1. A SHORT HISTORY OF CIVIL LAW DEVELOPMENT IN CHINA

It is impossible to understand Chinese civil law history without any knowledge of Confucianism. Having dominated Chinese thought for almost 2,500 years, Confucianism has strongly influenced all sectors of Chinese society. It is fair to say that

44. James Gordley, *Foundations of Private Law: Property, Tort, Contract, Unjust Enrichment*, Oxford University Press, 2006, 3.
45. *Ibid.*, 3.

Confucianism left little room or need for civil law in ancient China, and this section will start with a brief introduction to this philosophy.

1.1.1. Confucianism and the History of Chinese Civil Law before the Twentieth Century

Confucius (BC 551–479), arguably the most influential Chinese philosopher and seen as the founder of the teaching of Confucianism, was the scion of a noble family and started teaching in his early twenties.[46] His philosophy, which has deeply influenced thought and life in China, Japan, Korea and other Asian countries for 2,500 years, emphasized personal and governmental morality, social relationships, justice and sincerity.[47] His ethics focus on three concepts namely, righteousness (*yi*), morality (*li*)[48] and benevolence (*ren*).[49] Familial loyalty, ancestor worship, respect for elders and the family as the basis for an ideal government are the main principles or values of Confucianism.[50]

In the 5,000 years of Chinese legal history, numerous philosophical thoughts have in varying degrees influenced the development of law. For instance, the most famous rivals of Confucians were the Legalists,[51] who argued that strict law and rules were the only way to bring about peace and order. Mohists[52] argued that love

46. Roger T. Ames, Confucianism: Confucius (Kongzi, K'ung Tzu), in Antonio, S. Cua (ed.), *Encyclopedia of Chinese Philosophy*, Routledge, 2003, 58.
47. *Ibid.*, 58–64.
48. *Li*, was the main Confucianism concept to influence Chinese legal history. There are several English translations to this word, such as rules of proper conduct, morality, rules that inspire positive orderly conduct, reason, propriety, or ritual propriety. All these translations are reasonable, but it is difficult to find a suitable English word because the Chinese Character *li* includes the meaning of all these translations. In this dissertation, the term morality is used, even though morality is only a part of the meaning of *li*.
49. Antonio S. Cua, Confucianism: Ethics, in Cua (2003), *supra* n. 47, 72–78.
50. *Ibid.*
51. Legalism, which first appeared in BC 90, was the central governing idea of the *Qin* dynasty (BC 221–206). It made profound contributions to the unification of China under the first emperor *Qin Shihuang* (BC 259–210). Legalism upholds the rule of law and asserts that law rather than morality is the most reliable and useful instrument for ruling a state. Its most famous contributor, *Han Fei* (BC 280–233), argued that a ruler should govern the state by *fa* (law or principle), *shu* (method, tactic or art) and *shi* (legitimacy, power or charisma). Another contributor, *Guanzi,* considered the law to possess six characteristics: supremacy, compulsion, objectivity, normalization, unity and permanence. In later dynasties, legalism's influence waned and it ceased to be an independent school of thought since it was not consistent with the feudal hierarchy order. However, it continued to play an important role in Chinese legal history. From Cua (2003), *supra* n. 47, 277–280, 285–288, 361–363.
52. Mohism, a Chinese philosophy founded by *Mozi* (BC 470–391), was the major rival of Confucianism. It defines the morality as a constant moral guide that parallels utilitarianism and asserts that this moral guide must promote and encourage social behaviour that maximizes general utility. Mohism emphasizes the need for detachment from unreasoned emotions such as pleasure, anger, joy, sadness and love. The dispassionate intellect alone is necessary and sufficient for discovering the truth. It promotes universal love – an equal affection for all

was the only way to bring about order and Taoists[53] believed non-action was the only true way.[54] It has been widely accepted that Chinese legal philosophy was based essentially on Confucianism, which was re-established as a leading philosophy during the *Han* dynasty (BC 206–220 AD) by Emperor *Wu* (BC 140–87). It has since been the official state teaching and has dominated Chinese thought.[55]

Confucians believe in a society where all conduct themselves according to their position and status,[56] and where all know what to do and how to behave. Self-cultivation is considered the foundation.[57] Confucians also believe the rule of law can never bring about lasting peace and social stability, as it will only make people look for ways to circumvent the law. Morality, 'on the other hand, will instil in the people an inner sense of propriety and the accompanying sense of shame'.[58] It can make people aware of acts that are shameful and acts that are proper. And this makes 'possible an order which would be self-sustaining without outside enforcement or coercion'.[59] So confucians argue that the only way to create order out of chaos is to establish the value of morality.[60] This view has had profound and lasting impact on the traditional Chinese duty-oriented social structure.[61] Morality, however, is not arbitrary. It is considered to be in harmony with righteousness and benevolence.

'Chinese legal history is over two thousand years old and has chiefly been influenced by Confucianism history.'[62] Under its influence, civil law had not developed, although the concept and usage of contracts, known as *qiyue* (agreement), could be traced back to before the creation of Chinese characters (BC 1200–1050).[63] Sale, employment, barter and loan contracts existed as early as in the

individuals. Although Mohism disappeared during the *Qin* dynasty (BC 221–206), it deeply influenced Chinese history: its concept of universal love merged with the philosophy of Confucianism. From Cua (2003), *supra* n. 47, 453–480.

53. Taoism (or Daoism), along with Buddhism and Confucianism, has become one of the three major religious in China and has influenced East Asia for over 2,000 years. It started as a combination of psychology and philosophy, and it emphasizes compassion, moderation and humility. *Tao* (or *Dao*) can be translated as path or way, and is considered the influence that keeps the universe balanced and ordered. Taoist thought focuses on non-action (*wu wei*), spontaneity, humanism and emptiness. Non-action is the central concept of Taoism. It reveals the soft and invisible power within all things. Taoism also embraces a harmonious relationship with nature. Today, it is one of the most popular religions in China. From Cua (2003), *supra* n. 47, 202–213.
54. Chaibong Hahm, Confucianism and the Concept of Liberty, *Asia Europe Journal*, Springer-Verlag, 2006, 481.
55. R. David & J. E. C. Brierley, *Major Legal Systems in the World Today*, Stevens & Sons, 1985, 522.
56. Fuldien Li, Confucianism: Ethics and Law, in Cua (2003), *supra* n. 47, 80.
57. *Ibid.*
58. Hahm (2006), *supra* n. 55, 480–481.
59. *Ibid.*, p. 481.
60. Hahm (2006), *supra* n. 55, 478–479.
61. Fuldien Li, Confucianism: Ethics and Law, in Cua (2003), *supra* n. 47, 80.
62. Axel Hagedorn, Cultural Characteristics in the Chinese Contract Law: A Multidisciplinary Approach, thesis, VU University Amsterdam, 1996, 33.
63. Zhao Yuhong, Law of Contract, in Wang & Jone (1999), *supra* n. 9, 217–220.

Xizhou dynasty (BC 1066–771),[64] but there was no room for the development of a modern contract law system.[65] Law played a minor role in the traditional Chinese legal system.[66] Ancient China lacked the concept of separate civil and criminal branches of law. The statutes mainly focused on administrative and criminal matters.[67] Civil issues, in the *Qing* Code,[68] were considered 'minor matters' and were supposed to be dealt with by members of society themselves through extra-legal mechanisms.[69] There are several reasons for this.

First, ancient China was a centrally controlled feudal state and an agrarian country. Most farmers worked the land they lived on and it was not common for them to move frequently. Villagers knew each other well, were often related and social relationships mattered greatly to their survival. Some respectable or trusted persons could thus easily resolve civil conflicts through mediation or conciliation, whereas criminal law had to be systematic and strict to protect the ruling role of emperor and the feudal hierarchy.

Secondly, ancient China frequently implemented a closed-door policy to limit contacts with foreign countries. Historically, China was a closed and self-sufficient country and little attention was paid to the other countries of the world.[70]

Thirdly, traditional China favoured agriculture and discouraged commerce. Agriculture was regarded as providing the basis for the nation's survival and merchants were considered as diverting social wealth and labour from agriculture. The society therefore did not encourage commercial activities, which leads to the result that restrictions on commercial activities prevented the development of private law. Also, it was believed that commercial activities could disrupt normal social hierarchy and violate egalitarian ethics, firmly pinning merchants down to the lowest rung of the social ladder. The restrictions on the commercial activities therefore prevented the development of private law.

However, the ultimate reason to result the fact that civil matters were considered as minor issues has to do with cultural roots. It is commonly held that law is

---

64. Xiaoxin Ye, *zhong guo min fa shi* [*History of Chinese Civil Law*], Shanghai People's Press, 1993, 63–75.
65. Zhao Yuhong, Law of Contract, in Wang & Jone (1999), *supra* n. 9, 218.
66. Hagedorn (1996), *supra* n. 63, 58.
67. Yin-Ching chen, Civil Law Development: China and Taiwan, *Stanford Journal of East Asian Affairs*, vol. 2, Spring 2002, 9–10.
68. The *Qing* Code, also called the Great *Qing* Legal Code, was the legal code of the Qing dynasty (1644–1911 AD). It was based on the legal system structure of the *Ming* dynasty (1368–1644 AD). It was revised more than thirty times and it contained 1,907 statutes. It was conceived as criminal code, and civil issues were considered as minor matters. The *Qing* Code was the first written Chinese work to be translated directly into English (as Fundamental Laws of China, George Thomas Staunton, 1810). Although the code was mainly a criminal code, the British were still able to use it to resolve trading obstacles and issues remove obstacles to commerce. The English translation of the *Qing* Code became an important source for European Countries to understand the Chinese legal system and enabled them to make a profit from trading in China. From William C. Jones, *The Great Qing Code*, Oxford University Press, 1994.
69. Philip C. Huang, *Code, Custom, and Legal Practice in China*, Stanford University Press, 2001, 26.
70. Mo Zhang, *Chinese Contract Law Theory and Practice*, Martinus Nijhoff Publishers, 2006, 28.

part of a culture's way of expressing its sense of the order of things,[71] and Chinese legal tradition can be regarded as being founded on Confucianism. According to Confucianism, law (*fa*) deals with criminal and administrative cases, whilst morality is used for civil matters. Law and morality are indistinguishable.[72] The purpose of morality is to achieve social harmony. Confucianism is in fact very much an art of living in harmony with others, and neither written law nor written contracts can take its place.[73] Based on these thoughts, traditional Chinese society was full of social moralities that included but were not limited to the social network of relationships (*guanxi*) and human relationships (*renqing*), which played an essential role in resolving the civil issues.[74]

Culturally, traditional Chinese civil law is different from modern civil law. Modern civil law requires party autonomy, equal status and fault liability. In contrast, traditional China lacked these concepts. The Western concept of contract implies rights and obligations for the contracting parties, but the Chinese concept is 'only part of a relationship that goes far beyond a single agreement which is based on equality, mutual benefit and personal trust'.[75] So in China before the twentieth century, although the criminal codes were very systematic, the civil law was comparatively underdeveloped. It is worth mentioning that the extra-legal mechanisms, which are rooted in Chinese legal culture, have developed rapidly. Mediation, one of the extra-legal mechanisms, is culturally better suitable to the Chinese as it allows saving face, and it is preferable still:[76] it remains a compulsory procedure that must precede judicial decision.

1.1.2. The First Draft Civil Code

The first Chinese civil code was drafted in the early twentieth century. During the late *Qing* Dynasty (1840–1911), China's feudal society was in decline. Under a number of treaties with Western countries, the *Qing* government was forced to implement 'consular jurisdiction'.[77] Together with internal crises, such as

71. Lawrence Rosen, *Law as Culture: An Invitation*, Princeton University Press, 2006, 4–6.
72. Larusson & Sharp (1999), *supra* n. 30, 66.
73. *Ibid.*
74. Hagedorn (1996), *supra* n. 63, 25–33.
75. *Ibid.*, 25.
76. Bruno Zeller, CISG and China, in Michael R. Will, *CISG and China – An Intercontinental Exchange*, Universite de Geneve, 1999, 9.
77. Consular jurisdiction refers to a foreign consulate having jurisdiction according to its national law over its citizens residing in its colonies. Dating back to Roman Republic, it was first applied in the sixteenth century. At that time, Western businessmen who were living in the East voted to create a consulate arbitrating the internal commercial issues among themselves. Later, the Western countries extended this power to civil and criminal matters involving their expatriate citizens. In the Middle Era, European countries such as the Netherlands, Britain and Sweden exercised their consular jurisdiction both in civil and criminal matters over their citizens who were doing business in foreign countries. Until the nineteenth century, the West extended this jurisdiction through treaties to Asian and African countries. Impairing state sovereignty, it was

corruption and revolts, this was a major threat to the *Qing* dynasty. In order to maintain power, the government advocated a reform of the legal system inspired by Western practice.[78] So in order to save his dynasty and annul consular jurisdiction,[79] in 1902 the emperor *Guangxu* (1871–1908) issued an Imperial Edict ordering the revision of existing laws, and in 1907, the Office of Legal Revision was established. Three Chinese jurists, Shen Jiaben, Yu Liansan and Ying Rui, were appointed to carry out the civil code project.

The drafting process was started in 1907 and completed in 1911.[80] It was determined that the civil code had to: (1) focus on the most common legal principles in the world; (2) incorporate modern civil code theories from abroad; (3) respect national customs and traditions, especially regarding inheritance and marriage law; (4) and focus on the law of obligations and property law in order to distinguish this code from previous reforms. Under these four guiding principles, the first three books – General Principles, Law of Obligations and Property Law – were drafted by a Japanese jurist, Y.M. Matsuoka, who had been appointed by one of the Chinese jurists (*Shen Jiaben*). These three books were modelled on German civil code and influenced by Japanese civil law. The last two books – family and inheritance law – were drafted jointly by the Chinese jurists and ritual scholars. These two books reflected the spirit of the feudal state and included many customs. The grand total of articles in the five books is 1,569. But this civil code was never promulgated, as the *Qing* dynasty fell in 1911.[81] However, it is the first drafted civil code in Chinese legal history and it included a variety of custom law and traditions. It represents a major government attempt to establish a civil legal system modelled on modern European codes and is a partial departure from traditional laws.

Worth mentioning here is that when this civil code was being drafted, there was a nation-wide survey in the form of questionnaires regarding the customs citizens observed in daily life in order to ensure the draft code's consistency with national traditions. Surveys were conducted in all provinces and the outcomes were carefully considered. In this sense, the draft code has had a strong impact on Chinese legal history. Some scholars even consider that the development of contemporary Chinese civil law was mainly influenced by this draft civil code,[82] though limitations to individual freedom and subjugations of personal interests

---

first annulled in 1890 by Japan and by Turkey in 1923. Consular jurisdiction was first exercised in China by Britain in 1843 and by America in 1844. After the Second World War, the Chinese government dissolved it step by step. When the Republic of China was established in 1949, its government annulled all consular jurisdiction treaties. From Mengxue Wu, *mei guo zai hua lin shi cai pan quan bai nian shi* [A Hundred Years' History of Consular Jurisdiction by the USA in China], she hui ke xue wen xian chu ban she [Social Sciences Press], 1992.

78. Huixing Liang, zhong guo dui wai guo min fa de ji shou [The Reception of Foreign Civil Laws in China], *yue dan min shang fa* [*Journal of Yuefan Civil and Commercial Law*], vol. 3, 2003, 5–10.
79. Zejian Wang, min fa wu shi nian [The Fifty Years of Civil Law], *min fa xue shuo yu pan li yan jiu* [*The Theory of Civil Law and Cases*], vol. 5, 1991, 4–5.
80. Liang (2003), *supra* n. 79, 5–10.
81. Huang (2001), *supra* n. 70, 26.
82. Liang (2003), *supra* n. 79, 5–10; Wang (1991), *supra* n. 80, 4–5.

have essentially remained unchanged to this. The draft code is also considered the beginning, in Chinese legal history, of acknowledging the influence of foreign civil legal systems. By introducing German civil law principles, theories and reasoning to China, the draft civil code paved the way for the traditional Chinese legal system to transform into modern civil law legislation.

1.1.3. The First Implemented Civil Code

The second phase of Chinese civil law development occurred in the 1920s and 1930s. After the establishment of the Republic of China in 1912, the process of civil code revision progressed slowly. At the Washington Conference of 1922, the government brought up the issue of consular jurisdiction, and the conference decided to appoint some experts from Western countries to investigate whether the consular jurisdiction conflicted with national Chinese law. This decision accelerated the revision process of the Chinese civil code.[83] In 1925 the draft code, which was based on the *Qing* draft, was completed and it consisted of five books – General Principles, Law of Obligations, Property Law, Family Law and Inheritance Law – numbering 1,745 articles in all. The book on the law of obligations had changed considerably compared with the *Qing* draft, mainly incorporating the Swiss law of obligations.[84] This draft civil code was never enacted either, as in 1927 the National Government assumed power.

After the establishment of the National Government, the civil code was redrafted a second time, from 1928 to 1930. This National Civil Code consisted of 1,225 articles, and the five books dealt with General Principles, Law of Obligations, Property Law, Family Law and Inheritance Law respectively. It was based on the code drafted by the government of the Republic of China and some concept transplants from Japanese, Swiss and Soviet civil law.[85] It is the first implemented civil code in Chinese history, which today is still in force in Taiwan.[86] However, it transplanted numerous concepts and provisions from foreign civil law without considering their suitability for application in the Chinese context. Just like a hungry person is not choosy about his or her food, the government introduced whatever Western law it happened to find. Because of some resulting gaps between the legislation and practice, a large number of provisions could not be enforced at that time. Nevertheless, after several revisions, the civil code remains in force in Taiwan and plays a significant role in Taiwanese society. However, it is worth noting that the most significant achievement of this code is the successful creation of a comprehensive Chinese civil law vocabulary, while at the same time considerable emphasis was placed on public interest.[87]

83. *Ibid.*, 4–5.
84. *Ibid.*
85. *Ibid.*
86. Ma (1995), *supra* n. 32, 215.
87. Ling (2002), *supra* n. 10, 10–11.

1.1.4. The Development of the Civil Law in the Maoist Period

After the Chinese Communist Party came into power in 1949, the Republican legal system was abandoned and plans were made to establish a new socialist legal system.[88] In 1954, the National Committee ordered the drafting of a civil code. The resulting draft consisted of 525 articles in all.[89] The 1922 Soviet civil code was the main influence on this draft, which was obviously socialist in character. But the Anti-Rightist Movement and the 1958 Great Leap Forward overwhelmed the role of law in society. The Cultural Revolution of 1966 marked the start of a period when policy, not law, dominated Chinese society.

1.1.5. The Development of Contract Law in the 1980s

From 1978 onwards, China began to open its market to the world. In order to accelerate economic development, a law of contracts had to be implemented. So in 1981, 1985, 1986 and 1987, the Economic Contract Law, the Law on Economic Contracts Involving Foreign Interests, the General Principles of Civil Law and the Technology Contract Law respectively were adopted.

The Economic Contract Law of 1981 consisted of seven chapters: (1) general principles; (2) the establishment and performance of contracts; (3) changing and terminating contracts; (4) violations of contractual duties; (5) contractual disputes, mediation and arbitration; (6) supervision of contracts; and (7) supplementary provisions. Influenced by the economic law of Soviet Union, the law stressed that the establishment and performance of economic contracts must be in accordance with national plans, and that the administrative management has the power to affirm and avoid the contract.

In 1985, the Law on Economic Contracts Involving Foreign Interests was passed, which consisted of seven chapters: (1) general principles; (2) the establishment of contracts; (3) the performance and breach of contracts; (4) transfer of contracts; (5) modification, termination and dissolution of contracts; (6) dispute resolution; and (7) supplementary provisions. The common law and the 1980 United Nations Convention on Contracts for the International Sale of Goods (CISG) served as the basis for the structure and principles of this law, and the common law and international treaties have since had a profound impact on the Chinese legal system.

The 1986 GPCL consisted of nine chapters: (1) general principles; (2) citizens (natural persons); (3) legal persons; (4) civil juristic acts and agency; (5) civil rights; (6) civil liability; (7) limitation of action; (8) covered application of law in civil relations with foreigners; and (9) supplementary provisions. The framework and content of the GPCL were mainly influenced by the CISG. The GPCL

88. Article 17, Common Program of the People's Political Consultation Conference of China, adopted on 29 Sep. 1949 at the First People's Political Conference of China.
89. Liang (2003), *supra* n. 79, 5–10; Wang (1991), *supra* n. 80, 4–5.

has played a significant role in the development of China's market economy. It remains in force in China to this day and is even regarded as the basis for the uniform contract law that was passed in 1999. Also, it has been and is being widely applied in judicial practice where there is a vacuum in statutory law. Some scholars even considered it to be the Chinese civil code, as said by James Gordley: 'with the enactment of the Chinese Civil Code [which refers to GPCL], systems of private law modelled on those of the West will govern nearly the entire world.'[90]

In 1987, the Technology Contract Law was passed, which consisted of seven chapters: (1) general principles; (2) formation, performance, modification and termination of technology contracts; (3) technical development contracts; (4) technology transfer contracts; (5) technical consultancy contracts and technical service contracts; (6) arbitration and litigation of technology contract disputes; and (7) supplementary provisions.

Worth mentioning is that from the late 1970s to the mid-1980s, there was a fierce debate on whether economic law or civil law[91] should dominate the society (and although it has lost much of its fire, the debate continues to this day).[92] This debate directly influenced the notion of 'economic contract', which has socialist origins and had figured prominently in the socialist economic law regime. With the promulgation of the Economic Contract Law in 1981, the concept was officially adopted by the Chinese legislature. In the debate, many scholars held the view that economic contracts belong to the field of economic law, while non-economic contracts belong to the area of civil law.[93] Every court had separate economic and civil panels, which the Supreme Court only combined into a single civil panel around the year 2000. Without disregarding the influence of the concept of a socialist legal system and of a centrally planned economy, the advent of civil law may challenge Chinese cultural and historical traditions more radically than economic laws can or may have done, as civil law impacts more aspects of people's daily lives than economic law does.[94] As mentioned earlier, Confucianism advocates that civil matters be dealt with by means of morality whilst the law be used to resolve criminal and administrative cases, and it was therefore believed that civil law challenges the core principles of Confucianism more than economic law does.

---

90. James Gordley, *The Philosophical Origins of Modern Contract Doctrine*, Oxford Press, 1992, 1.
91. In civil law systems, a clear distinction is made between civil law (contracts, torts, property and family law) and economic law (antitrust rules and public regulation of private transactions). But in socialist states, this distinction is very vague since private and public law merge to some extent. In the 1980s, policy and administrative regulations played an essential role in economic development; it was believed that there should be no civil law in China because all means of production should be owned by the public in socialist societies and government interference should extend to civil activities. Even today in China, the boundaries between economic law and civil law are hazy and the debate continues. From Masanobu Kato, Civil and Economic Law in People's Republic of China, *The American Journal of Comparative Law*, vol. 30, 1982, 429–457.
92. Kato (1982), *supra* n. 92, 429–457.
93. Wang (1999), *supra* n. 7, 2.
94. Benjamin Gregg, The Modernization of Contemporary Chinese law, *The Review of Politics*, vol. 55, 1993, 466.

1.1.6. THE NEW UNIFORM CONTRACT LAW

From 1992 onwards, with the dramatic acceleration of economic reform, the concept of a socialist market economy began to replace a centrally planned economy. The three contract laws adopted in the 1980s – the Economic Contract Law, the Foreign Economic Contract Law and the Technology Contract Law – failed to meet the needs of China's development as a market economy,[95] the increasing scale and complexity of economic activities required a consistent uniform contract law to govern business transactions. Three features of the contract laws made them unsuitable to meet that need.

First, the three contract laws were the products of a socialist and centrally planned economy.[96] They emphasized the determinative and restrictive role of the state in the operation of economic contracts.[97] For instance, the Administration for Industry and Commerce (AIC) could validate economic contracts directly, and it thus had broad powers of intervention.[98] Also, economic contracts could only be concluded by legal persons and organizations,[99] whilst in a market economy, natural persons can also enter into economic contracts.

Secondly, there are numerous contradictions and inconsistencies among the three contract laws.[100] For example, both the Economic Contract law and the Foreign Economic Contract Law stated that the parties should observe the principles of equality and mutual benefit, whilst the Technology Contract Law required the principles of voluntariness, fairness, mutual benefit and good faith to be complied with.[101] Although it is argued that the three contract laws dealt with different topics, in modern civil society, party autonomy and social justice are fundamental values to be respected by all entities and individuals.

---

95. Wang (1999), *supra* n. 7, 3–8.
96. Lucie Cheng & Arthur Rosett, Contract with a Chinese Face: Socially Embedded Factors in the Transformation from Hierarchy to Market, 1978–1989, *Journal of Chinese Law*, 1991, 166.
97. Larusson & Sharp (1999), *supra* n. 30, 66–67.
98. Article 43 of the 1981 Economic Contract Law of the People's Republic of China: 'Administrative departments for industry and commerce of the people's governments at or above the county level and other competent departments shall, in accordance with their respective functions and duties stipulated by the laws, administrative rules and regulations, be responsible for the supervision over the performance of economic contracts.' In the Provisional Regulations of the State Administration for Industry and Commerce on the Confirmation and Handling of Invalid Economic Contracts, which was promulgated on 25 Jul. 1985 by the State Administration for Industry and Commerce, the Administration was empowered to declare contracts invalid.
99. Article 2 of the 1981 Economic Contract Law: 'This Law shall be applicable to contracts entered into between civil subjects of equal footing, that is, between legal persons or other economic organizations or self-employed industrial and commercial households or lease holding farm households for the purpose of realizing certain economic goals and defining the rights and obligations of the parties.'
100. Wang (1999), *supra* n. 7, 4–7.
101. Article 4 of the Technology Contract Law, Art. 5 of the Economic Contract Law and Art. 3 of the Foreign Economic Contract Law.

Lastly, the three contract laws lacked basic contract rules, such as that of offer and acceptance.[102] So with the development of its economy and the integration into the international market, wide gaps had opened up between the legislation governing economic activities and China's market economy development. Also, for the purpose of knocking on the door of the World Trade Organization (WTO),[103] a uniform contract law was called for.

On 15 March 1999, the uniform contract law (CLC) was adopted by the Ninth National People's Congress and it became effective on 1 October 1999.[104] The drafting process had started in 1993 and academic jurists completed the first draft manuscript in 1995.[105] In line with the drafting principles,[106] the

102. Wang (1999), *supra* n. 7, 5.

103. Feng Chen, The New Era of Chinese Contract Law: History, Development and A Comparative Analysis, *Brooklyn Journal of International Law*, vol. 27, 2001, 153–154.

104. Structurally, the CLC is divided into three parts: General Provisions, Specific Provisions and Supplementary Provisions (23 chapters comprising 428 Articles in all). The first part (General Provisions) has 8 chapters: General Provisions, Conclusion of Contracts, Effectiveness of Contracts, Performance of Contracts, Modification and Assignment of Contracts, Termination of the Rights and Obligations of Contracts, Liability for Breach of Contracts, Miscellaneous Provisions. The second part (Specific Provisions) contains 15 chapters on 15 types of contract: Sales; Supply and Use of Electricity, Water, Gas or Heating; Donations; Loans; Lease; Financial Lease; Hired Works; Construction Projects; Transport; Technology; Storage; Warehousing; Mandate; Commission Agency; Intermediation.

105. In 1993, the Commission of Legislative Affairs of the Standing Committee of the National People's Congress organized a conference to discuss merging of the three then current contract laws into a uniform contract law and appointed eight scholars to draft a proposal: Prof. Jiang Ping from China University of Political Science and Law, Prof. Huixing Liang from the Institute of Law of the Chinese Academy of Social Sciences, Prof. Liming Wang from Ren Ming University, Prof. Jianyuan Cui from Ji Lin University, Prof. Mingrui Guo from Yan Tai University, Justice Fan Li from the Supreme Court, Justice Xin He from the Beijing High Court and Prof. Guangxing Zhang from the Study of Jurisprudence. In January 1994, the Commission adopted the proposal drafted by these scholars and commissioned twelve law schools to draft a contract law: China University of Political Science and Law, Beijing University, Ren Ming University, the Institute of Law of the Chinese Academy of Social Sciences, the University of International Business and Economics, Ji Lin University, Yan Tai University, Wu Han University, Southwest University of Political Science and Law, Zhongnan University of Economics and Law, Northwest University of Political Science and Law, and East China University of Politics and Law. In November 1994, the drafts prepared by these universities were collected and finalized by Prof. Huixing Liang, Prof. Guangxing Zhang and Prof. Jingshen Fu. In January 1995, the draft contract law was remitted to the Commission. After four years of revision and six draft contract laws, the uniform contract law was finally adopted on 15 Mar. 1999 and it entered into forced on 1 Oct. 1999. From Liang (1996), *supra* n. 8.

106. The guiding principles for the drafting are as follows: (1) Taking into account reforms and the open-door policy, developing a socialist market economy and establishing a uniform law as well as integrating China's economy into the international market, the legislation must reflect China's own legal experience and learn widely from other developed countries in order to be consistent with international treaties and international customary laws, and reflect the common rules of a modern market economy. (2) Presenting the principle of party autonomy in order to protect the freedom of contract within the law, public order and social ethics, the legislation must not limit the freedom of contract without good reasons. (3) Considering the characteristics of law making and implementing, the legislation must meet the requirements of a

CLC's general provisions and the section on the sale contracts were primarily transplanted from international treaties, as the CLC drafting committee believed that these best reflect general principles accepted by most legal systems in the world. Another consideration was that the international practice would contribute to the Chinese contract law in manifesting the most common principles and customs in order to smoothly integrate China's economy into the international market. Except for transplanting from the international treaties, a number of concepts and provisions in the CLC were borrowed from the German Civil Code, Japanese civil law and Taiwan's Civil Code.[107] 'It [the CLC] is a hybrid of civil and common law literature.'[108]

Although the CLC borrowed numerous provisions from international treaties and other legal systems, the essential concept of party autonomy (freedom of contract) was hotly debated during the drafting process.[109] Even so, the CLC has diminished the import of such labels as 'socialist' and 'planned economy'. It is not only a milestone in Chinese civil law history, but also a significant step towards China's future enactment of a civil code. 'It can be expected to play a crucial role in regulating China's burgeoning market economy and in contributing to China's further legal development.'[110]

1.1.7. Chinese Property Law

After fourteen years of discussion, the Law of Real Rights was passed on 16 March 2007 and became effective on 1 October 2007. It had been the subject of a prolonged and sharp debate because of the incompatibility of Chinese socialism property law. In China, socialism referred to the ideology aiming to improve society through collective and egalitarian action,[111] which is at odds with the protection of individual property by the Law of Real Rights. Some scholars therefore insisted

---

successful socialist market economy, and be suitable to transforming situation a centrally planned economy into a market economy. (4) Considering the values of the contract law, which are economic efficiency, social justice, and transaction convenience and security. The legislation must focus on the development of productivity and social interests, protecting the interests of consumers and employees, safeguarding the social order in a market economy. It should reflect the characteristics of a modern market economy and facilitate both transactions and the forms and procedures for secure transactions. (5) The provisions must be operational; the phrasing must be simple and precise. From Guangxing Zhang, zhong hua ren ming guo he guo he tong fa de qi cao [Drafting the Contract Law of the People's Republic of China], *fa xue yan jiu* [Chinese Journal of Law], vol. 5, 1995, 4–7.

107. Wang (1991), *supra* n. 80, 4–5.
108. Mo Zhang, Freedom of Contract with Chinese Legal Characteristics: A Closer Look at China's New Contract Law, *Temple International and Comparative International Law*, vol. 14, 2000, 238.
109. Zhang (1995), *supra* n. 107, 12–13.
110. Wang (1999), *supra* n. 7, 1.
111. Mo Zhang, From Public to Private: The Newly Enacted Chinese Property Law and the Protection of Property Rights in China, Temple University Legal Studies Research Paper Series, No. 39, 2008, 7.

that the drafting of a property law diverged from China's constitutional law.[112] However, since the 1980s, China has opened the door to the world and from the 1990s onwards, it has implemented a market economy policy. Under the new economic regime, the property of citizens and foreign nationals is protected by law. This is likely to encourage them to exchange goods and services, and it will increase the prosperity of society. The property law is arguably consistent with current economic policy, and numerous scholars have argued that traditional meaning of socialism does not apply to modern China, with its market economy policy. Also, in 2004, the protection of private property was for the first time affirmed in constitutional law.[113] So the property law was finally implemented by the state after fourteen years' discussion.

However, the Law of Real Right has finally completed and it consists of five parts: (1) general principles; (2) ownership; (3) usufructuary rights; (4) security interest in property rights; and (5) possession. As some scholars suggest, it is a landmark in the Chinese legal history that will contribute to the future development of Chinese civil law.[114]

1.1.8. Chinese Tort Law

On 26 December 2009, the Standing Committee of the National People's Congress passed the tort law. It is composed of twelve chapters: (1) general provision; (2) liability and methods of assuming liability; (3) circumstances to waive and to mitigate liability; (4) specific provisions on tortfeasors; (5) product liability; (6) liability for motor vehicle traffic accident; (7) liability for medical malpractice; (8) liability for environmental pollution; (9) liability for ultrahazardous activity; (10) liability for harm caused by domestic animals; (11) liability for harm caused by objects; and (12) supplementary provisions. The implementation of the tort law in general outline completes the current civil law system in China, which by and large consists of the law of obligations, property law, family law, and inheritance law.

1.1.9. Chinese Civil Code

The current Chinese government started to work on constructing a civil code in the 1950s following the establishment of the People's Republic of China. But so far,

112. Xiantian Gong, yi bu wei bei xian fa he bei li she hui zhu yi ji ben yuan ze de wu quan fa cao an [A Drafted Law of Real Rights Deviating from the Basis Principle of Socialism], 2005.
113. Gebhard Marc Rehm & Hinrich Julius, The New Chinese Property Rights Law: An Evaluation from a Continental European Perspective, *Columbia Journal of Asia Law*, vol. 22, 2007, 177–182.
114. Huixing Liang, Some Opinions and Suggestions on the Draft of Real Property Law, *Front Law China*, vol. 2, 2007, 198–201.

a civil code has not been promulgated. Given the need for drastic social and political change and China's immense economic development, the Chinese legal community recognized the importance of adopting a civil code. In 1998, nine Chinese jurists were appointed to draft a civil code, and the drafting process was originally expected to be completed by the year 2010.[115] The national legislative committee later changed its plans and insisted on drafting the property law and the tort law first. However, drafting a civil code is a tremendous and complicated project that shall be undertaken gradually due to the fact that a civil code is closely connected to social life and economic development. Also, the civil code must reflect Chinese socialism, whilst at the same time using transplants from Western legal systems and the international treaties in order to clear obstacles to trade between China and the West. So a civil code needs to be drafted step by step. However, until now, three academic draft civil codes by Liang Huixing, Wang Liming and Xu Guodong respectively have been completed. From all these three draft civil codes, the uniform contract law has been directly incorporated into the civil code as essentially part of the law of obligations.

1.1.10. Conclusion

The Chinese legal history has long been dominated by the philosophy of Confucianism. Before the twentieth century, morality playing an essential role in traditional society, civil law was a modest factor at best. Before the 1980s, several civil codes were drafted but only the one designed in 1930s was actually implemented. These documents have facilitated and fostered the reception of Western law and the development of Chinese civil law. The *Qing* draft code in particular marked the start of an era of civil law development in China and laid the foundations of a modern Chinese contract law system. In the 1980s, as a result of the government's open-door policy, three contract laws were enacted as an impetus to economic development. However, these laws retained a strong socialist quality and they were often inconsistent with each other. Since the 1990s, the national Chinese economy has transformed into a market economy and China has (successfully) sought WTO membership. These developments necessitated a uniform contract law and in 1999, a new uniform contract law, the CLC, replaced the three contract laws of 1980s. The CLC has clearly been influenced by Western norms and international treaties, but it has retained two essential Confucianist tenets: the predominance of public interest and limitations to individual freedom. Currently, the Chinese civil code drafting process in ongoing and the code is expected to be implemented in the near future. The CLC will be incorporated in the section containing the law of obligations.

115. Wang (1999), *supra* n. 7, 1.

1.2. THE CONVERGENCE OF EUROPEAN CONTRACT LAW

> There shall not be one law at Rome, another at Athens, one now, another hereafter, but one everlasting and unalterable law shall govern all nations for all time.[116]

'Modern civil law was the product of three quite distinct historical influences: the Roman system of particular contracts; the late scholastic and natural law theories of fidelity, liberality, and commutative justice; and the nineteenth-century will theories.'[117] Since Roman times, there has been a systematic regime of contract law,[118] which has strongly influenced modern private law in Europe and even in most parts of the world. As the German Jurist Jhering said, Rome had conquered the world three times: first by force, second through religion and third by means of law, and the third may be the most peaceful and permanent conquest of all.[119] However, Roman jurists appeared to have little interest in theorizing. Despite a fair number of individual contract types in Roman law, no general theory was formed, and Roman jurists did not explain the structure and provisions of these contracts or what features all contracts had in common.[120] The construction of a theoretical framework underlying Roman law started in the eleventh century AD following the rediscovery of the texts of the *Corpus Iuris Civilis* compiled by Justinian in the sixth century AD.[121] Particularly until the fourteenth century, after the translation of Aristotle's *Metaphysics* and *Ethics,* and after the systematic application of Aristotelian philosophy to Christian theology by Thomas Aquinas, the post-glossators progressed to constructing a general theory of contract.[122] The Aristotelian concept of distributive and commutative justice was the basis of their construction, and the late scholastics analysed Roman contract law through three Aristotelian virtues: fidelity, liberality and commutative justice.[123] These virtues married Roman law with Aristotelian philosophy. However, as in the case of Confucianism in China, Aristotle's influence on private law did not extend beyond a philosophical discussion on moral virtue. Yet in contrast with Chinese contract law, modern European contract law fell on fertile ground.

However, in the seventeenth century, jurists rebuilt a theory that was distant from the Aristotle and Thomas philosophy, the result of which was the outcome of

116. Cicero, *De re publica* [On the Commonwealth], cited by Roy Goode, *Contract and Commercial Law: The Logic and Limits of Harmonisation*, 2003 METRO, Institute for Transnational Legal Research, 2.
117. James Gordley, *The Enforceability of Promise in European Contract Law*, Cambridge University Press, 2001, 10.
118. Andrew Borkowski, *Textbook on Roman Law*, Blackstone Press, 1997, 255–262.
119. John William Burgess, *The Foundations of Political Science*, Transaction Publishers, 1994, 38.
120. Gordley (1992), *supra* n. 91, 30–32.
121. Harold J. Berman, *Law and Revolution: The Formation of Western Legal Tradition*, Harvard University Press, 1983, 122–140.
122. *Ibid.*, pp. 245–248.
123. Gordley (2001), *supra* n. 118, 4–5.

the will theory of contract. But the will theory cannot explain many problems in the law of contract, and 'today, we have no generally recognized theory of contract'.[124]

In recent years, as a result of the establishment of a single European market in order to eliminate the barriers to competition between businesses, Europeanization of private law has been an intensively discussed topic since the 1990s.[125] The unification of contract law started in the field of consumer law through directives, the first one of which was issued in 1985.[126] The words unification, harmonization and convergence have often been used to distinguish various levels of Europeanization. While unification indicates that national legal systems completely disappear and a new and uniform law will be applied across all the Europe,[127] convergence reveals a more natural integration compared with the notion of harmonization that suggests a more active process of partial unification.[128] In this dissertation, convergence rather than harmonization or unification will be used.

In the process of private law Europeanization, the form of treaties, regulations, directives and recommendations, which the EU adopted, made a profound impact.[129] The case law from the European Court of Justice, the academic debate as well as educational projects have also contributed to the process of convergence. Amongst the available instruments, directives in particular have served to achieve a substantial level of integration among the laws of Member States, especially in the area of consumer law. Some observers believe that such regulation has contributed to the smooth operation of the internal market, having removed many obstacles to the free movement of persons, goods, services and capital, which resulted from differences between national laws.[130] However, the academic debate and political actions by the EU demonstrate that the present EC contract law rules, which form part of the *acquis communautaire,* are not satisfactory.[131] This is mainly due to the following four reasons.

First, European legislation has, even when seen over the last decades, only touched a tiny area of the veritable ocean of private law. Most of the directives, for

---

124. Gordley (1992), *supra* n. 91, 230–231.
125. Mark van Hoecke, The Harmonisation of Private Law in Europe: Some Misunderstandings, in Mark van Hoecke & Francois Ost, *The Harmonisation of European Private Law*, Hart Publishing, 2000, 1.
126. Council Directive 85/577/EEC of 20 Dec. 1985 to Protect the Consumer in Respect of Contracts Negotiated away from Business Premises.
127. Jan Smits, Convergence of Private Law in Europe: Towards a New *Ius Commune*?, in Esin Orucu & David Nelken, *Comparative Law: A Handbook*, Hart Publishing, 2007, 220.
128. Mark van Hoecke, The Harmonisation of Private Law in Europe: Some Misunderstandings, in Von Hoecke & Ost (2000), *supra* n. 126, 2–3.
129. Ewoud Hondius, European Private Law – Survey 2000–2002, *European Review of Private Law*, vol. 10, 2002, 865.
130. Arthur Hartkamp, Perspectives for the development of a European Civil Law, Paper presented to the Trento Conference of 15 Jul. 1999, 2–3.
131. Brigitta Lurger, The Future of European Contract Law between Freedom of Contract, Social Justice, and Market Rationality, *European Review of Contract Law*, vol. 5, 2005, 443.

instance, concern various individual aspects of consumer protection.[132] For full Europeanization of private law, more general principles and more areas would have to converge. It is worth noting that when Europeans speak of private law, they mostly mean the law of obligations, and sometimes include family law, other consumer law, labour law, etc.[133] But it is undeniable that contract law is an essential and significant part of any such convergence.

Secondly, the legal instruments adopted by the EU are not without flaws. The directives are often non-consistent and sometimes hinder rather than promote convergence.[134] Norms used in the directives are often rather vague, and notions employed by one directive cannot be transferred to others. Taking the notion of damage, for example, the ECJ held that the definition in the Package Travel Directive cannot be applied to the Product Liability Directive, with the result that different definitions of 'damage' operate for different sectors of law.[135] Furthermore, directives frequently adopt no more than a minimum level of protection of weaker parties, leaving intact higher levels of protection in many Member States, and a corresponding diversity between the domestic laws.

Thirdly, problems arising from the enforcement of the instruments make impact on the process of convergence. It is generally accepted that transposition is needed for implementation.[136] However, national courts often find it difficult to apply the abstract notion adopted in the directives to given cases. For example, the notion of good faith, which is employed, such as by the Unfair Terms Directive, will be more difficult to apply by lawyers from legal systems based on common law,[137] which can impair the effect of directives.

Finally, 'since a common legal background is lacking, the conceptual framework and the terminology of the directives are uncertain, and they do not present themselves as parts of an integrated legal system'.[138]

Therefore, although what has been done over the last decades has indeed stimulated the Europeanization of private law, a higher level of contract law convergence is still required for persons, goods, services and capital to move freely within the EU. And nowadays it has been argued that the Europeanization of private law can help shape the European citizenship and a community identity.[139]

In 1982, an independent body of experts, the Commission on European Contract Law headed by Professor Ole Lando and comprising twenty to twenty-five

---

132. Hartkamp (1999), *supra* n. 131, 2.
133. Duncan Kennedy, Thoughts on Coherence, Social Values and National Tradition in Private Law, in Hesselink (2006), *supra* n. 26, 9.
134. Smits (2001), *supra* n. 21, 4.
135. *Simone Leitner* Case, Case C-168/00, [2002] ECR I-2631.
136. Hondius (2002), *supra* n. 130, 865.
137. Jens Karsten & Ali R. Sinai, The Action Plan on European Contract Law: Perspectives for the Future of European Contract Law and EC Consumer Law, *Journal of Consumer Policy*, vol. 26, 2003, 160.
138. Hartkamp (1999), *supra* n. 131.
139. Hugh Collins, *The European Civil Code: The Way Forward*, Cambridge University Press, 2008b, 106–108.

members from all EU Member States, started to work on a European contract law.[140] The members were mostly academics some were practicing lawyers. They were not selected by any government and did not represent their countries officially. In 1995 Part One of the PECL, dealing with performance, non-performance and remedies, was published. Subsequently Parts One and Two, which cover the core rules of contract, formation, authority of agents, validity, interpretation, contents, performance, non-performance and remedies, were published in 1999, followed by Part Three in 2003, which covers plurality of parties, assignment of claims, substitution of new debt, transfer of contract, set-off, prescription, illegality, conditions and capitalization of interest. The objective of the PECL is to 'serve as a basis for the future European Code of Contracts. They could form the first step in the work [on a European civil code]'.[141] With the adoption of the PECL, contract law in the EU has converged to some extent, and a framework for further discussion is now available. But the PECL is a set of non-binding principles regarding contracts. Its scope remains rather narrow and it does not closely relate to other legislations at the EU level. When the PECL is chosen to apply to a contract, it may not suffice when disputes arise; opposing parties will often refer to other fields of laws, such as company law.

It is also argued that the PECL is lacking of the consumer or weaker party protection and thus does not really state the common rules of Europe. To some extent, the critical comments reveal the importance of weaker party protection in modern European contract law, and it is true to say that nowadays weaker party protection is shared by most European legal systems. It is also worth considering that the fundamental principle of good faith and fair dealing, which will be analysed in the second chapter, can be used to protect the weaker party. With the transformation from an individual oriented society into a socially oriented society, fair dealing often concerns substantive fairness. Also, there are various directives regarding consumer law, and the insufficiencies of the PECL could be overcome by merging these components of the *acquis communautaire*.[142] Even so, social justice has been advocated through a Manifesto to be absorbed into European private law, and the DCFR regards it as an underlying value it respects, as stated in the DCFR: 'Justice can also refer to protective justice – where protection is afforded, sometimes in a generalized preventative way, to those in a weak or vulnerable position.'[143]

From the end of the 1980s onwards, a more systematic convergence of European private law has been on the political agenda. Since 1989, the European Parliament has twice[144] taken the initiative to begin work on a European civil code. Under the Dutch presidency of the EU, in 1997 a conference on a European civil

140. Christian Twigg-Flesner, *The Europeanisation of Contract Law*, Routledge, 2008, 13–14.
141. Lando & Beale (2000b), *supra* n. 22, xvii.
142. Hans-W. Micklitz, The Principles of European Contract Law and the Protection of the Weaker Party, *Journal of Consumer Policy*, vol. 27, 2004, 339.
143. Von Bar & Clive (2009), *supra* n. 24, 41.
144. OJ EC 1989 C 158/400, OJ EC 1994 C 205/518.

code was held in Scheveningen in the Netherlands. Although the conference did not advocate the drafting of a European Code to bind all EU Member States, it was at this meeting that Christian von Bar began to set up the Study Group for a European Civil Code.[145] In 1999, the Tampere European Council called for an overall study on the need to approximate Member State's legislation in civil matters in order to eliminate obstacles to the smooth functioning of civil proceedings.[146] A major step taken by the European Commission (EC) was the publication of a Communication[147] to the Council and the Parliament on 11 July 2001 to request responses from academics, lawyers, legislators, and other stakeholders to investigate whether the diversity of contract law caused problems for business transactions and how to prepare legislation. Four options were presented in the Communication: (1) no community action, leaving the problem to the market; (2) the development of non-binding principles of European contract law; (3) improvement and consolidation of the existing private law; and (4) wide-ranging legislative actions.[148] In 2001 and 2002, the Commission received approximately 180 responses from academics and practitioners. The Commission responded to these contributions in February 2003 with its Action Plan[149] and partly reaffirmed its response in the 2004 Follow-Up Communication. According to the Action Plan, the following three strategies are highly desirable: (1) improve the coherence and consistence of the EC *acquis* in the field of contract law;[150] (2) promote the elaboration of the EU-wide standard contract terms;[151] and (3) further reflect on the need and value of a horizontal optional instrument.[152] In the Action Plan, the Commission also suggested drafting a Common Frame of Reference (CFR), whose aim is to provide fundamental principles, definitions and model rules that can assist in the improvement of the existing *acquis communautaire*, and might form the basis of an optional instrument.[153] However, whether the provisions of the CFR would be detailed or 'open-texture' remained unclear in the Action Plan. The Commission further substantiated the stated aim in its follow-up Communication to announce that the CFR should be adopted in 2009 following extensive consultation.[154] Even though the Commission officially disavowed the construction of a code, the possibility of the CFR being created raised many doubts

145. Hondius (2002), *supra* n. 130, 870.
146. SI (1999) 800.
147. European Commission Communication on European Contract Law Com (2001) 398.
148. *Ibid.*
149. A More Coherent European Contract Law – An Action Plan, COM (2003) 68 final, 12 Feb. 2003.
150. *Ibid.*, 15–20.
151. *Ibid.*, 21–23.
152. *Ibid.*, 23–25.
153. Hugh Beale, The European Commission's Common Frame of Reference Project: A Progress Report, *European Review of Contract Law*, vol. 2, 2006, 303–307.
154. Communication from the Commission to the European Parliament and the Council of 10 Nov. 2004 – European Contract Law and the Revision of the *Acquis*: The Way Forward, COM (2004) 651 final.

with academics and politicians alike.[155] In 2005, the Commission evaluated the consumer *acquis* in its First Annual Progress Report on European Contract Law and the *Acquis* Review,[156] which was corroborated at stakeholder meetings in 2006. As the creation of the CFR presented something of an obstacle to the Europeanization of contract law,[157] the review process of eight directives in the area of consumer contract law[158] was separated from the preparation of the CFR.[159] Some legal scholars hold that the *acquis* review of consumer law reveals that the Europeanization of private law a form of minimum harmonization, which has allowed Member States to divert from the standard, set by European legislation towards maximum harmonization, which indicates that no Member State can apply stricter rules than the ones laid down at the EU level.[160]

The Study Group on a European Civil Code (hereinafter Study Group) and the Research Group on the Existing EC Private Law (hereinafter *Acquis* Group) have made an enormous contribution to this convergence. The Study Group, a network of academic lawyers headed by Professor von Bar, has contributed to the Europeanization with its 'Principles of European Law', which, on the basis of the PECL, extends to the entire law of obligations and some aspects of property law. The aim of the *Acquis* Group is to restate the existing contract law as currently found in EC directives and regulations, and judgments of the European Court of Justice. Both Groups have jointly produced the recently published DCFR, which goes beyond the area covered by the PECL and includes specific contracts, torts, unjust enrichment, *negotiorum gestio* and securities in movable property.[161]

On 28 December 2007, the DCFR (interim outline edition) was presented to the EC.[162] 'The books II and III contain many rules derived from the Principles of European Contract Law.'[163] As '[t]he work of the Lando Commission has now been absorbed into the wider project being undertaken by the Study Group on a European Civil Code under the leadership of Professor Christian von Bar',[164] it is thus reasonable to say that the focus of this dissertation is on the contract law section of the DCFR. In 2009, the full edition of the DCFR was published, with some changes having been made to the first seven books of the interim edition, and the last three books, on the rights of movable goods, having been completed.

155. Nils Jansen & Reinhard Zimmermann, Restating the *Acquis Communautaire*? A Critical Examination of the 'Principles of the Existing EC Contract Law', *The Modern Law Review*, vol. 71, 2008, 507.
156. COM (2005) 456 final.
157. Jansen & Zimmermann (2008), *supra* n. 156, 508.
158. COM (2006) 744 final.
159. COM (2007) 447 final.
160. Vanessa Mak, Review of the Consumer *Acquis*: Towards Maximum Harmonization?, *European Review of Private Law*, vol. 1, 2009, 55–73.
161. Von Bar & Clive (2008), *supra* n. 27.
162. Jan Smits, *A European Law on Unjustified Enrichment? A Critical View of the Law of Restitution in the Draft Common Frame of Reference*, Paper presented at the Conference European Private Law Beyond the CFR at the Universitat de Lleida, 20–26 Oct. 2007, 1.
163. Von Bar & Clive (2008), *supra* n. 27, 24.
164. Goode (2003), *supra* n. 117, 10.

The goal of the DCFR is to serve as a draft for a CFR to be adopted by the European legislator.

However, because of many differences between the legal systems of the Member States, the preparation of the DCFR encountered various obstacles. It is widely accepted that in Europe, there are at least four categories of private law regimes.[165] The first one refers to the common law system of England and Ireland, in which judge-made law dominates. The second category is that of the traditional civil law countries, in which a civil code is functionally determined by the judges. Within this category, the private law systems based on the Code Napoleon, such as those of France, Belgium, Spain and Italy, and those based on the German civil code, for instance in Germany, Austria and the Netherlands are distinguished. The third group refers to the Scandinavian countries, such as Denmark and Sweden, and the last one concerns countries that have recently revised their civil codes – e.g., Poland, the Czech Republic, and Hungary. During the process of Europeanization, scholars have discussed several other forms of convergence to find out what approach will be the best for the EU. The first of these is the unification through international conventions.[166] In the past several years, the CISG has been ratified by nearly seventy-six countries, and it is believed that convergence through treaties of this kind could contribute to the Europeanization process. One problem with this kind of convergence is that in case of disputes there is no highest court to interpret the treaty authoritatively. Also, a treaty needs to be approved by the Member States' national parliaments in order for it to be legitimate. The second approach concerns natural spontaneous, convergence and is influenced by Hayek's theory.[167] The convergence of European private law is left to the natural competition of legal systems, the best of which will survive through selection by the market. However, Hayek's liberalism has been criticized for its rejection of extreme positivism and nationalism; a society built on a market economy combined with solidarity, fairness and loyalty is more suggested.[168] The third approach is the bottom-up method, creating a European private law through legal science and legal education.[169] The *ius commune* based on the Justinian code of Roman law had created a common legal scholarly tradition for Europe in the seventeenth and eighteenth centuries, so a new *ius commune* built on legal science and legal education, for example, the *Ius Commune* Research

165. Jan Smits, Convergence of Private Law in Europe: Towards a New *Ius Commune*?, in Orucu & Nelken (2007), *supra* n. 128, 219–221.
166. Jan Smits, Convergence of Private Law in Europe: Towards a New *Ius Commune*?, in Orucu & Nelken (2007), *supra* n. 128, 223–224.
167. Jan Smits, European Private Law: A Plea for a Spontaneous Legal Order, in Deirdre M. Curtin, *European Integration and Law*, Intersentia, 2006, 85–87.
168. Martijn W. Hesselink, A Spontaneous Order for Europe? Why Hayek's Libertarianism Is Not the Right Way forward for European Private Law, Centre for the Study of European Contract Law Working Paper Series No. 2008/07, 1–31.
169. Jan Smits, Convergence of Private Law in Europe: Towards a New *Ius Commune*?, in Orucu & Nelken (2007), *supra* n. 128, 229–231.

School can further contribute to the Europeanization of private law. The fourth approach involves drafting principle,[170] such as the PECL.

Currently, some other projects have also produced several scientific outcomes for the convergence of private laws, such as the book of *Good Faith in European Contract Law* edited by Zimmermann and Whittaker, and *Enforceability of Promises in European Contract Law* by James Gordley (Trento project), which aspire to help build a common European legal culture. Another group *ius commune* with its casebooks has also contributed for the common law of Europe. However, the difference between the Trento project and the DCFR/PECL is that the first one to provide 'a picture of the law existing in the European systems in a number of important areas which has to be as reliable and exact as possible', whereas the latter is to 'find out, on the basis of comparative research, which solution may best regulate certain legal problems in a common way, discarding at the same time the possibility that core divergence (and certainly not only details) might be justified on many grounds'.[171] In addition, Gandolfi started working on a Code of Contract Law around 1990, but compared with the DCFR/PECL, the Gandolfi Code has been drafted by a single person (and in French).[172] Besides these, some international model laws have also contributed to the process of Europeanization, particularly, the CISG has inspired the work on the PECL[173] and the DCFR has also considered the Unidroit Principle. But the DCRF/PECL are more concerned with presenting the common core of contract law in Europe, while the CISG/Unidroit Principle regard common rules at the international level. Of this scientific yield, the DCFR/PECL can be considered the best approach to studying European contract law (although the issue whether the DCFR/PECL can be legitimately presented as a common rule of Europe is still under discussion).

1.2.1. Academic Reasons

The convergence of European contract law started in the 1980s in the form of for example, directives and case law – the contract rules contained within that law can be regarded within the concept of European contract law. The DCFR, however, is a combination of existing EC contract rules and the remains, from which a general idea about European contract rules may be formed. The American Restatements of Law may serve as an example. Their purpose is to systematically state common rules of American law that have been accepted by most American states. In 1923, the American Law Institute was founded to make the common law simpler, more coherent and accessible. The first Restatement of Contracts was published in 1932, and work on the second edition started in 1951. Most of the Restatements are now

170. *Ibid.*, 231–233.
171. Nik J. de Boer, The Theoretical Foundations of the Common Core of European Private Law Project: A Critical Appraisal, *European Review of Private Law*, vol. 5, 2009, 842.
172. Hondius (2002), *supra* n. 130, 870–871.
173. Hartkamp (1999), *supra* n. 131, 3–4.

in their second edition, and some of them are in their third. Although the courts are not bound by them, the restatements, until 1 March 1995, had been cited 129,533 times throughout the United States,[174] and lawyers frequently cite the Restatements in their briefs.[175] These facts are proof to the success of the Restatements as a common core of American law.

The Lando Commission drew on the American experience with Restatements. The Restatement method has been adopted in the PECL, although their objectives differ: the Lando Commission attempts to present and restate a common core of European contract law, whereas the object of American Restatements is to clarify and simplify the law to meet social needs, to improve justice and to encourage the scientific legal works of American law. Above all, the Restatements present the rules that are accepted by most states. In Europe, however, it is difficult for national contract laws to be harmonized at the EU level, due to the diversity of legal systems, languages, societies, law finding procedures as well as (legal) cultures. The Lando Commission has been concerned with the diversity among different systems, but has also tried to present and restate a common core of European contract law.

1.2.2. Political Reasons

The purpose of the DCFR is to pave the way for the CFR. The Study Group is to meet the political aim of constructing a CFR (as advocated by the Action Plan), and the *Acquis* Group is 'supposed to formulate a system of European private law, with the primary and secondary acts of EC legislation as well as their judicial interpretation by the European Court of Justice as authoritative basis'.[176] Both groups have similar political aims, and the DCFR is very much a joint effort of the Study Group and the *Acquis* Group. It is true to say that until now there have been no other academic works with a stronger or at least official mandate from political organs or legislative instruments than the DCFR. Furthermore, the PECL has been invested with some political effects that parties within the EU can opt for. So focusing on the DCFR/PECL roughly equals looking into political instrument on contract law. However, the political fate of the DCFR is not quite certain. '[I]s it a stepping stone towards a European Civil Code, or at least a Contract Code? Or will it end up in the drawers of the Brussels bureaucracy?'[177] Yet the objective of the DCFR

174. Jens Karsten & Gosta Petri, Towards a Handbook on European Contract Law and Beyond: The Commission's 2004 Communication European Contract Law and the Revision of the *Acquis*: The Way Forward, *Journal of Consumer Policy*, vol. 28, 2005, 40.
175. Richard Hyland, The American Experience: Restatements, the UCC, Uniform Laws, and Transnational Coordination, in Arthur Hartkamp, Martijn Hesselink, Ewoud Hondius, Carla Joustra, Edgar du Perron & Muriel Veldman (eds), *Towards a European Civil Code*, Kluwer Law International, 2004, 59–60.
176. Jansen & Zimmermann (2008), *supra* n. 156, 509.
177. Ewoud Hondius, The Draft Common Frame of Reference: Building Block or Stumbling Block for a European Civil Code?, *European Review of Private Law*, vol. 4, 2009, 483.

drafting groups at least is clear: to make it 'function as a legislators' guide or toolbox'.[178]

1.2.3. Legal Reasons

In order to prepare a European civil code, it is necessary to have a common language for future discussions. The PECL provides some common principles and terms that can serve as a basis for future convergence, and most parts of the PECL have, with some modifications, found their way into the DCFR. So it is reasonable to say the DCFR/PECL can serves as a legal basis for the convergence of future European private law. But then, what about the counter-convergence argument of irreconcilable cultural differences? Opponents for the convergence have argued that European legal systems cannot converge as their underlying legal cultures make them fundamentally and incompatibly different.[179] With culture being described as 'frameworks of intangibles within which interpretive communities operate and which have normative force for these communities'.[180] Some legal scholars regard legal culture as the attitudes towards the law,[181] and opponents argue that the harmonization of law is only conceivable within a sufficiently homogeneous legal culture. Proponents, however, insist that every culture, including the legal culture, is an open and dynamic entity instead of a closed and static one so that preparing a civil code will lead to 'a complete rethinking of fundamental structures, distinctions, concepts and principles'.[182] In discussion about the relationship between national culture and law, three general strategies can be discerned.[183]

The first one denies the close relationship between law and national culture, which means that law and society are not closely related. The second one argues that law and national culture cannot be separated from each other. Pierre Legrand is one of the adherents of this strategy. The last one insists that the legal culture can influence people's behaviour, but not determine everything.

It seems reasonable to assume that underlying differences in legal culture result in system differences and that a European civil code cannot erase these differences. It is the same in Chinese private law. Although modern China has

178. Von Bar & Clive (2009), *supra* n. 24, 62.
179. Mark van Hoecke, The Harmonisation of Private Law in Europe: Some Misunderstandings, in Von Hoecke & Ost (2000), *supra* n. 126, 3.
180. Pierre Legrand, European Legal Systems Are Not Converging, *The International and Comparative Law Quarterly*, vol. 45, 1996, 56.
181. Jan M. Smits, Legal Culture as Mental Software, or: How to Overcome National Legal Culture?, in Thomas Wilhelmsson, Elina Paunio & Annika Pohjolainen, *Private Law and the Many Cultures of Europe*, Kluwer Law International, 2007, 141–152.
182. Mark van Hoecke, The Harmonisation of Private Law in Europe: Some Misunderstandings, in Von Hoecke & Ost (2000), *supra* n. 126, 5–10.
183. Jan M. Smits, Legal Culture as Mental Software, or: How to Overcome National Legal Culture?, in Wilhelmsson & Paunio & Pohjolainen (2007), *supra* n. 182, 145–147.

transplanted various concepts and legal reasoning from the West, Chinese private law still differs considerably from Western private law, because Chinese society is rooted in a different culture and history, and certain notions and provisions will thus be interpreted differently. On the other hand, convergences do not inevitably and exclusively imply that there should only be a uniform civil code in Europe; it can also mean that diversity is diminishing naturally as globalization progresses. The convergence advocated by the EC is a number of commonly shared principles instead of eliminating the diversity of national legal systems. Codification can then be understood as a framework within which diverse views may continue to flourish alongside a set of common principles. Another obvious example may be found from Roman times. In Roman law, *ius civile* dealt with issues involving only Roman citizens whereas *ius gentium* applied to all people regardless of their nationality. In today's Europe, a European civil code could be seen to some extent as *ius gentium* to govern all cross-boarder transactions within the EU, while national private law could be considered the *ius civile* for strictly national transactions. Both levels of law could coexist and not be incompatible. Moreover, 'the American experience suggests that the principal obstacle to [the] European codification maybe nothing more than an overly rigid understanding of what codification requires'.[184] The adoption of the PECL confirms that it is possible to have a code that consists of common principles.

1.2.4. Economic Reasons

The core essence of private law Europeanization in fact associates with the ideal of a single market. A converging contract law can encourage market transactions in theory, whereas differences in contract law structure and terminology, fundamental concepts, classifications, and legal policies can be seen as inimical to the efficient functioning of a single market. The DCFR/PECL could overcome these obstacles and contribute to a smooth functioning of the single market. EC legislation in the area of contract law has gone some way to removing obstacles from the free movement of persons, goods and services by way of convergence of contract laws. However, the economic reasons for convergence have been called into question because of the lack of empirical research, with some scholars arguing that in practice the diversity of private laws have not posed an obstacle to creating a single market, and this calls for empirical data to be collected. In recent years, the creation of a European identity and the promotion of social justice have substantially fostered the convergence of European private law.

The DCFR/PECL, then, contains a restatement of contract law rules common to all EU Member States. It establishes the basis of European private law convergence, which could offer guidance to legislators, national courts and academics, with sufficient autonomy for contracting parties, and a basis for community law to

184. Richard Hyland, The American Experience: Restatements, the UCC, Uniform Laws, and Transnational Coordination, in Hartkamp et al. (2004), *supra* n. 176, 70.

govern contracts.[185] But whether the DCFR/PECL will be successful as a common core of contract laws in Europe depends entirely on lawyers, judges and legislators who use them, and to what extent subsequent legislation will be inspired by them.

1.2.5. Conclusion

Roman private law and its centuries-long scholarly interpretation are the foundations of modern European private law. The Europeanization of modern private law is creating a more common European legal culture. Both the official instruments implemented by the EC and scholarly outputs make great contributions to works realizing a single market and social justice. Of the output in the field of contract law, the DCFR/PECL, a restatement of a common core of contract law rules within the EU, are favourably appreciated by the European legal community and they serve as the basis for the future contract law convergence. The DCFR, however, goes beyond the PECL and also covers the entire field of patrimonial law. However, it is argued '[as] the non-contractual branches of patrimonial law (tort, unjustified enrichment, transfer of property, real securities in movables) have developed much less homogeneously in the various European legal systems than the law of contract, the drafts published by the Study Group cannot claim to be a genuinely European text of reference in the same ways as the Principles of European Contract Law'.[186] Yet the law of contracts in the DCFR mainly derives from the PECL, which has been already received favourable attention by the legal society. It is therefore fair to say that the DCFR/PECL reveal the characteristics and values of and the development tendency in the law of contract in the EU.

1.3. COMPARATIVE CONCLUSION

Traditionally, China was dominated by the 'Morality' from Confucianism, and the modern concept of 'civil law' may not find its root in the Chinese legal history. On the contrary, in Europe, the private law had been developed comprehensively since the Roman times. During the medieval era, the jurists gave Roman private law a systematic philosophical basis. Founded on these developments, the modern contract law in Europe can be well constructed. Referring to the core element of contract law, which is freedom of contract, historically it was not recognized in China. But since the 1980s, when China opened its door to the world and with the implementation of 'market economy', the private law has developed sharply in order to be consistent with the economic needs. In contrast, in Europe, currently the Europeanization of private law has been hotly on agenda. In the past some decades, the EU has harmonized the private law through the means of treaties, directives,

185. Anthony Chamboredon, The Debate on a European Civil Code: For an 'Open Texture', in Von Hoecke & Ost (2000), *supra* n. 126, 92.
186. Jansen & Zimmermann (2008), *supra* n. 156, 506.

regulations, recommendations and ECJ cases. The academic works groups, such as the Lando Commission, the *Acquis* Group, the Gandolfi Code project, Trento Common Core project, *Ius Commune* Research School and the Study Group on European Civil Code etc. have substantively contributed to the Europeanization process. However, for the establishment of a single market and the construction of a European citizenship, a more coherent Europeanization is required. The political CFR thus has been advocated by the EU Commission. The DCFR, an outcome combined by the *Acquis* Group and the Study Group on a European Civil Code, tries to serve the political aims of Europeanization and attempts to be a toolbox for the European private law. Although the legitimacy and feasibility of the DCFR to be regarded as a common core of European private law are still under discussion, the author considers that it is the best approach until now to look into the contract law in Europe.

Chapter 2
Fundamental Principles of Modern Contract Laws[187]

Fundamental principles are abstractions from all the rules, and are the leading principles for the whole of contract law. Not only do they represent the essence and spirit of the law, but they are also the guiding principles for the drafting, interpreting, implementing and studying of the law.[188] These principles, in practice, could serve to guide or inform, or even act as the legal basis for the resolution of various contractual disputes.[189] This chapter therefore attempts to examine the CLC and the DCFR/PECL to reveal their fundamental elements.

2.1. FUNDAMENTAL PRINCIPLES OF CHINESE CONTRACT LAW

Like many other laws, the CLC contains certain fundamental principles that represent underlying policies, on the basis of which legislation is formulated and the law influenced.[190] Although the CLC consists of numerous transplanted terms and provisions of Western origin, significant elementary concepts in Western laws often carry a different meaning in Chinese law.[191] This subsection therefore attempts to discuss these to reveal their characteristics.

---

187. This chapter is revised, based on the article 'Towards a Social Value Convergence: a Comparative Study of Fundamental Principles of Contract Law in the EU and China', published on Oxford University Comparative Law Forum in December 2009.
188. Wang (1999), *supra* n. 7, 9.
189. *Ibid.*, 9.
190. Guodong Xu, *min fa ji ben yuan ze jie shi* [*Interpretation of Fundamental Principles of Civil Law*], China University of Political Science and Law Press, 1992, 8–15.
191. Larusson & Sharp (1999), *supra* n. 30, 67.

The following elements characterize fundamental principles in the CLC:

(1) Not only do the fundamental principles guide the rules of implementation, but also they can reflect the spirit as well as value orientation of contract law. They are determined by social and economic life, and guide all stages of a contract.
(2) They are uncertain, because they do not refer to the concrete rights and obligations of parties, with the effect that contractual parties cannot predict the precise consequences that these principles will have on their rights.
(3) They are mandatory rules, so contractual parties cannot exclude their application in contracts. Fundamental principles are part of mandatory statutory law that provides legitimacy to the judgment of a court.
(4) They serve for the interpretation of the law and may apply to specific cases where the law fails to govern specific rules.[192]

Although the principles of equal legal status between parties, of fairness, of respect for social ethics and morality and of obedience to the law and regulations are often regarded as fundamental to the CLC,[193] some scholars hold the view that 'contract law is primarily influenced by three major principles, namely freedom of contract, good faith and fostering transactions'.[194] Others such as Jiang Ping have argued that the designing of the CLC is based on the principles of uniformity, freedom of contract, protecting the interests of creditors and functionalism.[195] Some others also believe the fundamental principles of the CLC are equality, voluntariness, fairness, exchange of equivalent values, good faith and complying with the laws and policies of the state.[196] By combining these viewpoints with the guiding principles,[197] as well as the purpose of contract law, namely 'protecting the lawful

192. Ling (2002), *supra* n. 10, 39–54.
193. Chen (2001), *supra* n. 104, 169.
194. Wang (1999), *supra* n. 7, 2.
195. Ping Jiang, Drafting the Uniform Contract Law in China, *Columbia Journal of Asian Law*, 1996a, 245–255.
196. Zhao Yuhong, Law of Contract, in Wang & Jone (1999), *supra* n. 9, 227–228.
197. The guiding principles for the drafting are as follows: (1) Considering the conditions of reforming and the door-opening policy, developing socialist market economy, establishing the uniform and integrating into the international market, the legislation should conclude our own legal experience and learn widely from other developed countries in order to be consistent with the international treaties and custom laws, and reflect the common rules of modern economy market. (2) For presenting the principles of party autonomy in order to protect the freedom of contract within the law, public order and social ethics, the legislation should not limit the freedom of contract without serious proper reason. (3) Considering the era characteristics of law making and implementing, the legislation should be suitable to the requirements after the success of the socialist economy market, also shall be suitable to the transforming from the centrally planned economy to the market economy. (4) The values of the contract law are economic efficiency, social justice, convenience and security transaction. The legislation should focus on the development of productivity and social interests, protecting the interests of consumer and employee, safeguarding the social order of economy market. It should reflect the simply and rapid characteristic of modern market economy and

rights and interests of the contractual parties, safeguarding social and economic order and promoting socialist modernization',[198] the author in this dissertation believes that the fundamental principles of the CLC should be divided into the voluntary contract and socioeconomic valuation.

2.1.1. Voluntariness

The wording of Article 4 CLC implies that 'voluntariness' should be used rather than 'freedom of contract'.[199] One should remember that 'freedom of contract' was not accepted in China until very recently, in spite of the fact that since the beginning of the twentieth century, Chinese contract theory has been derived from the continental European and common law systems. However, the concept of freedom of contract has been gradually accepted in recent years. The reasons for this reluctance to adopt it are as follows:

First, 'freedom of contract', to a large extent, represents the concept of 'the individual' or 'liberty'. Most scholars agree that Chinese legal history and the spirit of modern law are influenced by Confucianism. However, Confucianism has no room for the development of liberty or individualism,[200] so it is thus reasonable to say that Confucianism is largely averse to 'freedom of contract'.

Secondly, since the establishment of the People's Republic of China in 1949, the strict running of the economy has been centrally planned, with the effect that it was impossible for individuals or business entities to have free access to the market. The economic plan and mandatory policies were playing an essential role at that time. Accordingly, it was impossible to recognize 'freedom of contract' as a fundamental principle under such a system.

Lastly, 'freedom of contract' has been criticized in China as a capitalist concept, which must be avoided by any socialist system.[201] In China, it has long been believed that the 'ideology of individualism' marks the main difference between capitalism and socialism. This belief continues to influence minds in China even today, which is why the CLC uses the notion of 'voluntariness' rather than that of 'freedom of contract' in the context of contract formation, reflecting the transformation from a centrally planned economy to a market economy, and considering the purpose of developing a socialist market economy.

---

convenience transaction as well as the form and procedure for the transaction security. (5) The provisions should be operational and the expression should be simple and exact. From Zhang (1995), *supra* n. 107, 4–7.

198. Article 1 CLC: 'This law is enacted with a view to protecting the lawful rights and interests of contracting parties, maintaining social and economic order and promoting socialist modernisation.'

199. Article 4 CLC: 'A party is entitled to enter into contract voluntary under the law, and no entity or individual may unlawfully interfere with such right.'

200. Hahm (2006), *supra* n. 55, 481.

201. Zhang (2006), *supra* n. 71, 242.

Basically, the principle of 'voluntariness' involves two elements: (1) the rights of contractual parties to enter into a contract voluntarily and within the limits of the law; and (2) the prohibition on others to interfere with the contract illegally. Admittedly, it is often believed in Chinese academic circles that 'voluntariness' is the same as 'freedom of contract'. However, the following will reveal the considerable differences that exist between these two notions.

First, concerning the content, 'freedom of contract' recognizes the autonomy of individuals to enter into a binding agreement, to choose the other contracting party, to determine the terms and contents of the agreement, to modify or terminate the contract by mutual consent, and to choose the form of a contract.[202] By contrast, 'voluntariness' is much narrower and essentially limited to the autonomy to enter into a contract.[203] And while 'freedom of contract' governs every stage of the contracting process, 'voluntariness' relates only to the initial stage of contract formation, giving parties a smaller amount of power to determine their affairs through agreements.

Secondly, concerning the essence, some scholars have argued that 'freedom of contract' focuses on maximum economic efficiency, promotes parties' ability to exercise their full creative potential and establishes appropriate business relationships that possess all the specific nuances required in such a relationship.[204] 'Voluntariness', by contrast, is subject to government intervention.[205]

Lastly, where background was concerned, 'freedom of contract' was historically derived from the consensus contract in Roman law, and became the cornerstone of modern contract law after the French Civil Code was adopted in 1804.[206] It represents the essence of a market economy, while 'voluntariness', which was derived from GPCL in 1986,[207] reflects the planned economy or the transition from the planned economy to the market economy.[208]

It is interesting to note that when the redrafting process for contract law began in 1993, an intensive debate arose over whether freedom of contract should be incorporated as a general principle. Some scholars held the view that, although the ideology had developed rapidly during the time of classical contract law, in the twentieth century many states strengthened their intervention in contracts, with the effect that this principle gradually declined. So, in Chinese contract law, the incorporation of necessary limitations into contractual freedom must be included in order to maintain the public interest and to protect the weaker parties.[209] This

202. Ping Jiang, lun xin he tong fa zhong de he tong zi you yuan ze yu cheng shi xing yong yuan ze [The Principles of Freedom of Contract and Good faith in New Contract Law], *zheng fa lun tan* [Politics and Law Forum], vol. 1, 1999c, 3–5.
203. *Ibid.*, 3–5.
204. Zhang (2006), *supra* n. 71, 246.
205. *Ibid.*
206. *Ibid.*, 241.
207. Article 4, GPCL: 'In civil activities, the principles of voluntariness, fairness, making compensation for equal value, honesty and credibility shall be observed.'
208. Jiang (1996a), *supra* n. 196, 245–255.
209. Jiang (1999c), *supra* n. 203, 3–5.

viewpoint, however, was criticized by most scholars, who insisted that although many developed nations have indeed strengthened intervention in contracts, the principle of 'freedom of contract' still remains fundamental. Considering the long Chinese history of intense centralized planning, the elimination of autonomy and intensive interference from the government in private law matters, an expansion of contractual freedom rather than further restrictions is what is needed by the markets.[210] Therefore, in the first drafting proposal in January 1995, 'freedom of contract' was stated as a general principle, namely, that 'the parties shall have the freedom of contract within the boundary of law and no unit, organization or individual shall unlawfully interfere with'.[211] This provision, however, was revised into 'the parties shall have the right equally and voluntarily to make contract according to law. None of the parties shall impose its own will on the other and no unit or individual shall unlawfully interfere with the parties' right' on 14 May 1997.[212] Later, on 20 August 1998, the provision was changed again to read 'a party is entitled to enter into a contract voluntarily under the law and no entity or individual may unlawfully interfere with such right', which was adopted in 1999.[213]

The history of this drafting process reveals that although 'voluntariness' eventually replaced contractual freedom, the basic notion of 'freedom of contract' has been widely accepted amongst academics. The concept of 'voluntariness' embodies the core essence of 'freedom of contract', which endows the contractual party with the autonomy and freedom to decide on the transactions they enter into, and contributes to bring about the efficient allocation of social and economic resources. However, due to the influence of Confucianism and a historically centrally planned economy, it is necessary for the state to exercise intervention measures to ensure that contracts are sufficiently fair and equal, and also that the parties' interests are not detrimental to the welfare of the state and society. Therefore, the CLC also imposes limitations on 'freedom of contract' to prevent its abuses, and for the state to regulate the economy as well as maintain public order.[214] Generally speaking, in Chinese contract law, 'freedom of contract' is reflected in the principle of voluntary contract, but limited to the following aspects:

(1) We look at the legal aspect. The CLC sets a number of mandatory rules that require the contract to be concluded consistently with the laws. Articles 3 to 7 specify the contract should be concluded voluntarily, in good faith and in accordance with fairness. These principles were made more specific through concrete doctrines such as validity of contract, so if a contract was made contrary to a general principle, then it was not

210. *Ibid.*, 3–5.
211. The Introduction to the Contract of Law of China and its Major Drafts, edited by the Civil Law Office, the Legal Affairs Committee of the Standing Committee of the National People's Congress, China Law Press, 2000, 8–18.
212. Zhang (2006), *supra* n. 71, 242.
213. *Ibid.*
214. Ling (2002), *supra* n. 10, 40–41.

enforceable. Except for the mandatory rules in the CLC, 'freedom of contract' should also be observed in other substantive and procedural laws and regulations. For example, government approval is needed for some kinds of contracts in China such as the joint venture contract, which has to be reviewed and approved by the state competent department in charge of foreign economic relations and trade.[215] Legal aspects limiting the freedom of contract in the CLC include all the mandatory rules provided in all the laws and administrative regulations concerning the contract or civil activities.

(2) We have the state aspect. Article 38 of the CLC requires that the contract should be concluded under mandatory state or public order plans that can be understood as a limitation from the state aspect, which includes rules pertaining to socioeconomic order, state mandatory plans, policy and administrative supervision, which are intended to maintain the interests of the state. In addition, although social ethics or social evaluations also play an essential role in Chinese society, they have never been defined precisely in either the CLC or the GPCL. But they are always used together with public order in many cases,[216] so public order serves as a limitation to individual freedom. As well as public order, policy is another important tool for enforcing state plans. It derives from the Communist Party and the government machine, and plays an essential role in limiting the freedom of contractual parties. Any contracts violating the interests of the state will not be enforceable.

2.1.2. Socioeconomic Valuation

'Socioeconomics' literally means involving social and economic factors. It is frequently used for areas of law closely connected to social issues, such as labour law. The present dissertation uses this terminology to describe Chinese contract law. It has been demonstrated above that the CLC reveals strong Chinese characteristics, even though it borrows numerous concepts and provisions from Western norms and international treaties. As law is generally embedded in culture, contract law reflects the social life of a particular people. In the case of Chinese contract law, the present author believes that certain characteristics have evolved from traditional social ethics and from the current economic situation. In the following parts, several fundamental CLC principles that are the result of such a socioeconomic valuation will be analysed.

215. Article 3, Law of People's Republic of China on Chinese Foreign Equity Joint Ventures, Revised on 1 Jul. 2003.
216. Zhang (2006), *supra* n. 71, 62.

2.1.2.1. Traditional Social Ethics

When performing obligations and rights under a contract, parties must adhere to the generally accepted moral, social and commercial standards in place: 'Confucianism made a practical importance to the Chinese traditional ethics, for twenty-five centuries it has been the life and spirit of the dragon kingdom.'[217] Even nowadays, Confucianism deeply influences the moral and social ethics of Chinese society. This part therefore attempts to analyse the principles of fairness, good faith and public interests from the roots of Confucianism.

2.1.2.1.1. Fairness

The principle of fairness requires equality in the values of respective obligations between the contractual parties and reasonableness in the allocation of risks, of which the function is primarily to prevent the stronger party from abusing its bargaining power and from imposing unconscionable terms on the weaker party. Fairness has its roots in the idea that 'the relation between the contractual parties shall be maintained to the extent that the rights and obligations are reasonably and justly allocated and shared',[218] which is consistent with the concept of righteousness (*yi*) found in Confucianism. From some current arguments, the Confucian idea of righteousness (*yi*) is similar to the notion of 'justice' in the West. As pointed out by John Rawls, justice is fairness,[219] and it is reasonable to say that the concept of righteousness (*yi*) in Confucianism, to some extent, also bears a resemblance to the Western notion of 'fairness'. In Confucianism, righteousness (*yi*) focuses principally on what is right or fitting, which depends on the reasonable judgment.[220] It may be construed as 'reasoned judgment concerning the right thing to do in particular exigencies',[221] or 'the oughtness of a situation which focuses mainly on the right act as appropriate to the particular situation that a moral agent confronts'.[222] Nevertheless, the virtue of righteousness (*yi*) constitutes the fundamental principle of morality, as it forms the necessary component to a virtuous life and 'restrains the inclinations towards material goods and desires of pleasure and comfort'.[223]

Righteousness (*yi*) is a guiding principle for all human relations,[224] and it is always trying to achieve a situation in which both sides are satisfied.[225] Under the

217. Keijiro Nakamura, The History and Spirit of Chinese Ethics, *International Journal of Ethics*, vol. 8, 1987, 86–87.
218. Zhang (2006), *supra* n. 71, 74.
219. John Rawls, *A Theory of Justice*, Belknap Press of Harvard University, 1999.
220. A.S. Cua, Yi (I) and Li: Rightness and Rites, in Cua (2003), *supra* n. 47, 842.
221. *Ibid.*
222. *Ibid.*, 333.
223. *Ibid.*, 842.
224. Sam Dragga, Ethical Intercultural Technical Communication: Looking through the Lens of Confucian Ethics, *Technical Communication Quarterly*, vol. 8, 1999, 369.
225. Quanyu Huang, Richard S. Andrulis & Tong Chen, *A Guide to Successful Business Relations with the Chinese: Opening the Great Wall's Gate*, International Business, 1994, 192–193.

basis of righteousness (*yi*) in Confucianism, both the GPCL and the CLC have treated the concept of 'fairness' as a fundamental principle. As stated in the GPCL, 'fairness and making equal compensation should be obeyed'.[226] The CLC also requires contractual parties to 'abide by the principle of fairness in defining the rights and obligations of each party'.[227]

In general, fairness concerns mainly the contents of the contract, with the purpose of achieving a balance in the rights and obligations between the parties,[228] while its function plays an essential role in Chinese contract law. The essence of fairness is to realize the 'social justice' in society, and it is even reasonable to say the achievement of 'social justice' is the driving force of traditional Chinese law.[229]

Since the notion of 'fairness' is difficult to define, it has been left to the courts to apply on a case-by-case basis. In judicial practice, two rules are commonly used for determining whether 'fairness' has been achieved. The first is the 'fair distribution of rights and obligation' rule,[230] under which a party is required to afford the duties that are proportionate to the rights this party has – or claims to have – under the contract. The issue concerning the remedies for invalid contracts, for instance, requires the party at fault to indemnify the other for its final loss sustained. If both parties are at fault, then both have to afford their liabilities respectively.[231] The other rule is 'reasonable and just allocation of risk'.[232] In business transactions, many unpredictable risks can materialize at any time. The principle of 'fairness' therefore requires the contractual parties to share the risks equally and justly. Taking the case of 'force majeure', for instance, both parties have to share the risks and damages fairly and justly according to the circumstances and performance of both parties.[233]

There can therefore be no doubt that 'fairness' as a fundamental principle in the CLC originates from the righteousness (*yi*) of Confucianism.

2.1.2.1.2. Good Faith

There is an express provision in the CLC that requires the parties to 'conduct themselves honourably, to perform their duties in a responsible way, to avoid abusing their rights, to follow the law and common business practice'.[234] The principle can find its roots in the concept of benevolence (*ren*), the most primary

226. Article 4, GPCL: 'In civil activities, the principles of voluntariness, fairness, making compensation for equal value, honesty and credibility shall be observed.'
227. Article 5 CLC: 'The parties shall observe the principle of fairness in determining their respective rights and duties.'
228. Zhang (2006), *supra* n. 71, 74.
229. Huang (2001), *supra* n. 70, 5–9.
230. Zhang (2006), *supra* n. 71, 73–76.
231. Article 58 CLC.
232. Zhang (2006), *supra* n. 71, 73–76.
233. Article 107–122 CLC.
234. Wang (1999), *supra* n. 7, 15.

virtue of Confucianism. *Ren* could also be construed as goodness or faithfulness.[235] The golden rule from Confucius could be used to explain the essential meaning of benevolence (*ren*): Do not do to others what you do not want them to do to you (*ji suo bu yu, wu shi yu ren*).

It is believed that 'Confucius is nothing more or less than the way that he as a particular person chose to live his life', of which the goal is to 'achieve the harmony and enjoyment for oneself and others through acting appropriately in those roles and relationships that constitute one'.[236] In order to achieve this harmony, the concept of benevolence (*ren*) plays an important role. Not only does it recognize the personal character as a consequence of cultivating one's relationships with others, but it is also fostered to deepen the relationship that takes on the responsibility and obligations of communal living and life.[237] Based on this essential concept, a man who achieves the standards of a gentleman (*junzi*[238]), which consists of trustworthiness and credibility as well as reliability, is considered to be the ideal sage. Confucius expected that all the human virtues – filial piety, fraternal love, loyalty and truthfulness – would need to be obtained to achieve appropriate relationships between people.[239]

Benevolence (*ren*) is not only rooted in everyday conduct, but also is an essential moral obligation for commercial business in China. The standard is applied in particular cases depending primarily on the nature of the contract and other mitigating circumstances. By tracing the principle of good faith, the GPCL recognized this traditional morality and business ethics in 1986, stipulating that 'honesty and credibility should be observed in the civil activities',[240] which was succeeded by the provision in the CLC whereby 'the parties shall abide by the principle of good faith in prescribing their rights and obligations'.[241]

However, similar to fairness, good faith has not been defined in the CLC, but is instead construed commonly as honesty and trustworthiness. Three functions of the principle of good faith in the CLC can be distinguished:

(1) It is a basic principle used to balance interests between parties and between the parties and society. As pointed out above, benevolence (*ren*) aims to harmonize relationships between persons, and advocates people to be honest with and responsible to others. So, in the CLC, the doctrines of pre-contractual liability, ancillary duties and post-contractual liability are incorporated,[242] which require the parties to obey the principle in every stage of the contract.

235. Dragga (1999), *supra* n. 225, 367.
236. Pei-jung Fu, Confucianism: Constructs of Classical Thought, in Cua (2003), *supra* n. 47, 67.
237. *Ibid.*, 68.
238. Junzi has been translated as 'superior man', 'noble man', 'gentleman', etc. In this paper, the author translated into 'gentleman'.
239. Pei-jung Fu, Confucianism: Constructs of Classical Thought, in Cua (2003), *supra* n. 47, 65.
240. Article 4, GPCL.
241. Article 5, CLC.
242. Jiang (1999c), *supra* n. 203, 8–12.

(2) The principle of good faith requires the parties to keep their word. As advocated by Confucianism, benevolence or faithfulness (*ren*) match one's words with one's deeds, and failure to deliver on a promise is thus a failure of morality.[243] Based on this ideology, the CLC therefore requires the parties to abide by the contract. Even if it is deficient in some way, the contractual parties still have to endeavour to alleviate the defects and try their utmost to perform their obligations.[244]

(3) While tremendous social and economic changes are occurring in China, many laws and regulations are not suitable for the current economic situation. The principle of good faith, however, could fill the legal vacuum and help to interpret contracts and laws, in order to achieve the necessary balance of interests between the parties.[245]

In many civil law countries, the principle of good faith has been considered since the 1970s, the highest guiding principle for the law of obligations. In China, it is also a significantly important principle because of both traditional ethics and current economic situations. Some scholars even compartmentalize good faith in the CLC into more detailed aspects:[246]

(1) before a contract is concluded, especially during the negotiations for an agreement, the parties have a duty to treat each other, and to cooperate to make the contract, in a good and faithful manner;
(2) after concluding the contract, the parties should take all the necessary steps to prepare and cooperate for the performance of the contract;
(3) while the contract is being performed, parties should assist each other and faithfully notify each other of relevant events;
(4) after the contract has been performed, the parties have an obligation to keep confidential any business secrets they have obtained from the other party during the contract period; and
(5) when a dispute arises which is related to the contract terms, the parties must interpret them in a truly fair and reasonable way, which respects the mutual benefits.

It is worth mentioning that in the first draft of the CLC, two additional provisions served to confirm the status of good faith, namely: (1) the principle of good faith can be relied on directly in a judgment when there is a vacuum in the law or if the application of a particular provision will be detrimental to social justice;[247] and

243. Dragga (1999), *supra* n. 225, 371.
244. Article 119 CLC: 'Where a party breached the contract, the other party shall take the appropriate measures to prevent further loss, where the other party sustained further loss due to its failure to take the appropriate measures; it may not claim damages for such further loss.'
245. Wang (1999), *supra* n. 7, 15–17.
246. Ping Jiang, *zhong hua ren min gong he guo he tong fa jing jie* [*A Detailed Explanation of Contract Law*], China University of Political Science and Law Press, 1999d, 6–8.
247. Huixing Liang, guan yu zhong guo tong yi he tong fa cao an di san gao [The Third Draft of Chinese Contract Law], *jin ji fa zhi* [*Economics and Law*], vol. 2, 1997, 49.

(2) the lower courts must refer the case to the Supreme Court for a preliminary ruling, as approval from the Supreme Court is required if the lower court resorts directly to the principle of good faith.[248] Eventually, though, these two provisions were deleted, as it was feared that they would give too much discretionary power to judges in a context of problematic judicial independence and therefore encourage possible judicial corruption. Nevertheless, this background reflects that the principle of good faith has been widely respected in the CLC.

2.1.2.1.3. Public Interest

In most legal systems, public interest is considered merely a limitation to the contractual parties' freedom. In the CLC, however, it is a fundamental principle for realizing the welfare of the state and society. In Western legal systems, the boundary of public interest is always defined in a narrow way, in order to respect the will and freedom of the parties, whilst in China the definition of public interest should be construed in a broad way to reflect the idea that socioeconomic order and mandatory state planning, as well as state policy, are vehicles for maintaining and realizing the welfare of the state.

Public interest is frequently used together with the concept of social ethics. The term 'social public interest' has been adopted in both the GPCL and the CLC. Generally, it is understood to include the concept of social morals and public order. Civil conduct shall be invalid if violating the public interest.[249] Scholars see all of the following as violating social public order: (a) damage to national interests; (b) hampering family relations; (c) violation of sexual morals; (d) violation or infringement of human rights or human dignity; (e) restriction of economic or business activities; (f) violation of fair competition; (g) illegal gambling; (h) infringement of consumer interests; (i) violation of labour protection; and (j) seeking usurious profits.[250] According to traditional culture, obedience to the public interest is a kind of morality for citizens – 'Familial loyalty, ancestor worship, respect for elders and the family as a fundamental basis for an ideal government' are the core principles advocated by Confucius.[251] In the family, the father has absolute power over his wife and children. Being respectful towards elders is seen as good morality that promotes harmonious family relationships. The family, rather than the individual, is regarded as the most basic and fundamental unit of society.[252] Confucianism advocates that we are living in the web of a big family – the state. In this big family, we have to be loyal to each other, which means that citizens should obey the ruler and individual interests must bow towards state

---

248. *Ibid.*
249. Article 54, GPCL: 'A civil conduct shall be the lawful act of a citizen or legal person to establish, change or terminate civil rights and obligations.'
250. Huixing Liang, shi chang jing ji yu gong xu liang shu yuan ze [Market Economy and the Principles of Public Order and Good Morals], *min shang fa lun cong* [Civil and Commercial Law Review], vol. 1, 1999, 57.
251. Hagedorn (1996), *supra* n. 63, 72.
252. Hahm (2006), *supra* n. 55, 487.

interests. The three cardinal principles advocated by Confucianism, which should be observed in order to maintain the stability of the country, are 'ruler over subject, father over son and husband over wife'.[253] Under this influence, it is acceptable that, in Chinese contract law, public interest precedes individual interests, and it is also understandable that policy and mandatory state plans, as well as socioeconomic order, are essential vehicles for limiting individual freedom, which in turn maintain and realize the public interest.

Worth mentioning is that from the establishment of the Republic of China in 1949 through to the 1980s, policy rather than law has been essential for maintaining the order and interests of the state. Even nowadays, it is reasonable to say that policy plays a significant role in society. However, it is unclear if there is any difference between state policy and party policy in Chinese law. In the words of Wang Hanbin, the former vice-chairman of the standing committee of the National People's Congress (NPC), the role of law in China is to establish 'a legal system with Chinese characteristics'.[254] And it is argued by some scholars that the policy of the Chinese Communist Party could dominate these Chinese characteristics.[255] The economic policies of the Chinese Communist Party, which include but are not limited to socioeconomic order and mandatory state plans, are mainly designed to accommodate the situation for the interests of the state or for the majority of its citizens.

It is generally accepted that policy is a supplementary source of law. In modern-day China, with its dramatic changes in the social and economic situations, policy can react flexibly to these changes and thus be a useful tool for the government to take measures in an area where the law is unclear.[256] However, two aspects make this use of policy somewhat problematic. The first is that policy is difficult to predict, so much so that it can make contracts uncertain.[257] Parties will require certain rules in order to predict their risks and interests before concluding the contract, whereas more unpredictable and uncertain elements shall be caused by policies. The second aspect concerns transparency. Generally speaking, most governmental policies in China take the form of internal documents, or are contained in the speeches of political leaders. On other occasions, they are not openly accessible to the public.[258] Nevertheless, in practice, these policies can be considered by judges and sometimes treated as ranking above the law. Even after the adoption of the GPCL, the People's Court frequently applied government policy to civil laws.[259]

---

253. Zhang (2006), *supra* n. 71, 54.
254. Hanbin Wang, NPC Creates Good Legal Environment for Reform and Opening-up, Interview with Wang Hanbin, vice-chairman of the Standing Committee of the NPC, *China Law*, vol. 1, 1995, 57–60.
255. Hogedorn (1996), 17–18.
256. Zhang (2006), *supra* n. 71, 82.
257. *Ibid.*
258. *Ibid.*
259. Ling (2002), *supra* n. 10, 37.

The requirement to observe the public interest was incorporated into the GPCL in 1986. Article 6 required that civil activities must be in compliance with state policies, while Article 7 stipulated that civil activities must respect social ethics and must not harm the public interest, undermine state economic plans or disrupt the socioeconomic order. One could, of course, argue that these provisions are simply the consequence of the centrally planned economy in the 1980s, but the CLC was designed in the latter part of the last century. It attempts to reflect social life and economic changes at the turn of the twenty-first century, in particular China's changing attitude towards a market economy. Nonetheless, several provisions still serve to strengthen the status of public interests. For example, Article 7 of the CLC requires parties to abide by administrative regulations as well as social ethics, and not to disrupt the socioeconomic order or harm public interests. One can therefore say that the domination of the state over private autonomy results mainly from traditional ethics, and Confucianism still dominates modern Chinese society and social life.

It is interesting to note that the role of the Administration of Industry and Commerce (AIC) was debated during the drafting of the CLC. In the previous three contract law drafts in the 1980s, the AIC had broad power to supervise contracts not detrimental to the public interest. They could even invalidate a contract they believed to be harmful to the state or society, but with the development of the rule of law, some scholars argued that the power of administration should be curbed, and that only courts should be allowed to declare a contract void. Therefore, the drafting committee decided to give no such ongoing power to the administration. However, the AIC argued as follows in favour of it retaining its power to supervise contracts:[260]

(1) Chinese state-owned enterprises frequently failed to take responsible care of state assets, causing enormous losses. Their business operation should therefore be supervised for the protection of state assets;
(2) Chinese enterprises were often poorly managed. Their lack of self-discipline and self-protection often caused unnecessary losses, which required the AIC to supervise;
(3) the courts did not have sufficient resources to deal with all the problems, and judicial remedies did not compensate for the loss of state interests.

It is obvious to see the administrative organization merely consider their own interests and try to absorb their interests into the law in order to legitimate their intervention. Therefore, Article 127 CLC eventually stipulated that the 'AIC shall be responsible for monitoring and dealing with any illegal act which harms state interests and public interest in accordance with the laws and regulations.' However, this provision was too vague. While it endowed the AIC with the right to supervise contracts, it failed to spell out in which way and in which areas the AIC could supervise contracts. This lacuna remains open to this day.

260. *Ibid.*, 48.

2.1.2.2. Current Economic Situation

Modern Chinese contract law is not only influenced by Confucianism, but also inspired by the current economic situation. China has opened its doors to the world and is willing to integrate into an international market. Consequently, some concepts and provisions have had to be transplanted from other legal systems in order to diminish obstacles in cross-border transactions. There can be no doubt that the CLC is also influenced by this current economic situation. The following subsection will attempt to analyse two fundamental principles of the CLC that have resulted from the current economic situation, namely equality and the promotion of business transactions.

2.1.2.2.1. Equality

Inequality between certain groups of persons was advocated by Confucianism, such as the father having absolute power over his wife and children and the emperor having absolute power over his citizens. Women should respect men, younger persons should respect elders, and only the oldest son shall succeed to the authority of the family, etc. These strict hierarchy and descent lines are part of morality (*Li*), which is consistent with the needs of a ruler in a feudal state. So, to some extent, this is the reason why Confucianism has been the official philosophical thought and teaching since the *Han* Dynasty (BC 206–220 AD). Under the priority of this philosophy and public interests, it was extremely difficult for a private company during the 1980s to be treated equally with a state-owned enterprise. It is particularly true that the government had a clear preference for protecting state-owned enterprises, because their interests were directly interrelated. Due to the fact that judicial power is not independent in China, it is understandable why equality was not respected in the previous contract laws and practice of the 1980s.

However, with the development of the economy and with China knocking on the door of the WTO, all parties willing to enter into the contract are now to be treated equally. It is true to say that the market calls for equality between the contractual parties. The principle of equality has thus been incorporated into the CLC as a fundamental principle. It includes three aspects:[261]

The first is equal capacity. In previous economic contract law, only legal persons had the right to conclude what was referred to as the 'economic contract', a contract established for economic purposes. However, all parties in a market require the same capacity to contract, and it is reasonable for those involved to have an economic purpose. So the CLC endowed all the parties, including natural persons, legal persons and other organizations, with the same capacity to enter into a contract.[262]

261. Liming Wang, *he tong fa yan jiu* [*Study in Contract Law*], People's University Publisher, vol. 2, 2002, 25–60.
262. Article 2 CLC: 'Contract, as referred to in this Law, is an agreement whereby natural persons, legal persons or other organisations, as equal parties, establish, modify and extinguish relationships of civil rights and duties.'

The second is equal legal standing. All parties are required to negotiate and conclude the contract voluntarily. In practice, though, many large-scale companies or monopolies could conclude contracts without negotiation with other parties, or use their superior bargaining position for concluding unequal contracts. This was frequently observed for consumer contracts. So, in order to maintain the equal legal standings of all parties and to ensure that contracts were based on true consent and manifest mutual benefits, the CLC provided that a party to a contract could require the court or arbitration tribunal to amend or rescind the contract if it was apparently unreasonable at the time of concluding.[263] The party that supplied the standard terms had to be given more responsibility to inform about the contract.[264]

The last requirement is equal treatment. As stated above, in the past, private companies were treated differently from state-owned companies, both before the contract was concluded and after disputes arose. For instance, the state-owned company would often be the preferred choice at the conclusion of the contract, and after a dispute arises, it would receive better treatments by the judges. The principle of equality requires not only the equal legal status of the parties before a contract is made, but also equal treatment once disputes arise after the conclusion of a contract. In current China, with its underlying socialist orientation, there are still many state-owned companies. If courts or arbitration tribunals treat state-owned companies better in the adjudication of disputes, parties will be very reluctant to enter into contracts with state-owned companies, which in turn will be harmful to economic development. Therefore, courts or arbitration tribunals are required to treat all parties equally, without considering the owner's status.

Therefore, equality, an underlying principle in the CLC, is required at every stage of the contract, from negotiation to dispute resolution. It serves as a logical premise that reflects the notion of autonomy and freedom inasmuch that contractual parties in a free market should compete and cooperate on an equal footing.[265]

2.1.2.2.2. Promotion Business Transactions

Like many other countries at the time, ancient China implemented a policy of 'emphasize agriculture while restraining commerce', a policy rooted in the legal culture. When the central planning of the economy introduced after the establishment of the People's Republic of China in 1949 was gradually replaced and the CLC drafted, most members of the drafting committee argued that contract law should set out the fundamental legal rules, which govern market transactions. It was believed that the promotion of business transactions had been ignored in China

263. Article 54 CLC.
264. Article 41 CLC: 'If a dispute arises over the understanding of a standard term, the term shall be interpreted in accordance with the usual understanding of the term. If there are two or more interpretations of a standard term, the interpretation that is unfavourable to the party that supplies the standard term shall be adopted. If there is an inconsistency between a standard term and a non-standard term, the non-standard term shall prevail.'
265. Ling (2002), *supra* n. 10, 41–42.

for such a long time that it should be incorporated in the new unified contract law, in order to accelerate economic development.[266]

According to some scholars, there are three aims for the promotion of business transactions in the CLC.[267] The first is to promote the development of a market economy, under which 'contractual relationships constitute the most basic legal relationships' and 'a fundamental objective of contract law must be to foster and encourage the transactions'.[268]

The second is that the promotion of business transactions contributes to increased efficiency and social wealth, as '[t]his is not only because different entities and individuals can satisfy their needs for different goods or services and their desire to increase their wealth only through the transactions, but also because only through freely negotiated transactions can resources be distributed optimally and utilized most efficiency'.[269] In most societies, the market serves as the principal mechanism for the production and distribution of wealth,[270] and contract law is in existence to facilitate efficient exchange and repair market failures. The CLC thus attempts to contribute to the creation of social wealth, by promoting efficient transactions.[271]

The last aim is to protect the freedom of contract. Promoting business transactions is consistent with the wills of the parties, and it encourages people to negotiate freely for the contract according to their wills. As a result, most scholars advocate that the principle of promoting business transactions should be incorporated into the CLC.

Promoting business transactions is also a guiding principle for drafting. It has found its way into the CLC in at least the following aspects:

(1) Formation of the contract. Previous contract laws operated without the notions of offer and acceptance. The CLC, however, adopts offer and acceptance as the main elements of contract formation under the principle of promoting business transactions, on the grounds that they make business transactions more convenient and efficiency. Also, previous contract laws used chiefly formal elements such as signatures for establishing a contract. In contrast, the CLC allows contracts to be established by conduct, namely performance.
(2) Invalid contracts. In the GPCL, seven situations could invalidate civil activities,[272] but their scope was too wide. Invalidity was used for contract

266. Lixing Yang & Shaofeng Zhang, On A Few Problems in Making Laws of Unified Contract-comments on the Problems Deserving Attention in Making of Unified Contract Discussed in the Annual Meeting of Civil Law and Economic Law Research Society of China Law Science Society and Hainan Academic Seminar, Law of Hebei, vol. 3, 1996, 3.
267. Wang (1999), *supra* n. 7, 23–33.
268. *Ibid.*
269. *Ibid.*
270. Collins (2008a), *supra* n. 5, 1–5.
271. Hesselink & Vries (2001), *supra* n. 4, 80.
272. Article 58 GPCL: ;Civil acts in the following categories shall be null and void: (1) those performed by a person without capacity for civil conduct; (2) those that according to law may

termination to a degree that was harmful to the economic development. This was remedied in the CLC. For some of the situations in which the GPCL envisaged invalidity, the CLC provides that certain terms are amended or the contract rescinded instead of invalidated, if the contract was entered into by fraud or duress, or by taking advantage of the other party.[273] It is interesting to note that the CLC also distinguishes between *invalid contracts* and *contracts with pending validity*. For instance, a contract concluded by an agent without any authority, or who exceeds his authority, or whose authority has lapsed, will be valid after the ratification by the principal.[274]

(3) Interpretation of the contract. Previous contract laws lacked rules on interpretation. In practice, contracts were generally held to be invalid when their content was too vague. The CLC adopts a rule of interpretation that allows such contracts to stand, thus making business transactions more predictable and certain.[275]

It is worth mentioning that business transactions must be legal and not harmful to public interests. The CLC encourages only lawful transactions, which means that the transactions must be voluntary, within the law and regulations, and must reflect the true intentions of the parties.

2.2. FUNDAMENTAL PRINCIPLES OF EUROPEAN CONTRACT LAW

> That [fundamental principles] suggests that it may have been meant to denote essentially abstract basic values. The model rules of course build on such fundamental principles in any event, whether they are stated or not.[276]

Rough speaking, there are several characteristics for the underlying fundamental principles in the DCFR/PECL:

(1) they are shared by most European legal systems and are evidenced in most European national contract laws;

---

not be independently performed by a person with limited capacity for civil conduct; (3) those performed by a person against his true intentions as a result of cheating, coercion or exploitation of his unfavourable position by the other party; (4) those that performed through malicious collusion are detrimental to the interest of the state, collection or third party; (5) those that violate the law or public interest; (6) economic contracts that violate the state's mandatory plans; (7) those that performed under the guise of legitimate acts conceal illegitimate purposes.;

273. Article 54 CLC.
274. *Ibid.*
275. Huixing Liang, he tong de jie shi gui ze [The Interpretation Rule of Contracts], *min shang fa lun cong* [*Civil and Commercial Law Review*], vol. 6, 1997, 539–545.
276. Von Bar & Clive (2009), *supra* n. 24, 5.

(2) fundamental principles are the leading rules of the DCFR/PECL. They are used to guide the drafting and interpretation of all the provisions of contract law;
(3) they are mandatory principles by nature, which as such cannot be excluded by the parties in their contract;
(4) the DCFR/PECL reflects modern contract law. Its fundamental principles reveal some features of modern contract law and manifest the valuation of modern society;
(5) fundamental principles are required in all stages of a contract. They are required in the formation, performance, the exercise of the rights of the parties and the enforcement of their duties.

The general, binding principles of the PECL include 'freedom of contract', good faith and fair dealing, the duty to cooperate, duty of care and reasonableness.[277] However, the duty to cooperate and the duty of care are the more specific reflections of good faith and fair dealing, which means they just make the principles of good faith and fair dealing more concrete. The same can be said for reasonableness, inasmuch that it is also a concrete expression of fair dealing – it is the status of outcome that the value of fair dealing pursues. In the DCFR, the headings of freedom, security, justice and efficiency are suggested as underlying principles.[278] Notwithstanding this point, it shall be noted that the underlying principles in the DCFR cover not only contract law, but also non-contractual obligations such as unjust enrichment, tort law and property law. So, when referring to the law of contract, the principles of freedom, good faith and fair dealing are more fundamental than the ideas of *security* and *efficiency*, due to the fact that they are not only written in the *introduction* of the DCFR, but also expressly stated in the contents of the DCFR through the means of concrete provisions. Article I.-1:103 is the rule on 'good faith and fair dealing', while Article II.-1:102 is about 'freedom of contract'. This part therefore attempts to describe the three most fundamental principles evidenced in DCFR/PECL, which are 'freedom of contract', good faith and fair dealing.

2.2.1. Freedom of Contract

Like most national legal systems in Europe, the DCFR/PECL acknowledges the right of both legal and natural persons to decide with whom they will enter into a contract and to determine its contents.[279] The idea of freedom reveals that individuals should be given the choice of whether they should enter into the contract, and they should also be allowed to choose freely the provisions of their contract.[280] 'It sees in the general licence to enter binding contracts an enhancement of freedom

277. Chapter 1: General Provisions, PECL.
278. Von Bar & Clive (2009), *supra* n. 24, 7–10.
279. Lando & Beale (2000b), *supra* n. 22, 99.
280. Collins (2008a), *supra* n. 5, 25.

since this facility permits the new forms of cooperative endeavours which last over a period of time.'[281]

'Freedom of contract' was rooted in the will theory of classical contract law in the eighteenth and nineteenth centuries, and was attractive to both civil and common lawyers at that time.[282] Since the establishment of classical contract law, the essential purpose of the law of contract has focused upon the free choices of individuals.[283] Before this time, lawyers focused instead on the discussion of contract law in terms of promise rather than the consensus and wills of the contract. Only around the turn of the nineteenth century did lawyers and judges begin to focus on the will or consensus of the contracting parties. As expressed by Morton J. Horwitz, 'modern contract law is fundamentally a creature of the nineteenth century'.[284] There are at least three reasons for this rapid development of 'freedom of contract' during this century:

> The first concerns the division of labour. While the Industrial Revolution brought fundamental changes to economic and business development, there was an increasing demand for the transfer of property from some members of the community to the others, and for the performance of services by members of the community for other people. Contract law is about a variety of relationships and concerns economic changes such as buying and selling, employment and service, lending and borrowing. In short, it serves the market in its quest to distribute the wealth and resources of society. Until the nineteenth century, however, existing contract law was inadequate in meeting the new requirements of these developments, as it lacked the 'necessary generality' and 'emphasized procedure rather than substance'.[285] Lawyers thus required the books that treated contract law as a whole to analyse the general principles and illustrate these principles to deal with practical issues.[286] Jurists, therefore, were working again to theorize the law of contract in these centuries.
>
> Secondly, the work of Adam Smith changed the attitude of lawyers' thinking about contracts.[287] The free market serves as the basis of free choice for private parties to make their own contracts on their own terms, which is the central feature of classical contract law, and 'its influence is to be found in every corner'.[288] The legal *laissez-faire* ideal means the law should interfere in private life as little as possible. Its objectives, which are to enable people to realize their will or, in a more detailed definition, to leave them to get on with their business, to conduct their commercial affairs as they think best, to lead

---

281. *Ibid.*
282. Gordley (2001), *supra* n. 118, 16.
283. Collins (2008a), *supra* n. 5, 6–7.
284. Morton J. Horwitz, the Historical Foundations of Modern Contract Law, *Harvard Law Review*, vol. 87, 1974, 917.
285. P.S. Atiyah, *The Rise and Fall of Freedom of Contract*, Clarendon Press: Oxford, 1979, 398.
286. *Ibid.*
287. M.P. Furmston, *Law of Contract*, Oxford University Press, 2006, 13.
288. Atiyah (1979), *supra* n. 286, 408.

their own lives without interference by the government and so on, have been rooted in the thinking of society.[289] The notion assumes that the parties are the best judges of their own needs and circumstances, and they will calculate the risks to enter into the bargain. Contract law theory that had been in development since the eleventh century, however, obviously adopted the ideology of paternalism, which conflicted with the ideal of free market. The jurists in the nineteenth century, hence, tried to distance themselves from Aristotle's philosophy, and subsequently established a new theory known as the 'will theory of contract'.

Lastly, it is necessary to note that philosophical thoughts from the sixteenth to the eighteenth centuries provided a foundation for the outcome of the 'will theory of contract'. According to Atiyah, the idea of 'will theory' was promoted by natural lawyers, especially Grotius, Pufendorf, Bentham and Pothier.[290] While John Locke argued similarly that political obligations derived their legitimacy from the social contract to which the people gave an implied assent, judges argued that private obligations depended mainly on the private contracts to which contractual parties endowed with an implied consent.[291] Moreover, 'social contract theory' created a convenient environment for the development of 'freedom of contract'. There is little doubt that contract law was designed to provide for the enforcement of private arrangements agreed upon by relevant parties. Based on this philosophical foundation, at least according to Gordley, common lawyers in the nineteenth century built a doctrinal system for the first time.[292] Furthermore, drafters of the French civil code borrowed almost two-thirds of the code and nearly all the provisions on contracts from the natural school, while German jurists concentrated on building a doctrinal system as perfectly as they could manage.[293] Natural law thoughts, no doubt, created an intellectual environment for the concept of will to be widely accepted.

As reflected in the theory, contracts are entered into by the will or mutual consent of the parties involved. Although contractual liability stems from a meeting of minds, it does not mean the parties have indeed agreed in their innermost minds or that they have actually agreed or at least intended to agree. Mutual assent is measured only by the words and other forms of conduct of the parties, which could lead a reasonable person to assume they have agreed. This is an objective test. The commitments are enforceable because of the 'will' of the promisor to choose to be bound by his commitment, and he cannot complain about force being used against him as he 'intended that such force could be used when [he] made the commitment'.[294]

---

289. P.S. Atiyah & Stephen A. Smith, *Atiyah's Introduction to the Law of Contract*, Clarendon Press, 2005, 8.
290. *Ibid.*, 7.
291. *Ibid.*, 10.
292. Gordley (1992), *supra* n. 91, 4–5.
293. *Ibid.*
294. Randy E. Barnett, A Consent Theory of Contract, *Columbia Law Review*, 1986, 269–275.

The PECL subscribes to freedom of contract, as evidenced in Article 1:102 whereby parties are free to enter into contracts and to determine their contents. This is one of the cardinal principles of the PECL. Not only is it a convenient way to understand the economic virtues of the free market system, as contract law governs the rules for the exchange of wealth produced and allocated by the market, but it also manifests the legitimacy of the state in that its power is limited in order to maximize, respect and even enforce the liberty of citizens. Traditionally, the vague notions of 'public policy' or 'good morals' have been used as limitations to 'freedom of contract'. Nevertheless, the importance and value, as well as standards employed, are rather vague and uninformative.[295] Since the twentieth century, when the protection of weaker parties and fundamental rights began to play a greater role, various limitations have been imposed on that freedom. While the PECL acknowledges 'freedom of contract', it also states that this freedom is restricted by the requirements of good faith and fair dealing, and also by mandatory rules, which include national, supranational and international rules.[296]

The DCFR adopts the same approach as the PECL and recognizes freedom of contract as a fundamental principle of contract law. As stated in the introduction to the DCFR, 'as a rule, natural and legal persons should be free to decide whether or not to contract and with whom to contract. They should also be free to agree on the terms of their contract. This basic idea is recognized in the DCFR'.[297] In the DCFR, freedom is promoted from two aspects – the first through the assumption of party autonomy, which should be respected unless there is a good reason to intervene, and the second which is to enhance the capabilities of people to do things and 'make it easier and less costly for them to enter into well-regulated legal relationships'.[298] Article II.-1:102 expressly integrates this fundamental rule into the concrete provisions of the DCFR.

However, in modern contract law, the meaning of 'freedom' has changed somewhat when compared to that prevailing at the time of classical contract law. Nowadays, social elements are widely included in order to maintain justice within a society, for instance to protect the consumers in the contract, to protect small- and medium-sized enterprises (SMEs). The notion of social justice therefore is understood as a significant element that limits contractual freedom. Under the DCFR, a contract infringing the interests of particular third persons or society is obviously a ground on which a legislator shall invalidate. Besides this, the DCFR sets six other situations as limitations to freedom, which are: (1) interventions when consent is defective: when the party is not free or has been misinformed, such as under a situation of duress or unfair exploitation, the contract may not be

295. George A. Bermann, *Party Autonomy: Constitutional and International Law Limits in Comparative Perspective*, Juris Publishing, 2002, 1–3.
296. Ulrich Schroeter, Freedom of Contract: Comparison between Provisions of the CISG (Article 6) and Counterpart Provisions of the PECL, *The Vindobona Journal of International Commercial Law and Arbitration*, vol. 6, 2002, 262.
297. Von Bar & Clive (2008), *supra* n. 27, 18.
298. *Ibid.*, 38.

enforced; (2) restrictions on the freedom to choose a contracting party: any discrimination based on gender, race or ethnic origin is prohibited; (3) restrictions on freedom to withhold information at the pre-contractual stage: a party has remedy if the full information was not provided when concluding the contract; (4) information as to the terms of the contract: if the party is not fully aware of the content of contracts, or it is not fully understood, such as under a standard contract, the term can then be modified or invalidated; (5) correcting inequality of bargaining power; and (6) minimum intervention: in general terms, the parties, particularly the consumer, shall be provided with sufficient information. However, sometimes they cannot effectively make use of this information, in which case certain minimum rights shall be justified to provide the other party with sufficient guidance to efficiently arrange its affairs.

Generally speaking, three different models are described to limit the freedom of contract in Europe, which are the paternalistic, social and perfectionist models.[299] In the DCFR/PECL, it is also reasonable to outline them as follows:

(1) We look at the paternalistic model. Traditionally, the state can interfere with an individual's free choice if 'its intervention is legitimated by the superior moral authority of the law and is restricted to very narrow ambits.'[300] Paternalism is the most traditional model for restricting the individual's freedom to contract. It refers to the circumstance in which the state will set the contracts aside if the integrity of the state or the fundamental rights of individuals are infringed. Mandatory rules in the sense of the DCFR/PECL and national laws are basically included in this model.[301] They are meant to have a mandatory nature from which the parties cannot deviate,[302] but most rules in the DCFR are default rules, with only a few fundamental principles mandatory by nature. The same as the PECL, Article 1:103 acknowledges that the effect should be given to the mandatory rules of national, supranational and international law, which are applicable irrespective of the law governing the contract. Article II.-7:302 DCFR and Article 15:102 PECL also set the effects of those contracts infringing the mandatory rules of national laws: 'All European systems deal with contracts which contravene some rule of law, as opposed to contracts which are contrary to fundamental principles of morality or public policy.'[303] In addition, basically, they are used to

299. Maria Rosaria Marella, The Old and the New Limits to Freedom of Contract in Europe, *European Review of Contract Law*, vol. 2, 2006, 257–274.

300. *Ibid.*, 261.

301. F.W. Grosheide, Scope of the Principles, in Danny Busch & Ewoud Hondius & Hugo van Kooten & Harriët Schelhaas, *The Principles of European Contract Law (Part III) and Dutch Law: A Commentary II*, Kluwer Law International, 2006, 35.

302. *Ibid.*

303. Ole Lando & Eric Clive & Andre Prum & Reinhard Zimmermann, *Principles of European Contract Law: Part III*, Kluwer Law International, 2003, 219.

'protect the public interest in efficiency, morality or equity that might or might not be overlap with the interests of the parties'.[304] Furthermore, as revealed in Article II.-1:102 DCFR and Article 1:102 PECL, freedom of contract should also be restricted to the requirement of good faith and fair dealing. In both the DCFR/PECL and national laws, numerous mandatory provisions provide the requirements of good faith and fair dealing in a more concrete circumstance through the doctrine of validity, undue influence, etc. For example, if the contract was made under the influence of threat or enforced power, then the contract should be modified or deemed invalid.

(2) We address the social model. The social model, mainly derived from the pressure present in social and economic conditions, is a critique of the individualism of private law.[305] The difference between paternalism and socialism is that the first one refers to the limitations outside the market, while the latter makes relations inside the market, which shall 'conform to a solidarity rationale'.[306] The social model is manifested mostly from weaker party protection, as the achievement of the well-being of society has been frequently regarded as one of the most significant aims that contract law should pursue. 'Social justice' or 'social solidarity' has been used often to describe this ideal achievement. Article 4:110 PECL concerning unfair terms is in fact in place to correct the structural inequality of bargaining power between the poor and the rich. However, it is often argued in the PECL that the weaker party protection has not been absorbed, or is insufficient.[307] After being advocated by the Study Group on Social Justice in European Private Law,[308] the DCFR has fully noticed the issue, and the promotion of solidarity and social responsibility has been made one of the overriding principles and primary functions of the DCFR.[309] Worth mentioning at this juncture is that the consideration of the social model to restrict the freedom of contract is one of the most obvious places to make the distinction between modern contract law and classical contract law. Traditionally, an individual deemed to be the best judge of his own interest was allowed to pursue his own interest, whereas, in modern times, social justice has been imposed on all contractual parties.

(3) We examine the perfectionist model. With the adoption of the European Convention on Human Rights and Fundamental Freedoms in 1950, and the European Charter of Fundamental Rights in 2000, it is notable that in

304. Marella (2006), *supra* n. 300, 258.
305. Duncan Kennedy, Thoughts on Coherence, Social Values and National Tradition in Private Law, in Hesselink (2006), *supra* n. 26, 19.
306. Marella (2006), *supra* n. 300, 266.
307. Micklitz (2004), *supra* n. 143, 339–356.
308. Study Group (2004), *supra* n. 2, 653–674.
309. Von Bar & Clive (2009), *supra* n. 24, 8.

> recent case law the ECJ has recognized that fundamental rights could serve as a justification to restrict the EC freedoms that result from the prohibition of a certain commercial activity with a cross-border element in a Member State.[310] Among these fundamental rights, human dignity is an essential value that plays an important part in current European contract law. The *Omega* case[311] is an obvious example inasmuch that the court held that the objective of human dignity protection could lead to national courts restricting the freedom to provide services by holding that a certain cross-border element is contrary to good morals on the basis that it infringes the fundamental rights recognized in the EU.[312] The influence of fundamental rights has not only appeared in this case, but also in other cases such as the *Courage* case or the *Manfredi* case, wherein fundamental rights endowed by constitutional laws or international treaties have played an important role. It is even argued that the consitutionalization of contract law is a tendency of modern European contract law. The DCFR has completely followed this trend. Article II.-1:102 of DCFR states clearly that party autonomy, as an expression of freedom of contract, is not absolute, as it still has to be restricted by the non-infringement of fundamental rights, legality and social conditions, similar to the PECL.[313]

In conclusion, freedom of contract is a fundamental principle in the DCFR/PECL. It endows contracting parties with the freedom to choose the other party, to determine whether to conclude the contract or not, and to decide its contents. However, this freedom must be interpreted together with its limitations. Traditionally, paternalism is an essential tool available for the state to interfere with the self-determination of individuals through the doctrines of illegality, public policy and immorality. Since the nineteenth century, pressure from society to maintain social solidarity has produced major restrictions. The balance of bargaining power between the parties is, remarkably, a reflection of the social model. In modern contract law, fundamental rights expressed in national constitutional instruments and international conventions have been advocated as a new limitation to the freedom of contract. In recent years, human dignity in particular has played an important role in protecting the basic values of society. The DCFR/PECL, on the one hand, recognizes freedom of contract as a fundamental principle for achieving the functioning of the free market and the construction of European citizenship, while on the other hand all three models that limit the freedom for a rational market have been also integrated.

---

310. Olha Cherednychenko, Fundamental Rights and Contract Law, *European Review of Contract Law*, vol. 4, 2006, 801.
311. [2004] OJ EC C 300/3 [ECJ].
312. Cherednychenko (2006), *supra* n. 311, 501–502.
313. Von Bar & Clive (2009), *supra* n. 24, 129–131.

2.2.2. Good Faith

As Aristotle pointed out, *if good faith has been taken away, all intercourse among men ceases to exist.*[314]

Good faith has been considered a vitally important ingredient in modern contract law: 'The draftsmen of the PECL appear to have regarded it as part of the common core of European contract law.'[315] However, as the notion is connected closely with the ethical standards of the community, and has been regarded as injecting moral notions into law, the meaning of good faith differs considerably according to different scholars. Some academics define it as 'an expectation of each party to a contract that the other will honestly and fairly perform his duties under the contract in a manner that is acceptable in the trade community'.[316] In the DCFR, good faith is defined as 'a mental attitude characterised by honesty and an absence of knowledge that an apparent situation is not the true situation'.[317]

Not only are there numerous ways in which good faith can be defined, but these can also vary considerably over time. In Roman law, good faith, or bona fides, was always 'associated with trustworthiness, conscientiousness and honourable conduct'.[318] Cicero gave a complete definition of good faith as follows:

> These words, good faith, have a very broad meaning. They express all the honest sentiments of a good conscience, without requiring a scrupulousness which could turn selflessness into sacrifice; the law banishes from contracts ruses and clever manoeuvres, dishonest dealings, fraudulent calculations, dissimulations and perfidious simulations, and malice, which under the guise of prudence and skill, takes advantages of credulity, simplicity and ignorance.[319]

However, medieval jurists spoke of good faith in contract law as the description of three types of conduct expected by the parties.[320] Firstly, one must keep his words as a matter of faith, equity and the *ius gentium*. The term '*pacta sunt servanda*' is the reflection of this notion. Secondly, a party to a contract must not take advantage of the other by misleading that party or by the use of unequal bargaining power.

---

314. William Tetley, Good Faith in Contract Particularly in the Contracts of Arbitration and Chartering, the text is available at: <www.mcgill.ca/files/maritimelaw/goodfaith.pdf> (last accessed in March 2010).
315. Reinhard Zimmermann & Simon Whittaker, *Good Faith in European Contract Law*, Cambridge University Press, 2000, xiii.
316. P.J. Powers, Defining the Indefinable: Good Faith and the United Nations Convention on the Contracts for the International Sale of Goods, *Journal of Law and Commerce*, 18, 1999, 333.
317. Von Bar & Clive (2009), *supra* n. 24, 72.
318. H.A. Rommen, *The Natural Law, A Study in Legal and Social History and Philosophy*, B. Herder Book Co., 1947, 117.
319. De Off, 3, 17, cited by Association Henri Capitant des Amis de la, Societe de Legislation Comparee, *European Contract Law: Materials for a Common Frame of Reference: Terminology, Guiding Principles, Model Rules,* European Law Publisher, 2008, 152.
320. James Gordley, Good Faith in Contract in the Medieval ius commune, in Zimmermann & Whittaker (2000), *supra* n. 316, 93–106.

Thirdly, both parties must fulfil such obligations that an honest person could be expected to, even if they are not expressed in the contract.

As pointed out by Gordley, the jurist Baldus (1327–1400) associated good faith with equity and conscience.[321] The requirement of good faith, as posited by Baldus, was that 'no one should be enriched at another's expense'.[322] He argued that the judge should take account of good faith in a contract for two purposes: the first to know whether contracts are binding, and the second to know what the parties' obligations are and whether they have been fulfilled.[323] From this interpretation and analysis, the essence or substantive element of good faith can be concluded reasonably as 'just and honest conduct'.

The French scholar Domat (1625–1696) declared 'by the law of nature and by our customs, every contract is *bonae fidei*, because honesty and integrity hath and ought to have in all contracts the full extent the equity can demand'.[324] However, good faith did not have the philosophical basis until the German philosopher Immanuel Kant, one of the great moralists of the Enlightenment, established his own slant on the notion.[325] Kant regarded good faith as a categorical imperative wherein acts consistent with the status of people as free and rational beings are morally right and need to be carried out to inspire mutual confidence in society, which leads ultimately to the promotion of happiness.

Nowadays, in most civil legal systems, good faith is recognized as a fundamental principle in making and carrying out contracts.[326] It requires each contractual party to act reasonably and extends the obligation. That a party should take the other's interests into account is often interpreted in modern contract laws.[327] For example, contractual parties owe each other a pre-contractual duty to negotiate fairly and honestly. Furthermore, each party may not seek for their own profits without considering the other's interests. However, the notion of good faith is an open norm, and in practice, it is not easy to clarify its scope. Generally speaking, there is a distinction between subjective good faith and objective good faith. The first is always regarded as a subjective state of mind, while the latter is normally considered a norm for the conduct of parties. In common law systems, historically, good faith was not given legal recognition.[328] However, it is argued

321. *Ibid.*, 108.
322. *Ibid.*
323. *Ibid.*, p. 109.
324. William Strahan, The Civil Law in Its Natural Order: Together with the Public Law, vol. I, London 1722, 45, cited by Simon Whittaker & Reinhard Zimmermann, Good Faith in European Contract Law: Surveying the Legal Landscape, in Zimmermann & Whittaker (2000), *supra* n. 316, 32.
325. Ole Lando, Is Good Faith an Over-Arching General Clause in the Principles of European Contract Law?, *European Review of Private Law*, vol. 6, 2007, 842.
326. Article 1134 s. 3 French Civil Code; 242 German Civil Code; Art. 2 Swiss Civil Code; Arts 1175 and 1375 Italian Civil Code; Art. 762, s. 2, Portuguese Civil Code; Art. 288 Greek Civil Code; Arts 6:2 & 6:248 Dutch Civil Code.
327. Martijn W. Hesselink, The Concept of Good Faith, in Hartkamp, Hesselink, Hondius, Joustra, du Perron and Veldman (2004), 472.
328. Atiyah & Smith (2005), *supra* n. 290, 213.

that in many cases the implied term 'reasonable expectations of honest people', which is perhaps the closest substitute in common law that has been found for the notion of good faith in the civil legal system,[329] has been used to establish the same standard of good faith in particular circumstances.[330] In addition, various specific rules under common law achieve the same result as the requirement of good faith in civil law systems, such as the requirement of equity.

The DCFR/PECL establishes good faith as a basic principle running through the principles from the formation to the enforcement of a contract.[331] Roughly speaking, the notion of good faith has at least three functions in the DCFR/PECL and in most European countries:[332]

(1) Interpretative: as circumstances often change considerably in practice, and there are often some ambiguities in the contract, good faith is thus regarded as a yardstick for the interpretation to protect the justified expectation of contractual parties. It is an efficient way of implementing the 'spirit of bargain' and recognizing the minimum principles of fairness and honesty.
(2) Supplementary: as contractual parties cannot express all the circumstances in the contract, good faith is therefore considered an implied term to supplement the contract in determining the nature and scope of justified expectations.
(3) Restrictive: good faith also has a restrictive function in that when a rule binding upon the parties does not apply to the full extent, or in a given circumstance that is unacceptable to a reasonable person, then the judges can apply this principle to restrict the scope of bargaining.

The notion of good faith can be linked to several PECL rules, such as those that acknowledge pre-contractual liability, duty of information, ancillary duties and post-contractual liability. These have been deduced, to a large extent, from the notion of good faith. A similar observation can be made about the DCFR.[333] Article I.-1:103 expressly recognizes the idea of 'good faith' as one of the general principles of the DCFR. The standard of conduct through 'honesty, openness and consideration for the interests of the other party to the transaction or relationship in question' is required from all parties.[334] However, good faith is placed together with fair dealing in the DCFR/PECL, expressed in such a way that good faith refers to 'a subjective state of mind generally characterized by honesty and a lack of knowledge that an apparent situation is not the true situation'.[335] It is concerned

329. William (2010).
330. *Ibid.*
331. Lando & Beale (2000b), *supra* n. 22, 114.
332. E. Allan Farnsworth, Duties of Good Faith and Fair Dealing under the Unidroit Principles, Relevant International Conventions, and National Laws, the text is available at: <http://tldb.uni-koeln.de/php/pub_show_document.php?pubdocid=122100> (last accessed in May 2010).
333. Article I.-1:103 DCFR.
334. Von Bar & Clive (2009), *supra* n. 24, 89.
335. *Ibid.*

merely with the subjective sense. Under the DCFR/PECL, the requirement of good faith has been set in every stage of a contract, such as in the pre-contractual stage, whereby the negotiation must be consistent with good faith and not be broken off contrary to good faith. In the performance stage, care for the other's interest is demanded, while after the completion of a contract, confidentiality shall be obeyed implicitly. It can thus be said that good faith, the recognition of moral rights in the law, acts as an overarching principle in the DCFR/PECL.

2.2.3. Fair Dealing

Good faith and fair dealing are always combined into one notion and often considered as a single rule in the DCFR/PECL. It has been argued by some scholars that the reason for this combination is to make it less irritable for the English legal community, as 'good faith' is not accepted widely by English lawyers.[336] However, it is possible to make a distinction between these two notions, as pointed out in the DCFR, whereby the only notion of good faith refers to the subjective sense.[337] So, it is reasonable to say that good faith focuses on the minds of the parties, whereas fair dealing emphasizes their conduct.[338]

The concept of fair dealing is, to a certain extent, linked to the notion of fairness. Some scholars even argue that the notion of fair dealing is a typical translation of fairness from the Anglo-American world,[339] and that the terms 'fair dealing' and 'fairness' are closely related. However, there should be some differences between the two concepts, as the first concentrates on the process of bargaining and the latter on the outcome(s) of bargaining.

Traditionally, fair dealing was more concerned with will deficiencies such as threat, mistake, abuse of circumstances, etc. Nevertheless, in modern contract law, some new limitations to the freedom of contract, for instance lack of bargaining power, duty to inform, duty of care, right to withdraw, mandatory rules, etc., have been integrated, the essence of which in fact is to achieve the fair dealing of all parties involved into the contract.

The principle of fair dealing has played an essential role in the process of European contract law convergence. Since the second half of the 1980s, the EC has adopted numerous directives that aim to protect the interests of consumers. The first directive, commonly referred to as the Doorstep Selling Directive, was adopted in 1985,[340] and was followed by, amongst others, the Consumer Credit

336. Marjorie Hoch, Is Fair Dealing A Workable Concept for European Contract Law, *Global Jurist Topics*, vol. 5, 2005, 17–18.
337. Von Bar & Clive (2009), *supra* n. 24, 89.
338. Lando & Beale (2000b), *supra* n. 22, 112–116.
339. G.P. Fletcher, Comparative Law as A Subversive Discipline, *American Journal of Comparative law*, 1998, 5–40.
340. Directive 85/5777/EEC of 20 Dec. 1985 to protect the consumer in respect of contracts negotiated away from business premises.

Directive in 1987,[341] the Unfair Contract Terms Directive in 1993,[342] the Timeshare Directive in 1994,[343] the Distance Selling Directive in 1997,[344] the Injunctions Directive in 1998,[345] the Consumer Guarantees Directive in 1999,[346] the Distance Selling of Financial Services Directive in 2002,[347] Unfair Commercial Practices in 2005[348] and the Misleading and Comparative Advertising Directive in 2006.[349] The main purposes of these directives were to improve the protection of consumers or weaker parties in Member States through the duty of information, the right to cancel within a certain time after the closing, etc., and to improve the functioning of the internal market.[350] Weak party protection was set up ultimately to achieve fair dealing in the society.

Nowadays, it is widely accepted that 'in order to achieve distributive justice, [we] must impose standards of fairness in contracts'.[351] It is generally held that modern contract law has been shifting from procedural fairness, which ensures there is no undue influence, to substantive fairness, which concerns a fair outcome. The traditional view, whereby the main purpose of contract law is to enforce the contract instead of ensuring the fairness of the contract, has been criticized in recent years.[352] The DCFR/PECL therefore acknowledges the doctrine of fair dealing as one of the tools for achieving fairness, and considers it one of the most overarching and fundamental of values. Generally speaking, fair dealing includes both procedural and substantive fairness, explained as follows:

(1) Substantive fairness: The DCFR/PECL provides that unfair terms that have not been individually negotiated are invalid.[353] A term that has not been individually negotiated is considered unfair if it causes a significant imbalance between the parties. This provision extends the scope of application of the general clause of the EC directive on the Unfair Terms in Consumer Contracts (1993).[354] Another example for substantive

341. Directive 87/102/EEC of 22 Dec. 1986 for the approximation of the laws, regulations and administrative provisions of the Member States concerning consumer credit.
342. Directive 93/13EEC of 5 Apr. 1993 on unfair terms in consumer contracts.
343. Directive 94/47/EEC of 26 Oct. 1994 on the protection of purchasers in respect of certain aspects of contracts relating to the purchase of the right to use immovable properties on a timeshare basis.
344. Directive 97/7/EC of 20 May 1997 on protection of consumers in respect of distance contracts.
345. Directive 98/27/EC of 25 May 1998 on injunctions for the protection of consumers' interests.
346. Directive 1999/44/EC of 25 May 1999 on certain aspects of the sale of consumer goods and associated guarantees.
347. Directive 2002/65/EC of 23 Sep. 2002 concerning the distance marketing of consumer financial services.
348. Directive 2005/29/EC of 11 May 2005 concerning unfair business-to-consumer commercial practices in the internal market.
349. Directive 2006/114/EC of 12 Dec. 2006 concerning misleading and comparative advertising.
350. Brigitta Lurger, The 'Social' Side of Contract Law and the New Principles of Regard and Fairness, in Hartkamp, Hesselink, Hondius, Joustra, du Perron and Veldman (2004), 272.
351. *Ibid.*
352. Hoch (2005), *supra* n. 337, 32–33.
353. Article 4:110 PECL; Art. II.-9:403 DCFR.
354. Lando & Beale (2000b), *supra* n. 22, 266.

fairness in the DCFR/PECL, also in line with the laws of most EU Member States, is the doctrine of change of circumstances, which is used to correct any injustice that results from an imbalance caused by supervening events. Acknowledgements of these doctrines are examples of reflecting the shifting discourse from the classical fairness concept to the modern notion.

(2) Procedural fairness: In line with classical contract law, the DCFR/PECL employs notions of fairness to scrutinize the process of bargaining. It ensures that contracts are not unfair as a result of procedural impropriety during the negotiation procedure through the doctrines of, amongst others, fraud, misrepresentation, duress and undue influence.

Compared with the PECL, the DCFR expressly makes the protection of weaker parties' interests one of its ultimate aims. This is also expressed through the concrete provisions that the weaker party's interest needs to be protected.[355] Originally, the aim of the internal market philosophy was to improve, simplify and promote cross-border trade and competition within the EU. However, nowadays, weaker party protection has been absorbed gradually into this internal market philosophy, which can be plainly observed in the DCFR. The same as good faith, fair dealing is thus a fundamental principle in the DCFR/PECL.

2.3. COMPARATIVE CONCLUSION

In modern accounts of contract law, we cannot ignore that the foundation of the traditional conception of contract law was based on the idea of facilitating free choice. It is an essential tool for understanding market relations and legitimizing legal decisions. Private law convergence arguably serves two functions – one is the functioning of an integrated market, while the other constructs a European citizen.[356] For the second reason, the Europeanization of private law to establish the relationship between the individual and the community in Europe, and regarding contract law, the relationship between them is concerned mainly with the definition of freedom of contract and its limitations.[357] In the DCFR/PECL, the concept of freedom of contract is accepted widely, which is reflected in Article II.-1:102 DCFR under the heading 'party autonomy', and Article 1: 102 PECL, which stipulates that parties are free to enter into a contract and to determine its contents. However, there are still some restrictions. Traditionally, the vague notions of 'public policy' or 'good morals' have been placed as outer limitations to the freedom of contract, although their importance and value, as well as the standards employed, are rather vague and uninformative.[358] Since the twentieth century, with the wide use of

355. Von Bar & Clive (2009), *supra* n. 24, 508.
356. Marella (2006), *supra* n. 300, 257–258.
357. *Ibid.*
358. Bermann (2002), *supra* n. 296, 1–3.

standard contracts, weaker party protection, environmental protection and the influence of fundamental rights, varieties of limitations to freedom have emerged. Generally speaking, the restrictions to the DCFR/PECL may be included in the paternalistic model, social model and perfectionist model.

When comparing the DCFR/PECL with the CLC, it is logical to say that contractual parties are endowed with more freedom in the DCFR/PECL, which is revealed by the principle of 'freedom of contract'. The CLC, rather than acknowledging freedom of contract, uses instead the expression 'contract voluntariness', the scope of which is within freedom of contract. The latter acknowledges the freedom to choose contractual parties and to conclude and determine the contents of a contract, whereas contract voluntariness only grants the freedom to choose the contractual parties and conclude the contract. Further, under the CLC, restriction from the social and economic order is a primary limitation to the freedom of contractual parties. The ideology of freedom in Chinese legal history has not been as widely absorbed in the legal history of ancient China compared with Europe. China implemented the policy 'Emphasise Agriculture while restraining Commerce' for a long time, and the dominant-thinking school of Confucianism also limited individual freedom. Lacking traditional foundations, it is extremely difficult for current Chinese contract law to develop the values of 'freedom of contract' compared with how the DCFR/PECL has dealt with this subject. However, in order to satisfy the requirements of economic development and globalization, limited freedom has to be recognized in the CLC. The party could enjoy the freedom prescribed by the government that the 'bird in the cage' could be used to describe it in the CLC.[359]

Party autonomy serves as a basic value for the freedom of contract. From the comparisons of 'freedom of contract', it is reasonable to conclude that party autonomy in the CLC has not been endowed as widely as it has in the DCFR/PECL. Restrictions to party autonomy are due mainly to a great variety of aims that need to be implemented by contract law. Generally speaking, 'good faith' and 'fair dealing' are the two most fundamental principles restricting party autonomy in both the CLC and the DCFR/PECL.

In China, 'good faith' originates from the moral standards of Confucianism, which was used to maintain hierarchal order in society and was deep rooted in Chinese culture, whereas in European contract law 'good faith' helps commercial development, as the bona fides are associated closely with commercial elements. Nowadays, in both the EU and China, the spirit of good faith has been integrated into society, and is now closely associated with commercial practice. Both contract laws therefore recognize 'good faith' as an overarching principle – a primary value for restricting party autonomy in the EU and China.

The same could be observed from the notion of fair dealing, the idea of which has a close relationship with substantive fairness and procedural fairness. Traditionally in Europe, procedural fairness has been referred to more, especially through the doctrine of will deficiencies, whereas in modern contract law, the

359. Zhang (2006), *supra* n. 71, 60.

substantive fairness has been integrated more, particularly from the protection of weak parties. Conversely, traditional China has lacked procedural fairness, and it is even logical to say the whole legal system was to achieve a fair outcome of the judgment which concerns with substantive fairness, no matter if the procedure was reasonable or not. Revealed from contract law in the past, Chinese private law lacked recognition of the equal status of contractual parties, and weaker party protection was highly advocated by society, which still existed before the 1990s. However, with the transformation of the country into the market economy, the importance of procedural fairness has been gradually recognized as a significant element in guaranteeing that substantive fairness can be achieved. In sum, modern Chinese contract law is shifting its focus from substantive fairness to procedural fairness, whereas European contract law is moving from procedural fairness to substantive fairness. From this perspective, it is reasonable to state that the social values of the West are somehow meeting those of the East.

Except for the above two main restrictions to party autonomy, in the CLC socioeconomic value is still a major limitation, which consists of traditional social ethics and current economic situations. The maintenance of the public interest is a highly socialist characteristic. Although public interest is often implemented as a restriction to autonomy by all states, in China it is interpreted differently. The instrumental means through the laws, contractual parties shall not violate policies and all other documentation issued by the Communist Party, because all of these instruments are in place to maintain the interests of the state. This is consistent with the historical and cultural roots whereby Confucianism advocated individuals' interests should be subject to the state. Worthy of mention is that, in modern times, social justice has gradually become a significant element in restricting party autonomy in European private law. It is thus reasonable to say that, in China, the autonomy of individuals is extended progressively with the development of the economy, whereas in the Western countries party autonomy is gradually restricted for the well-being of society.

Chapter 3

Comparison of Several Doctrines

3.1. INTERPRETATION

Two of the main functions of contract law are arguably: to permit the parties to exercise their autonomy within the contract as they wish, and to protect the certainty of business transactions in a free market.[360] In an ideal world, the parties shall explicitly express in their contract, the remedies to all the situations that may occur in the future, and make these very clear in the agreement. However, in reality, due to lack of information, time, sufficient ability, or money, the parties often leave or do not realize the ambiguity of the words or unregulated matters in terms of their contract. This often requires the court to provide a solution and allocate rights and obligations to the parties, and make the transactions a certainty.

Also, from the economic perspective, the negotiation of a complete contract induces more costs, and parties may rationally not prefer economizing on the negotiations to complete the contracts by providing for a contingency and thus reducing their costs of negotiation.[361] So an incomplete contract with gaps is often left open for the judges, and it is true to say the interpretation in fact is needed for all the contracts.

However, during the process of interpretation, the role of courts' intervention in the contract inevitably results in undermining the individuals' autonomy, since the interpretation that the court applies, intrudes frequently on the parties' freedom in determining the contents of the contract. The judges may choose to dig out the subjective intentions common to the parties, or they may decide to interpret clauses based on the objective expressions in their contracts. The selection of either option reveals whether party autonomy or the certainty of business is more respected.

---

360. Lawrence M. Solan, Contract as Agreement, *Notre Dame Law Review*, vol. 353, 2007, 101–102.

361. Richard A. Posner, The Law and Economics of Contract Interpretation, Chicago John M. Olin Law & Economics Working Paper No. 229 (2D Series), 2004, 2–3.

The contract interpretation is ultimately to balance the value of autonomy and ensure the certainty of business transactions through determining the ambiguous terms and filling the gaps in the contract.[362] However, as distinct from other issues involving formation, validity and remedies, the interpretation of contracts has often been neglected or has been given relatively little attention.[363]

Arising from the fact that contract interpretation is actually an intervention undertaken by the judges to ascertain the meaning of ambiguities or omissions, the relationship between the role of judges and the function of party autonomy in the process of interpretation can be revealed through the doctrine.[364] This section thus attempts to analyse the differences in contract interpretation in the EU and China to reveal which jurisdiction shows greater respect to party autonomy during the interpretation process. Three research questions: is there any difference in the contract interpretation between the DCFR/PECL and the CLC? Assuming there were, then, can the different functions and roles of party autonomy resulting from the historical roots explain these differences? If not, what is the reason? This question will be answered subsequently.

3.1.1. European Contract Law

As to the interpretation of contracts, some scholars have forwarded several different opinions for systematic analysis. Kornet argues that three categories: ordinary interpretation, constructive interpretation and supplementation of the contract could be discerned.[365] Ordinary interpretation means determining the meaning of actual expressions by the parties according to the words used in the contract. Constructive interpretation is to make a logical conclusion through considering the contract as a whole, the aims and purposes of the contract, and other relevant circumstances. And the supplementation aspect refers to supplementing the contract with a solution stemming from sources outside of the contract, such as from the principle of good faith. However, Kötz thought of four distinctions, which should be made such as subjective interpretation, objective interpretation, constructive interpretation, and the maxims of interpretation.[366]

Generally speaking, objectivism and subjectivism are the two basic elements for interpretation. The first one 'objectivism' is based on the 'expression theory', which gives precedence to the external fact that the words have actually been expressed in contrast to unexpressed intentions.[367] The underlying reason is to

362. Steven J. Burton, *Elements of Contract Interpretation*, Oxford University Press, 2008, 2–4.
363. Posner (2004), *supra* n. 362, 1.
364. *Ibid.*, 2–3.
365. Nicole Kornet, *Contract Interpretation and Gap Filling: Comparative and Theoretical Perspectives*, Intersentia, 2006, 231–265.
366. Hein Kötz & Axel Flessener, *European Contract Law, Vol. 1: Formation, Validity, and Content of Contracts; Contract and Third Parties*, Clarendon Press, 1997, 106–123.
367. Hein Kötz, Interpretation and Contents, in Hugh Beale, Arthur Hartkamp, Hein Kötz & Denis Tallon, *Cases, Materials and Text on Contract Law*, Hart Publishing, 2002, 556.

protect the reliance on what others actually say instead of what they meant to say in order to accommodate the needs of a commercial market. This approach was originally adopted in ancient Roman law and in the pre-eighteenth century period.[368] Under this approach, the judge sought to interpret the contract through the external phenomena, and lawyers were convinced that the inward things should be left to God for determination, while the Law of Man could only regard the evidentiary.[369] To ascertain the meaning of what the parties have agreed to, the 'officious bystander' test is adopted which means it shall be interpreted according to the understanding of a reasonable man, who is supposed to be in the situation of the addressee and who understands the words in the circumstances.[370] Simply speaking, the interpretation had to be consistent with the reasonable expectations of a reasonable man who had been placed in the same situation.

The other aspect 'subjectivism' was founded on the 'will theory', which was coherent with the principle of party autonomy. It is argued that the legal obligation arises from the free wills of individuals, and the interpretation should be placed on the intention of parties.[371] As Savigny said, 'we must regard the intention as the only important and effective thing, even if, being internal and invisible, we need some sign by which to recognize it'.[372] However, subjectivism did not dominate legal literature until the late nineteenth century.[373] This approach has been mainly adopted in civil law countries like the Netherlands, Germany, etc. It is worth mentioning that the fact of common intentions is a psychological point and that it is impossible for us to look into the innermost intentions of the parties. What subjective interpretation intends to do is to seek common intentions of the parties, which are actually attributed to the contract.

The conflicts between the two theories have had some significance in the days gone by, but nowadays, most countries hover between the subjective and objective interpretations.[374] It is rare to find a legal system strictly sticking to one theory in modern contract law. The only difference lies in which theory prevails over the other, and the conflict between two theories lies in that if the intention was found out to be different from the expression, which one would dominate. In most of the continental countries, the subjective interpretation has been primarily adopted and the intention takes precedence over the expression, whereas in common law countries, expression prevails. Regarding the role of the judges under subjective interpretation, they take the contractual parties' understanding as their starting point, which is contrary to the objective approach where the judges adopt the

368. Joseph M. Perillo, The Origins of the Objective Theory of Contract Formation and Interpretation, *Fordham Law Review*, vol. 69, No. 2, 2000, 14–25.
369. Posner (2004), *supra* n. 362, 15–17.
370. Hein Kötz, Interpretation and Contents, in Beale et al. (2002), *supra* n. 368, 585–587.
371. David Charny, Hypothetical Bargains: The Normative Structure of Contract Interpretation, *Michigan Law Review*, vol. 89, 1991, 1823–1828.
372. Kötz & Flessener (1997), *supra* n. 367, 107.
373. *Ibid.*, 108.
374. *Ibid.*, p. 112.

position of an objective third party as their starting point.[375] However, what has to be emphasized is that both the subjective and objective interpretations give effect to the intentions of parties, the only difference is whether this intention is assessed subjectively or objectively,[376] as said by Lord Steyn in the Judgment of *Deutsche Genossenschaftsbank v. Burnhope*: 'It is true the objective of the construction of a contract is to give effect to the intention of the parties. But our law of construction is based on an objective theory. The methodology is not to probe the real intentions of the parties but to ascertain the contextual meaning of the relevant contractual language. Intention is determined by reference to express rather than actual intention.'[377] But it is reasonable to say the subjective interpretation is more favourable to party autonomy, whereas the objective interpretation is more concerned about the certainty of business transactions.

Chapter VIII in Book II of the DCFR and Chapter V of the PECL are concerned with the doctrine of interpretation. Article II.-8:101 DCFR/5:101 PECL deals with the general rules, which focus on the common intentions of the parties, and Article II.-8:102 DCFR /5:102 PECL is about the relevant circumstances, which should be considered for the interpretation. Article II.-8:103 DCFR/ 5:103 PECL is the *contra proferentem* rule, while Article II.-8:104 DCFR/5:104 PECL gives effect to the terms, which have been individually negotiated rather than those which have not. Article II.-8:105 DCFR/5:105 PECL provides that the contract has to be interpreted as a whole, and Article II.-8:106 DCFR/5:106 PECL stipulates that the interpretation should be preferred to the one which could render the contract lawful, while Article II.-8:107 DCFR/5:107 PECL is about the preferences with regard to the versions of the contract, which were drafted in different languages. This subsection is intended to describe these rules in the DCFR/PECL.

3.1.1.1. Common Intention

As is widely accepted most of legal systems nowadays combine both the subjective and objective interpretation, the DCFR/PECL also follows this tendency. The DCFR/PECL firstly acknowledges that the interpretation should seek the common intention of the parties through the subjective way, which is set out in Article II.-8:101(1) DCFR/5:101(1) PECL. The assumption for this provision flows from the will theory of contract, the essence of which considers the contract to be a result of the mutual intentions of the parties.[378] Ascertaining the intentions of the parties is believed to be in accordance with the presumption that the economic function of efficiency is to achieve for the greatest interest through the compliance with individual preferences.[379] Self-determination requires the state

375. Kornet (2006), *supra* n. 366, 234.
376. Ewan McKendrick, *The Creation of A European Law of Contracts*, Kluwer, 2004, 28.
377. *Deutsche Genossenschaftsbank v. Burnhope* [1995] 1 W.L.R. 1580; Cited by Kim Lewison, *The Interpretation of Contracts*, London: Sweet & Maxwell, 2004, 20.
378. Lando & Beale (2000b), *supra* n. 22, 288–290.
379. Claus-Wilhelm Canaris & Hans Christoph Grigoleit, Interpretation of Contracts, in Hartkamp et al. (2004), *supra* n. 176, 445–448.

to respect the autonomy of the parties. The judges are thus encouraged to seek out common intentions of the parties at the time of framing of the contract, which expressly demonstrates that mutual consent should be respected by the judges.[380]

Article II.-8:101 DCFR/5:101 PECL thus further states that the interpretations should respect the common intentions even if they are different from the literal meanings. However, it is argued that this provision in fact is contrary to objective interpretation, which is adopted in English Law.[381] In England, lawyers traditionally believed the intentions could only be judged from the outward documents created for the commercial certainty and the factual matrix of the contract, so the words ought to be interpreted according to this outward meaning.[382] But since the approach of the continental legal system and common law was quite different, it is reasonable to say they are sometimes even contrary to each other. If the DCRF was effective, the question arises whether this rule would impair the effect of literal interpretation on English law.

It often happens that if one party assigns a particularly different meaning to the words or if the party uses the words wrongly, and the other party is not unaware of the actual intentions, then in that situation, Article II.-8:101(2) DCFR/5:102(2) PECL states that the meaning attributed to the words by the first party should be considered for interpretation. This rule is actually a more specific rule based on the aspect that common intention prevails over the literal meaning, and this has been widely recognized. Although in the common law system, the objective interpretation dominates in general, yet under this situation, if the particularly different meaning attributed to the words is clearly stated and the other party is not unaware of it, then, the judges interpret the contract according to what has been clearly stated in the contract.[383]

Except for the subjective interpretation, the DCFR/PECL also combines with the objective method of adopting the rule of 'officious bystander' mentioned in Article II.-8:101(3) DCFR/5:101(3) PECL. As stated in those provisions, the interpretation should be given according to the understanding of a reasonable person in the same circumstances, where the subjective method cannot discover the intentions of the parties concerned. This rule actually supplements the subjective interpretation, and it is true to say that in the DCFR/PECL, the subjective interpretation dominates. Therefore, on the one hand it reveals party autonomy is more respected, as the contract is considered to be the result of mutual intentions but on the other hand, if the mutual intentions cannot be discovered, then, the objective method taken by a external view according to the criteria of reasonableness and good faith will be adopted, which demonstrates the values of maintaining market certainty and keeping the fairness between the parties in place. In sum, the choosing of subjective or objective interpretations reveals which is more respected, whether party autonomy or the certainty of business transactions and fairness between

380. Lando & Beale (2000b), *supra* n. 22, 289–292.
381. McKendrick (2004), *supra* n. 377, 31–32.
382. Hein Kötz, Interpretation and Contents, in Beale et al. (2002), *supra* n. 368, 578–579.
383. *Ibid.*, p. 566.

parties. However, it is true to say that all these values shall be considered at the same level, or even if it is argued that autonomy will be more dramatic, all the values are considered nonetheless important and should be integrated. It is not often that a current system will adhere to only one method of interpretation. Most of the systems hover between subjective and objective interpretations, as all the values of autonomy, business certainty and fairness between parties need to be balanced and taken into account.

However, compared with the PECL on the rule of the 'officious bystander', the DCFR supplements another provision on the exception of privity of contract. Traditionally, neither additional obligations nor any enforceable rights may be given to a person who is not a party to the contract, since the rights and obligations of those who have not consented to the agreement cannot be affected. But many national rules nowadays permit the extension of the contract to the parties who did not sign it, such as the extension to the agency.[384] Under this circumstance, if the contract is extended to a third party who has never consented to it, then, when interpreting the contract, the DCFR requires the judges to adopt the rule of the 'officious bystander'. This supplemented-rule in fact is to maintain some fairness among the parties. It is obviously unfair if the subjective method of interpretation according to the common intention of the parties which signed the contract was extended to those who were not party to the contract, as they have not even consented to the agreement. Although for the signatory parties, the subjective interpretation will be the best approach for them, as their mutual intentions will be respected it would also be unfair to the non-signatory party. In order to be fair to all the parties, the objective method according to the reasonableness shall be used. It is worth mentioning that in the Netherlands, for the collective employment contracts (CAOs), the interpretation is restricted to the 'information that is publicly available for all parties involved'.[385] From this perspective, it is reasonable to say that under the DCFR, fairness is a limitation to party autonomy, since its subjective interpretation is not effective when the contract is extended to a third non-signatory party, and the aim of the extension of 'officious bystander' is to maintain (substantive) fairness among the parties.

3.1.1.2. Relevant Matters

Article II.-8:102 DCFR/5:102 PECL sets out the circumstances which have to be taken into account when seeking common intentions of the parties, which are (a) preliminary negotiations; (b) subsequent conduct; (c) practices established between the parties; (d) meaning commonly given; (d) nature and purpose of the contract; (e) usages; (f) good faith and fair dealing. All these circumstances are matters, which may be relevant for the determination of either the common intentions or the reasonable meanings of the contract for judges. It is correct to say in fact that the common intentions of the parties can only be assumed by the judges, as

384. Collins (2008a), *supra* n. 5, 302–308.
385. Kornet (2006), *supra* n. 366, 39.

one cannot enter the inner minds of the parties to see what they really think. However, in order to make this hypothetical intention reveal the real common intention, all the circumstances of making the contract should be considered. So the DCFR/PECL clearly states all the relevant matters for the judges to interpret the contract. However, it is true to say that the first three circumstances are more closely relevant for subjective interpretation since the common intentions can be easily revealed from the communications and behaviours of the parties, which include negotiations, subsequent conduct and practices between the parties. But for the objective interpretation, the last three circumstances are more relevant, since objective interpretation refers to clear ambiguities or fill the gaps through the views of a reasonable person. So it is true to say that the usages, the meanings commonly given, and the nature and purpose of the contract are more important for a reasonable man, as he does not have to dig out the mutual intentions of the parties. However, it shall be noted that in the common law system, in order to maintain the certainty of transactions, pre-contractual negotiations are not reliable as a guide to the interpretation of a formal contract document.[386] But the DCFR/PECL still sets the preliminary negotiations as relevant circumstances, which clearly demonstrates that the judges are encouraged to dig out the mutual intentions of the parties, since common intentions can often be better revealed after considering the documents of prior negotiations. However, if the parties make it clear that documents of previous negotiations will not be used for interpretation, then, this common intention shall be respected. It is thus true to say the DCFR/PECL is more in favour of subjective interpretation, which is 'justified by the principle of party autonomy',[387] since it allows the judges to draw conclusions as to the intentions of the parties after taking into account all the circumstances, in particular the prior negotiations and subsequent conduct.

3.1.1.3. *Contra proferentem* Rule

Contra proferentem rule means the unclear term to be construed against the party who is responsible for the drafting. Generally speaking, three elements are constituted for the rule, which are: (a) doubt the meaning of a contract term: the rule only applies when there is a dispute on the meaning of the term, and both parties understand it differently; (b) not individually negotiated: the term is normally drawn-up unilaterally by one party without negotiation; (c) against the party who supplied it: the rule makes it certain that the term is to be interpreted against the party who is the author of the clause or the party using the clause drafted by a third person.[388] This provision applies not only against the author of the contract, but also against the one who supplies the pre-drafted contract. In the classical

386. Von Bar & Clive (2009), *supra* n. 24, 563.
387. K. Zweigert & H. Kötz, *An Introduction to Comparative Law*, Clarendon Press, 1998, 401.
388. C. Mak, Liability for Negotiations, in Danny Busch, Ewoud Hondius, Hugo van Kooten, Harriët Schelhaas & Wendy Schrama (eds), *The Principles of European Contract Law and Dutch Law: A Commentary*, Kluwer Law International, 2002, 250.

contract law, the strict performance of the contract was demonstrated as respecting the autonomy of the parties; but in modern contract law, the maintenance of substantive fairness is a primary ethic to limit the freedom, which can obviously be seen from the *contra proferentem* rule. In the pre-supplied contract, an imbalanced bargaining position often existed, and for the achievement of substantive fairness between the parties; the law had to be in favour of the party, which was weaker in the bargaining process. So the *contra proferentem* rule has been set to achieve substantive fairness between the parties, under the rule of which the judges can simply interpret the contract against the party who supplied it instead of digging out the common intention. From this perspective, it is true to say *contra proferentem* is an exception to subjective interpretation, and (substantive) fairness is a limitation to party autonomy. The rule has been adopted through Article II.-8:103 DCFR/5:103 PECL. Besides this, the DCFR goes even further and extends the rule to the application of the case where the contract has been concluded under the dominant influence of a party even if it has been negotiated.[389] This extended rule does not apply only to the contract between business and consumers, but it is also applicable to the contract between a professional company and a non-professional party. It is true to say that even in the negotiated contract, if a party may dominantly influence the contract, then, it shall also be interpreted against this party. Hence, it is reasonable to say that when compared with the PECL, the DCFR is even more extensive and integrating in terms of the contractual (substantive) fairness.

3.1.1.4. Legal-Effect Preference to the Individually Negotiated Terms

The principle of interpretation is to rely on the ability of the court to recognize 'which parts of a contract are general terms not chosen by the parties, and which have been specially negotiated'.[390] However, for some years, numerous types of contracts were made on the standard forms, and various printed words were frequently altered or omitted by the contractual parties. Under this situation, 'the object sought to be achieved in construing any contract is to ascertain what the mutual intentions of the parties were as to the legal obligations each assumed by the contractual words in which they sought to express them'.[391] Article II.-8:104 DCFR/5:104 PECL follows this rule to give the effect of preference to the individually negotiated terms rather than the standard terms or those, which have not been negotiated when both are in conflict with each other. This provision is consistent with subjective interpretation, which demonstrates that party autonomy is highly respected, since the individually negotiated terms are in the best position to find out the mutual intentions of the parties. Except for the individually negotiated terms, preference is also given to the modifications made to a printed contract

389. Von Bar & Clive (2009), *supra* n. 24, 565.
390. Lewison (2004), *supra* n. 378, 307.
391. *Pioneer Shipping Ltd v. B.T.P. Tioxide Ltd*, [1982] A.C. 724; Cited by Lewison (2004), *supra* n. 378, 19.

either by writing in hand or in other ways, as it is assumed the modifications are always negotiated and they may reflect the mutual intentions of the parties better.[392] It is thus true to say the prevalence of individually negotiated terms is a more specific rule of subjective interpretation, and its purpose is to respect mutual intentions and the autonomy of the parties.

3.1.1.5. Reference to Contract as a Whole

Due to the fact that the same word or clause may be understood differently in different parts of the same contract, a term shall be construed coherently after taking the whole contract into account. The judges may not isolate clauses from each other and interpret them out of context.[393] Article II.-8:105 DCFR/5:105 PECL provides a guideline to complement the main rules of interpretation in Article II.-8:101 and 102 DCFR/ 5:101 &102 PECL. It is true to say this provision is an additional rule to help the judges discern the common intentions of the parties, or to give a reasonable interpretation through a reasonable person. It is worth mentioning that taking the contract as a whole also applies to the groups of contracts under which, the contract or the term shall be construed after considering the entire framework of contracts coherently.[394]

3.1.1.6. Terms to Be Given Effect

For the contract, it sometimes happens that there are two methods of interpreting the ambiguities in which one way of interpretation could render the contract invalid and the other, on the contrary, would make it valid. If the judge seeks out the common intentions between the parties under the provisions of Article II.-8:101 DCFR/5:101 PECL, then the interpretation will perhaps render the contract invalid. In such an event, Article II.-8:106 DCFR/5:106 PECL makes it certain that the preference, which makes the contract valid should be chosen by the judges. This rule is found in the French, Belgium, Italian, Spanish and Luxembourg codes as well as in the case laws of Germany and England.[395] Since one of the functions of contract law is to maintain the certainty of business transactions, the frequent invalidity will cause an uncertainty in the market. However, on the other hand, the rule supporting the preference for a valid contract may impair the effect of party autonomy, if the common intentions were found to render a contract invalid. It is thus true to say the preference for the validity of the contract is an exception to subjective interpretation and its purpose is to maintain the certainty of market transactions. From this perspective therefore, the functions of economic

392. Lando & Beale (2000b), *supra* n. 22, 295.
393. Von Bar & Clive (2009), *supra* n. 24, 568.
394. C. Mak, Liability for Negotiations, in Busch, Hondius, van Kooten, Schelhaas & Schrama (2002), *supra* n. 389, 254.
395. Lando & Beale (2000b), *supra* n. 22, 297.

development or its efficiency can be regarded as a limitation to party autonomy, or an incentive for the interpretations.[396]

3.1.1.7. Linguistic Discrepancies

The DCFR/PECL mainly deals with cross-border transactions within the EU, and it is normal for a contract to be drafted in several versions of different languages. As discrepancies often occur between these different versions, it is seen that the meaning of a word or a term is not consistent between one language and the other, therefore, the question arises in accordance – with which version, should the words be interpreted or which version should prevail.

Article II.-8:107 DCFR/5:107 PECL acknowledges that preference should be given to the version in which the contract was originally drawn up since it is assumed the original draft is likely to express the common intentions of the parties mostly.[397] From this perspective, it is true to say this rule is consistent with subjective interpretation since both rules seek mutual intentions of the parties. However, if in the contract, different versions are provided to be treated equally, the interpretation, it is argued, will be decided according to the version that corresponds better to the common intentions of the parties.[398] This provision actually is the extension of Article II.-8:101 DCFR/5:101 PECL. It is worth mentioning that this provision shall be read 'along with the *contra proferentem* rule if the original version was drafted by one of the parties'.[399]

3.1.2. Chinese Contract Law

For a long time in Chinese legal history, the rules on contract interpretation were found lacking. In ancient China, the '*Yamen*' [government] combined both the administrative with judicial powers, and there was no single judicial unit.[400] The judge was the head of the '*Yamen*' and was also the governor. Specific contract interpretation rules were not needed, as mostly the 'Exact Confession by Torture' (*xing xun bi gong*) had been used for thousands of years in ancient China.[401] What mattered to the head of the '*Yamen*' was to find the 'truth' of the parties.

Even in the contract laws of the 1980s, it is seen that the doctrine of contract interpretation had not been adopted. After the implementation of the CLC, it was the first time that the interpretation rules were written in Chinese law. Under the CLC, there are two provisions regarding the contract interpretation, which are

396. Avery Wiener Katz, Contract Formation and Interpretation, *New Palgrave Dictionary of Economics and the Law*, 1998, 8–11.
397. Lando & Beale (2000b), *supra* n. 22, 298.
398. *Ibid.*, 298.
399. Von Bar & Clive (2009), *supra* n. 24, 571.
400. Huang (2001), *supra* n. 70, 185–189.
401. J. Chen, *Chinese Law: Towards an Understanding of Chinese Law, Its Nature and Development*, Kluwer Law International, 1999, 219–222.

Articles 41[402] and 125.[403] According to the CLC, judges issue their interpretations based on three concepts, which form the core principles.

3.1.2.1. True Meaning

As it has been widely accepted in China, contractual obligation arises primarily from the agreement between parties, and the interpretation is thus the means of defining the scope of contractual obligations under the principle of party autonomy.[404] The function and role of judges, during this process, is to seek common intentions that the contractual parties had agreed upon.[405] Article 125 thus acknowledges that the interpretation is to determine the 'true meaning', which should be sought according to the relevant provisions of the contract, the purpose, the transaction usage and the principle of good faith. It is fair to say the 'true meaning' is the core essence the judges have to dig out for their interpretation. Regarding the definition of 'true meaning', some scholars argue that it is equivalent to the meaning of 'common intention' in the West; but as mentioned above, in Chinese history, the 'truth' was the principal elements, which the head of the '*Yamen*' had to dig out. So it is true to say the notion of 'true meaning' has come down from Chinese history, although in modern contract law it has the same meaning as 'common intentions'.[406]

The approach to finding this 'common intention', is unclear in the CLC. Some Chinese scholars argue that the interpretation rule combines both the objective expressions and subjective intentions,[407] while some others think the subjective interpretation is primarily adopted, and the understanding from a third, reasonable party is immaterial for the judges.[408] Since the CLC does not make

402. Article 41 CLC: 'If a dispute arises over the understanding of a standard term, the term shall be interpreted in accordance with the usual understanding of the term. If there are two or more interpretations of a standard term, the interpretation that is unfavourable to the party that supplies the standard term shall be adopted. If there is an inconsistency between a standard term and a non-standard term, the non-standard term shall prevail.'
403. Article 125 CLC:

> (1) If there is a dispute between the parties over the understanding of a term of the contract, the true meaning of that term shall be determined in light of the words and expressions used in the contract, the related terms in the contract, the purpose of the contract, the usage of transaction and the principle of good faith. (2) Where a contract is drawn up in two or more languages and it is agreed that all versions are equally authentic, the words and expressions used in all versions shall be presumed to have the same meaning. Where the words and expressions of different language versions are not consistent with each other, they shall interpret in light of the purpose of the contract.

404. Wang (2002), *supra* n. 262, 405–412.
405. Jiang Ping, *zhong guo xing he tong fa quan shu* [*Encyclopedia of Contract Law of China*], zhong guo ren ming gong an da xue chu ban she [People's Public Security University Press], 1999e, 205–207.
406. Ling (2002), *supra* n. 10, 226–227.
407. Zhang (2006), *supra* n. 71, 130.
408. Ling (2002), *supra* n. 10, 226.

clear the approach adopted to seek the 'true meaning', for the discussion of this issue, the case of *ShanXi Machinery Import & Export Corp.* (hereinafter seller) *v. ShanXi Petroleum & Chemical Material Supply & Marking Co., Ltd* (hereinafter buyer)[409] will be a good example to reveal the approach adopted in Chinese law. In this case, both parties agreed in the contract 'the goods should arrive in Shanghai Harbour no later than 5 July 1993 to deliver after the customs declaration, inspection and quarantine' in the blank of 'delivery time and quantity'. But in fact, the goods arrived in Shanghai Harbour on 25 July and passed the inspection on 25 August before finally arriving on 28 August. The buyer informed the seller of his intentions to terminate the contract when it was found that the goods had not been delivered on 5 July, and then refused to accept the goods on 28 August. The buyer lodged a suit in the ShanXi High Court to request a termination of contract and remedial measures for the breach of contract by the seller. In this case, the ShanXi High Court found the fact that the contract was valid, and the seller should have delivered the goods before 5 July. The buyer was thus held to have the right to terminate the contract since the seller had failed to deliver it on time. However, in the appellate court, the judges reversed the judgment of ShanXi High Court and held that 5 July, meant the time when the goods should have arrived at Shanghai Harbour rather than be delivered to the buyer. So now it meant that the seller would have to pay the late remedial fees according to the contract, since the goods had arrived at Shanghai Harbour before 5 July. But the buyer could not terminate the contract and was told to accept the goods. Therefore, the buyer was held liable for a breach of contract.

The main issue in this case is in the literal Chinese expressions. The provision of the time of 5 July 1993 is rather ambiguous as there could be two meanings which are: (1) the goods should have been delivered before 5 July 1993; (2) the goods should have arrived in Shanghai Customs for the customs declaration, inspection and quarantine before 5 July 1993. The ShanXi High Court interpreted the term according to the fact that the time was written below the blank space provided for 'delivery time and place', which was in contrast with the interpretation rules. The appellate court considered the whole contract instead of interpreting the provisions according to the information printed on the blank space provided.[410] Although this case occurred before the implementation of the CLC, to some extent it reveals the interpretation under Chinese contract law, which makes seeking subjective intentions of the parties, and the literal expressions of the contract, immaterial. However, it should be noted that the 'true meaning' is not to dig out what the inner thoughts of the parties are, but to rely on the declared intentions, except if the declaration is defective.[411] This reflection may be also observed from the Academic Draft of Contract Law, which was implemented to take over from the CLC after some revisions. In the academic draft one, this provision was expressed,

409. The case was cited by Huixing Liang in the book of *min shang fa lun cong* [*Civil and Commercial Law Review*], vol. 6, 1996a.

410. *Ibid.*

411. Ling (2002), *supra* n. 10, 226.

as 'in the interpretation of a contract, the common and true intention of the parties shall be sought rather than the literal meaning of the words or expressions'.[412] From this original provision, it is obvious that the purpose of interpretation was to find the common intentions of the parties through the subjective approach.

3.1.2.2. Purpose of Contract

Another crucial element in the interpretation under the CLC is the definition of 'purpose of contract', which does not mean the particular purpose for which the contractual parties entered into the contract, but refers to the general economic and social effects which the contractual parties are pursuing.[413] For example, in the sales contract, generally speaking, one party is pursuing money while the other is in it for the objects.[414] However, in fact, both parties possibly have some other purposes for entering into the contract. But the general purpose can only be the one that both parties are normally pursuing. Also, due to the fact that the purpose of the parties may have changed with the development of practical market situations; the 'purpose of contract' only concerns the aims at the time when the parties entered into the contract instead of the time when the contract was performed.

The notion of the purpose of contract is significantly important in the CLC for proper interpretation. Article 125 sets out that if the words or clauses in two or more different versions of languages are not consistent in the contract and the parties agree that all versions have the same authority, then, the purpose of contract shall be used to determine the 'true meaning'. As the true meaning is a concept similar to common intentions, and China primarily chooses the subjective interpretation, it is thus true to say the purpose of contract is of utmost relevance to find out the true meaning of the parties.

Besides this, according to some scholars, the concept of the 'purpose of contract' could also be extended to the interpretation in favour of the valid contract.[415] This means if two interpretations could be adopted, but one would invalidate the contract while the other would validate it; the latter interpretation would be chosen to make it consistent with the purpose of contract, as mostly the parties enter into the contract for the purpose of business transactions rather than to conclude an invalid contract.

From the above explanation of the purpose of contract, it is true to say the scope and the meaning of the notion has been extended to some more concrete situations. However, it is still a rather vague concept in the CLC since China lacked the rules of interpretation in its long history. And it is reasonable to say the general rules of interpretation could not be implemented functionally, and the vague notions were difficult for the judges to adopt in practice. The future Chinese

412. *Ibid.*
413. Wang (2002), *supra* n. 262, 435.
414. *Ibid.*
415. *Ibid.*

civil code, it is hoped, shall make all these concepts and the interpretation strategies as well as the rules more specific and detailed.

3.1.2.3. *Contra proferentem* Rule

The *contra proferentem* rule in the CLC has been transplanted from the Western countries and Article 41 makes it certain that for a standard term, if there are two or more interpretations, then the interpretations shall be unfavourable to the party which drafts it. This rule in fact is a limitation to the subjective interpretation, which seeks to find out the true meaning of the parties under the CLC. According to this rule, the judges do not have to find out the true intentions of the parties for the standard contract, and the only way they can do this is by simply interpreting against the party, which supplied it. The *contra proferentem* rule has been widely accepted to maintain the contractual fairness between the parties. It is true to say that fairness also limits party autonomy in the CLC. However, this rule is only limited to the standard contract in China.

3.1.3. Comparison

The CLC was the first time when a contract interpretation rule was written in Chinese Law, the rules of which had been transplanted from the Western legal systems, and the 'true meaning' was the core essence the judges had to dig out for proper interpretation. By contrast, in the West, the academics have constructed a fruitful basis for the development of modern contract law, and the rules on interpretation of the contract are rather systematic. It is correct to say the judges have to seek the common intentions of the parties when construing the contract in almost all the legal systems. But the approach differs between the continental countries and common law countries. Traditionally, subjective interpretation and objective interpretation are the two main approaches based on the will and expression theories. However, nowadays most of the countries combine both approaches. The DCFR/PECL also follows this tendency. Under the DCFR/PECL, the subjective approach is mainly adopted to seek out the common intentions of both parties. If the common intentions cannot be found under this approach, then the understanding according to a reasonable person shall be used. However, when compared with the CLC, there are some differences as mentioned below:

3.1.3.1. Common Intention versus True Meaning

'Common intention' is the core element that judges have to seek for interpretation under the DCFR/PECL, whilst the 'true meaning' is set out under the CLC as a supreme essence of its interpretation. The 'true meaning' in fact is drawn from Chinese history, which said that the '*Yamen*' often searched for the truth through the 'Exact Confession by Torture'. However, in modern Chinese law, it is argued the 'true meaning' under the CLC is equivalent to the 'common intention' listed in the DCFR/PECL, as the CLC nowadays also believes party autonomy is an overriding principle of private law, and the 'true meaning' is to seek the mutual intentions of the parties. But the approach to dig out the common intentions between both systems differs slightly. The DCFR/PECL ascertains that the subjective interpretation is the main rule for the judges to discern the common intentions, which shall be supplemented by the objective interpretation if it cannot be found out through the previous approach. It is true to say the DCFR/PECL combines both approaches to dig out the common intentions of the parties. However, under the CLC, it is unclear which approach has been adopted; but, from the case laws analysed, it is true to say the subjective interpretation prevails over the expression. However, whether the objective approach is also adopted under the CLC or whether the 'true meaning' cannot be found out by the subjective interpretation is indicative of a gap in the practice.

3.1.3.2. Relevant Circumstances

Under the DCFR/PECL, the relevant circumstances to search for the 'common intention' are: (a) preliminary negotiations; (b) subsequent conduct; (c) practices established between the parties; (d) meaning commonly given; (d) nature and purpose of the contract; (e) usages; (f) good faith and fair dealing. But in the CLC, the true meaning shall be dug out according to: (a) expression and words; (b) relevant provisions; (c) purpose of contract; (d) usage of transactions; and (e) good faith. The main difference in the relevant circumstances for interpretation between the DCFR/PECL and the CLC is whether the preliminary negotiations and subsequent conduct can be used to determine the common intentions. Under the DCFR/PECL, both the preliminary negotiations and subsequent conduct are set as the relevant circumstances since it is assumed that the mutual intentions of the parties can be better revealed through the individual communications. On the contrary, the documents from prior negotiations and subsequent conduct are not within the purview of circumstances that the judges have to consider in the CLC. From this perspective, it is true to say that although both the DCFR/PECL and the CLC adopt the subjective interpretations, which adhere to party autonomy, the DCFR/PECL pays more attention to the communications between the parties.

3.1.3.3. *Contra proferentem* Rule

Both the DCFR/PECL and the CLC adopt the *contra proferentem* rule to make it certain that the interpretation will be against the person who drafts the term if both parties understand it differently. However, the rule in the CLC is only restricted to the standard term, whereas the DCFR extends this rule also, to the dominant influence of one party, which brings about the conclusion of the contract, which has been negotiated. This rule has proved to be an exception to subjective interpretation for the purpose of maintaining the contractual (substantive) fairness. From this perspective, it is true to say contractual fairness in the DCFR/PECL than in the CLC, has a wider scope of limiting party autonomy.

3.1.3.4. Linguistic Discrepancies

Both the DCFR/PECL and the CLC take the situation of linguistic discrepancies for international transactions into account, and set out the rules for the interpretation if the terms or words are inconsistent during these versions. The DCFR/PECL makes it clear that if all the versions have equal effect, then, the interpretation shall be in accordance with the contract in its original language. However, the CLC sets the true meaning as the measure for the judges under this circumstance. It is thus reasonable to say that both the CLC and the DCFR/PECL try to find out the common intentions of the parties, but when compared, the rules under the DCFR/PECL are more concrete than in the CLC, and it is easier for the party to foresee the remedies when disputes arise.

Therefore, two dramatic striking points can be observed from the comparison. The first one refers to the historical and cultural influences of the CLC. Although the provisions regarding the interpretation in the CLC actually are mostly transplanted from the international treaties, the core concept – true meaning – under the CLC is drawn from its own history. Although in academics, it is described as being equivalent to common intention, since China is not a case law country, it is difficult to know how this term is practically understood by the judges. But at least from different terminology, it is true to conclude that Chinese history and culture still exercise some influence on the current CLC. The second point concerns the modern meaning of party autonomy, which is primarily restricted by contractual fairness. Under the DCFR, the application of *contra proferentem* is extended to the contract, which is dominantly influenced by a party, whereas the CLC only restricts it to the standard terms. Both dramatic differences can be reasonably explained by the different roles and functions of party autonomy that is rooted in the local history and culture. Since in ancient China, the doctrine of interpretation was lacking in history, the judges would find out the truth through exacting confessions using torture instead of digging out the common intentions (a reflection of party autonomy). So it is true to say that party autonomy had not been generally recognized at that time. Influenced by this history, the true meaning is adopted in the CLC as a core principle rather than the notion of common intentions. However, the modern meaning of party autonomy is not only about freedom, and its limitations, but should also be connected to good faith and fair dealing. From this perspective, the modern meaning of party autonomy under the CLC is seen to lack deep integration as compared to the DCFR, which can be demonstrated through the extension of *contra proferentem* rules to the dominant influences of a party under the DCFR.

3.2. PRE-CONTRACTUAL LIABILITY

As revealed by the merits of party autonomy, parties are free to enter into or break-off the negotiations and are free to decide whether or not to conclude a contract. According to the classical contract law, parties are usually not bound by any agreement before the formation of the contract, and the number of extra-contractual obligations it was seen, were rather limited to be enforced by the judges.[416] However, in recent decades, it has often been assumed that the doctrine of 'offer and acceptance' is not sufficient to govern the process of contract formation, since the legal and ethical rules should have been established among the business community before the contract was concluded. Especially in modern business transactions, parties usually enter into rounds of negotiations and there are successions of draft agreements aimed at maximizing expected economic outcomes. Sometimes a draft agreement is suggested as a 'preliminary agreement' and if the transaction turns out to be profitable after uncertainty is resolved, the parties go on to make their agreement more concrete and certain.

Rudolph von Jhering, the first scholar to recognize the liability of a falsity party during the process of negotiation, argued that a party, which induced another to rely on the conclusion of a valid contract could be liable for *culpa in contrahendo*.[417] However, he only dealt with situations where a party was lead to conclude an invalid contract by the other's fault in the negotiation stage, but without any mention to the liability for negotiations broken-off. Only in 1906, the Neapolitan magistrate Gabriele Fagella started to discuss the liability for broken-off negotiations. He distinguished the negotiation process into three stages, which were, the period before the offer had been drafted, the period during which the offer was being drafted and the period after the offer had been made.[418] He accepted that the negotiating party could be liable in all these stages, the opinion of which was also recognized by the French lawyer Raymond Saleilles and later enforced by German lawyers to supplement the doctrine of *culpa in contrahendo*.[419] Nowadays, 'all legal systems are moving in the same direction of imposing on the parties the obligation to behave fairly when conducting negotiation; violation of such obligation leading to imposition of pre-contractual liability'.[420] The balanced relationship between the freedom to the contract and respect for the interest of the other party could be found through this doctrine.[421] This section is therefore intended to describe the differences in pre-contractual liability between the DCFR/PECL and the CLC, and the reason for these differences will also be analysed subsequently.

3.2.1. European Contract Law

As argued by some scholars, such as Atiyah, extra-contractual duties can be divided into negative duties, positive duties and reliance-based duties. According

416. Atiyah & Smith (2005), *supra* n. 290, 85.
417. Alyona N. Kucher, Pre-contractual Liability: Protecting the Rights of the Parties Engaged in Negotiations, the text is available at: <http://centers.law.nyu.edu/jeanmonnet/fellowsforum/Kucher-paper.rtf> (last accessed in May 2010), 10.
418. Martijn Hesselink, Pre-contractual Good Faith, in Beale et al. (2002), *supra* n. 368, 237–238.
419. *Ibid.*
420. Kucher (2010), *supra* n. 418, 10.
421. Martijn Hesselink, Pre-contractual Good Faith, in Beale et al. (2002), *supra* n. 368, 238.

to his opinion, 'negative duties' mean the duties of not harming another's person, property or liberty, and 'positive duties' are to assist or benefit another person, whilst 'reliance-based duties' refer to the loss suffered by someone who detrimentally relied on the belief that a contract would be created, where the belief was not induced by a misstatement and the reliance did not benefit the others.[422] But some others described it more specifically, and several duties within this general category are argued as being contrary to good faith and fair dealing which are conducting parallel negotiations, negotiating without intending to conclude a contract, knowingly concluding an invalid contract, not giving adequate information, disclosing confidential information, and causing physical harm to the other party in the course of negotiations.[423] Chapter III in Book II of DCFR deals with the marketing and pre-contractual duties. Within this category are five sections: (1) information duties; (2) duty to prevent input errors and acknowledge receipt; (3) negotiation and confidentiality duties; (4) unsolicited goods or services; and (5) damages for breach of duty. This subsection will describe three specific duties of: duty of information, negotiation in accordance with good faith and fair dealing, and duty of confidentiality.

3.2.1.1. Information Duty

One of the most significant specific duties in the negotiation stage is that of the negotiating party which may have to inform each other adequately about the material facts. Information duty is 'of exceptional significant in European contract law'.[424] Article II.-3:101 DCFR deals with the duty of disclosing information about goods, other assets and services, under which the business-to-business contract and the business-to non-business contract are distinctly rendered. In the first type of contract, the disclosure of information not deviating from 'good commercial practice' is required; while in the latter, the disclosure of sufficient information under 'normal circumstances' is demanded. The duty in fact does not require full or positive disclosure, but merely requires disclosing all the information that can be reasonably expected by the other party.

It is worth mentioning that the disclosure of adequate information during the negotiation process is different from the duties in the event of a mistake or fraud. In the latter case, the party could be held liable after the conclusion of the contract and one of the consequences is to avoid the contract, if the party's failure to disclose material information either in the pre-contractual stage or in the contract itself leads to the conclusion of the contract. But the first one only refers to the liability of false party, which does not disclose adequate information, and which leads the others to continue the negotiations but without concluding the contract.

---

422. Atiyah & Smith (2005), *supra* n. 290, 86–92.
423. Martijn Hesselink, Pre-contractual Good Faith, in Beale et al. (2002), *supra* n. 368, 238.
424. Reiner Schulze, Precontractual Duties and Conclusion of Contract in European Law, *European Review of Private Law*, vol. 6, 2005, 847.

Take an example, before concluding the contract, one party breaks-off the negotiations as he notices there is some material information that has not been disclosed by the other party and if he knows this early, he will not continue the negotiation. In this case, the false party could be held liable for the pre-contractual disclosure duty. But if the party knows that the non-disclosure of material information after the contract has been concluded, then the case will be within the category of a fraud or mistake.

However, the duty regulated under Article II.-3:101 DCFR is only imposed on businesses engaged in the supply of goods, other assets and services.[425] But it is not a generalization of the law of contracts. Articles II.-3:102 to II.-3:107 also regard the specific duties applied to the relations between businesses and consumers.[426] The reason that the information duty has not been widely integrated into the general rules of contract is due to the sharp differences between the continental countries and common law countries.[427] In the common law system, the disclosure duty is based on the principle of equity whereas in civil law system, it is derived from pre-contractual good faith. Due to this dramatic difference, it is difficult for the DCFR to broadly integrate the information duty as a generalization of contract law. However, regarding the area of consumer law, numerous directives have already imposed the duty on the parties, and it is true to say that the information duty can be found out as a general principle in the existing EC consumer law.[428] So the DCFR mainly builds on the common traditions of the Member States and on the autonomous principles of the *acquis communautaire*,[429] and only brings out the duty of information into the consumer contract law.

3.2.1.2. Negotiation in Accordance with Good Faith and Fair Dealing

Article II.-3:301 DCFR/2:301 PECL does not only entitle the freedom to negotiate, but also recognizes the general duty of pre-contractual good faith during the negotiation process that both parties have to take each other's interest into account. The negotiation in accordance with good faith and fair dealing is required in the DCFR/PECL. Article II.-3:301(2) and (4) DCFR makes it concrete that breaking-off negotiation and negotiation with no real intention are the two specific situations for breaching of pre-contractual duties. These duties may not be excluded or limited by the parties in their contract. From the comments of DCFR/PECL, the drafting committee describes these duties in more concrete situations, which are: (a) entering into negotiation knowing that a contract will not be concluded;

425. Von Bar & Clive (2009), *supra* n. 24, 200–201.
426. Schulze (2005), *supra* n. 425, 849.
427. Thomas Wilhelmsson & Christian Twigg-Flesner, Pre-Contractual Information Duties in the *Acquis Communautaire*, *European Review of Contract Law*, vol. 4, 2006, 443–444.
428. Carlo Castronovo, Information Duties and Precontractual Good Faith, *European Review of Private Law*, vol. 4, 2009, 363–365.
429. Schulze (2005), *supra* n. 425, 841.

(b) continuing negotiations after one has decided not to conclude the contract; and
(c) breaking off negotiations contrary to good faith and fair dealing.[430]

However, as pointed out above, the liability for concluding an invalid contract was first recognized by Jhering through his article in 1861. And nowadays, it is widely recognized a party, which knows or should know that the contract will be invalid but without warning the other party, to be held for the reliance damages, as he failed to act in accordance with the duty to care, which had been established by the initiation of contractual negotiation between the parties.[431] It is worth mentioning that the provision of Article II.-3:301 DCFR/2:301 PECL is similar to the Article 2.1.15 Unidroit Principle of International Commercial Contracts (hereinafter Unidroit Principles). However, in the illustrations of Article 2.1.15 Unidroit Principles, it states:

> A, who is negotiating with B for the promotion of the purchase of military equipment by the armed forces of B's country, learns that B will not receive the necessary export license from its own governmental authorities, a prerequisite for permission to pay B's fees. A does not reveal this fact to B and finally concludes the contract, which, however, cannot be enforced by reason of the missing licenses. A is liable to B for the costs incurred after A had learned of the impossibility of obtaining the required licenses.[432]

It is obvious that a party shall be liable if it leads to the conclusion of an invalid contract by its fault under the Unidroit Principle. However, in the comments of DCFR/PECL, this situation has not been explicitly illustrated.

For the remedies of pre-contractual liability, in the previous practice, the ECJ took the view that the damages were related to the matter of tort for the purposes of Brussels Convention.[433] So under the DCFR, if the party negotiates contrary to good faith and fair dealing, the non-contractual liability arising out of damages caused to another, these can be claimed. Besides this, the contractual damages are alternative solutions for the claim, which means the party can claim the damages based on either a non-contractual or contractual basis.[434] Regarding their damages, a distinction is made between the reliance (negative) interest and the expectation (positive) interest. The first refers to the financial equivalent of what the plaintiff would have had if no negotiations had taken place, whereas the latter means the financial equivalent of what the plaintiff would have had if a valid contract had been concluded.[435] However, under the DCFR/PECL, the party, which breaches the pre-contractual duties shall compensate the losses, which include expenses incurred, work done, and loss of business made in reliance of the expected contract.

430. Von Bar & Clive (2009), *supra* n. 24, 247–248.
431. Case BGH, 29 Jan. 1965, NJW 65.813.
432. UNIDROIT Principles of International Commercial Contracts with Official Commentary [1994].
433. Von Bar & Clive (2009), *supra* n. 24, 262.
434. *Ibid.*, 248.
435. Martijn Hesselink, Pre-contractual Good Faith, in Beale et al. (2002), *supra* n. 368, 250–251.

It is true to say the DCFR/PECL acknowledges the 'positive interest' or 'expectation interest' that is 'reasonably expected as a consequence of the absence or incorrectness of the information'.[436]

3.2.1.3. Duty of Confidentiality

Generally speaking, parties, which negotiate a contract normally have no obligation to treat the information they have exchanged during the negotiations, as confidential. However, some information given to the other party may be declared as secret or may not be used by the other party. If this duty has been violated, the damages shall be compensated for the liability. Article II.-3:302 DCFR/2:302 PECL explicitly acknowledges the non-disclosure of confidential information duty, and clearly defines the 'confidential information' arising from, either the nature or the circumstances in which it is obtained. The party can expressly declare that the information they released is confidential and require the other party not to disclose this to others or use it for their own benefit. If the information is not expressly declared to be secret, then the implied duty shall also be complied with if the other party knows or can be reasonably expected to know that the the information is confidential. The implied duty can be derived from the character of the information, or from the status of professional parties. The duty of confidentiality is an important part of the pre-contractual liability under the DCFR/PECL. For the breach of this duty, the injured party may claim the benefits that the person in breach has received through the disclosure of the information or the using of it. If the injured party has suffered some losses, then he can also claim for the compensation of his losses to the party in breach.

3.2.2. Chinese Contract Law

Under the principle of voluntariness, parties are free to negotiate a contract, and decide whether to enter into the negotiation or continue their negotiation. However, in modern contract law, it is widely accepted that good faith and fair dealing are significant principles to limit the individual's freedom. Pre-contractual liability requires the parties to negotiate in accordance with good faith and fair dealing. The CLC, like most of the current legal systems, has accepted the pre-contractual liability to impose sanctions on the party, which violates the principle of good faith and causes the other party to suffer damages during the negotiation process. In fact, as early as in the Law of Economic Contracts Involving Foreign Interest, the party could be held reliable for the loss suffered by the other party if it was responsible for the invalidation of a contract.[437] Also, the GPCL provides that the party who is

436. Von Bar & Clive (2008), *supra* n. 27, 111.

437. Article 11, Law of The People's Republic of China on Economic Contracts Involving Foreign Interest, Adopted at the Tenth Session of the Standing Committee of the Sixth National People's Congress, promulgated on 21 Mar. 1985.

at fault shall compensate for the other's loss if the legal act was null or void.[438] These two provisions from the 1980s can be regarded as a basis for the development of pre-contractual liability in the CLC. However, both provisions were under the title of validity of contract instead of pre-contractual liability in the 1980s. It is true to say at that time in China, the pre-contractual liability had not been widely known yet. It was only after the 1990s, that the doctrine started to transplant from the Western countries. It was the first time that the CLC explicitly integrated it into Chinese law. According to Articles 42 and 43 of the CLC, there are four circumstances under which the party can be held liable, which are described below.

3.2.2.1. Negotiating in Bad Faith under the Pretext of Concluding a Contract

Article 42(1) holds that if a party negotiates in bad faith under the pretext of concluding a contract, then it shall be liable for the compensation. This provision in fact has been borrowed from the international treaties,[439] as in the Unidroit Principles, Article 2.1.15 states the party, which negotiates or breaks-off negotiations in bad faith should be liable. The essence of this provision in CLC is the concept of 'bad faith' that should include two elements, the first of which is that the party has no intention of concluding the contract whereas the second is that the party has the purpose of causing damages to the other party. However, it should be distinct from the situation where a party enters into the negotiations lacking knowledge of the market. If during the negotiations, the party becomes more knowledgeable about the market or about some changes in the company itself and decides to break-off the negotiation, then it cannot be liable for negotiating in bad faith.

3.2.2.2. Deliberately Concealing Important Facts Relating to the Conclusion of the Contract or Deliberately Providing False Information

Article 42(2) recognizes the duty of disclosure in the negotiation stages. Parties have to disclose adequate information to the others to ascertain their determination of whether to enter into a contract or continue their negotiations. The information required to be disclosed is a material fact relevant to the conclusion of the contract. It is true to say that under the situation, if a party concludes the contract based on some false information or some other information that it did not know, and if it knows the truth, it will not enter into the contract or continue its negotiation, then, it can claim the liability of compensation. It should be noted that under the doctrine of fraud, concealing information deliberately or providing false information could make the contract void. However, it is different from the pre-contractual liability in the following perspectives: (a) time: the pre-contractual liability should be held before the conclusion of the contract which means there should be no contract in

438. Article 61, GPCL.
439. Wang (2002), *supra* n. 262, 332–333.

existence, while the liability for fraud can only be held after the conclusion of the contract; (b) foundation: the liability for pre-contractual stage is based on the principle of good faith, while the liability for fraud is based on the contract; (c) effect: for the contractual liability, the effect is to compensate for the losses whereas for the effect of fraud, the contracts are generally held to be avoided or adapted.

3.2.2.3. Disclosing or Inappropriately Exploiting Business Secret

Article 43 of CLC recognizes the obligation of keeping business secrets during the negotiation stage. It holds that no matter if the contract was concluded or not, the business secret received by the party during the negotiation of the contract cannot be disclosed or improperly used. It is taken as an important part of the pre-contractual liability. However, the CLC does not give the definition of 'business secret', which has to be sought from the Anti-Unfair Competition Law,[440] under which business secret refers to the technical information or business information which is unknown to the public, and which could bring about economic benefits to the entitled person, have practical utility and in respect of which the entitled person takes measures to protect its secrecy.[441] From this provision, it is true to say there are four requirements that determine what a business secret is: (a) it is unknown to the public which expresses the fact that the information could not be obtained directly from the public channels; (b) it could bring the economic benefit to the owner, as it is widely accepted that the 'economic benefit' is the subjective test; (c) it has practical utility; and (d) the owner takes some measures to keep it a secret.

3.2.2.4. Other Activities Violating the Principle of Good Faith

Article 42(3) CLC gives a broad scope and content of pre-contractual liability. It provides that other activities violating the principle of good faith in the course of negotiations can be deemed as violating the pre-contractual duties. However, as the provision is too broad to exercise in practice, some scholars describe it more specifically. The pre-contractual liabilities are argued to include the following situations:[442] (a) obligation not to withdraw an offer without a due reason; (b) obligation to inform; (c) obligation to operate and assist; (d) obligation to be faithful; (e) obligation to keep secret; and (f) obligation not to abuse the freedom of the contract.

Therefore, it is true to say that under the CLC, there are three factors for the judges to determine the pre-contractual liability which are (a) violation of good faith: The requirement of good faith derives from what is expected from a reasonable person on the basis of moral, social and commercial standards in the society.

---

440. Anti-Unfair Competition Law of the People's Republic of China, Adopted by the Third Session of the Standing Committee of the Eighth National People's Congress on 2 Sep. 1993.
441. Article 10, Anti-Unfair Competition Law.
442. Wang (2002), *supra* n. 262, 312–313.

A prerequisite for pre-contractual liability requires the negotiations to be contrary with good faith; (b) subjective fault: in order to claim the pre-contractual liability, the defaulting party has to present the case that it acted either intentionally or negligently in breaching the duty; and (c) loss of reliance interest: the aggrieved party has to show it suffered losses due to the defaulting parties' breach of duty.

The elements that consist of the pre-contractual liability in the CLC can be reasonably concluded to a 'fault' and a 'loss'. For the 'fault', the party must demonstrate that it acted either intentionally or negligently when violating the pre-contractual duties.[443] If the party was held liable, the other party could choose either to sue on a contractual liability or on tort liability.[444] As to the 'loss', the injured party must show it suffered some losses due to the other's breach. However, the CLC only states that the party with failure to comply with pre-contractual obligations should pay the 'loss' without any provisions on which loss can be claimed. But as argued by some scholars, if the party was held liable for the pre-contractual compensation, then the injured party may claim damages for the reliance on the contract being concluded, which includes 'actual expenditure incurred in the negotiation and preparation for the performance of the contract and lost opportunities of alternative contracts with other persons'.[445]

3.2.3. Comparison

Freedom of contract entitles the parties to negotiate freely for the contract, which is a reflection of party autonomy. However, in modern times with the development of society, the concept of party autonomy has changed its meaning. It does not only refer to the self-determination, but the concept of good faith and fair dealing which also exercise a significant restriction to limit party autonomy. Under this tendency, as early as in 1861, Jhering discussed the liability for *culpa in contrahendo*. He argued that a party should be liable if he induced another party to rely on the conclusion of a valid contract. Based on this argument, the pre-contractual liability has been developed and widely accepted. Traditionally, the liabilities for broken-off negotiations and negotiating with no intention to conclude a contract are arguably the most two important elements.

Nowadays, the duty of information, duty to care and duty of confidentiality are generally of exceptional significance in contract laws. Under the DCFR, the pre-contractual liability, which is integrated includes: duty of information, negotiation in accordance with good faith and fair dealing, and duty of confidentiality. Broken-off negotiation and negotiation with no intention to conclude the contracts are specific situations, which are contrary to good faith and fair dealing. For claiming liability, parties can choose either the contractual liability or the non-contractual liability, and the party in breach shall compensate for the damages to the injured

443. Ling (2002), *supra* n. 10, 214.
444. Zhang (2006), *supra* n. 71, 85.
445. Ling (2002), *supra* n. 10, 215.

party, which can amount to the expectation interest. However, in the CLC, the pre-contractual liability has been formally transplanted since the 1990s, although in the contract laws of 1980s, the liability of an invalid contract induced by a party's fault had been already recognized under the title of Validity. In the CLC, four situations can be held reliable which are: (a) negotiating in bad faith under the pretext of concluding a contract; (b) concealing deliberately important facts relating to the conclusion of contract or providing deliberately false information; (c) disclosing or inappropriately exploiting business secret; and (d) other activities violating the principle of good faith. Generally speaking, both the DCFR and the CLC have the same rule that the negotiations shall not be contrary to good faith and fair dealing, otherwise the damages can be claimed. Within this category, both laws explicitly state that broken-off negotiations and negotiating with no intentions to conclude the contract are two particular situations for incurring liability.

However, a considerable difference in pre-contractual liability between the DCFR and the CLC may be found in information duty. In the DCFR, the information duty is only imposed on the businesses engaged in the supply of goods, other assets and services. It is not as generalized for all contract laws, and its scope is only limited to the consumer contracts or the businesses. However, in the CLC, the duty of information can be applied to the general contracts also. The reason resulting in this difference can be found in the fact that it is difficult for the DCFR to integrate the information duty into the general contract laws, due to the dramatic difference between the continental and common law systems. At the EC level, the duty of information has been only imposed on the consumer contracts. The DCFR may only represent the common rules of Europe or restate the existing EC law. But the duty of information cannot be found within either category, so that the DCFR cannot apply it to the general contracts. On the contrary, in China, pre-contractual liability started getting constructed since the 1990s and there existed no obstacle to its construction. So in China, the duty of information can be extended to the general contracts. Beside this, another difference maybe found from the standard to measure the information duty. Under the DCFR, the information duty is determined as what the other person can reasonably expect for the business-to-non-business contract, and non-deviation from good commercial practice for business-to-business contract, whereas in the CLC a deliberate intention is required for both these. It is true to say the standard in the CLC is higher than in the DCFR, for in the latter, any non-disclosure of the information the other party should expect, will be satisfied without any deliberate intention, whereas in the first, a deliberate intention is demanded. This difference may be reasonably explained by the broadly integrated weaker party protection norms listed in the DCFR, as the substantive fairness rules are nowadays more widely integrated in European contract law.

3.3. CONTRACT VALIDITY

It is generally accepted that when parties indicate their assent for a transaction, the contract is concluded. However, the binding effect of a contract does not generate from the mere assent of parties, but from the operation of law, which implies that contractual parties should comply with certain requirements of law in order to make their contracts legal. This section considers various situations in which the apparent agreement concluded by the parties will not be treated as fully effective for a variety of reasons. Generally speaking, the issue of validity includes three aspects: (1) incapacity, illegal and immoral contracts; (2) traditional deficiencies of wills, which contain mistakes, fraud and threats; (3) the most recent movement on weaker party protection which is crucially revealed from the imbalanced bargaining power, abuse of circumstances, information duties, and unfair exploitation. However, the DCFR/PECL does not deal with the issue of capacity, because 'it is more a matter of the law of persons than of contract proper'.[446] And illegality and immorality are treated through the effects of an infringement of fundamental principles or mandatory rules under the DCFR.[447] Since fundamental principles and mandatory rules are two of the most significant restrictions to party autonomy, in this dissertation, they will be analysed in two separate sections. Therefore, this section will only describe the traditional deficiencies of wills containing mistakes, fraud, and threats, and the most recent movements on weak party protection, which is mainly revealed from the protection against imbalanced bargaining. The research questions on whether there is any difference between the European and Chinese contract laws in the contract validity, and whether party autonomy can explain these differences will be analysed subsequently.

3.3.1. Mistake

All legal systems acknowledge that the contract could be void if the consent was defective. Mistake is one of the grounds, which is widely accepted to annul a contract. In a broad sense, it refers to 'some misapprehension about the subject matter of the contract or the circumstances, or as to the terms of the contract'.[448] The remedies of mistake are often allowed for the parties to escape from the agreement, which on the one hand may lead to the impairment of business certainty, and on the other hand it may reveal that the contract is a creation of mutual intention of the parties, and if this intention does not exist, then the parties shall not be obliged to undertake any obligations, which is ultimately to respect the autonomy or self-determination of the parties. Mistake thus strikes a fair balance between party autonomy and the protection of market certainty. This subsection attempts to compare the differences in mistake between the DCFR/PECL and the CLC in order to reveal how party autonomy is limited by mistake on both sides.

---

446. Lando & Beale (2000b), *supra* n. 22, 227.
447. Von Bar & Clive (2009), *supra* n. 24, 451.
448. Hugh Beale & John Harrington, Fraud, Mistake and Misrepresentation, in Beale et al. (2002), *supra* n. 368, 343.

3.3.1.1. European Contract Law

'The principle of freedom of contract suggests that a party should not be bound to a contract unless its consent to it was informed.'[449] It happens frequently that a party enters into a contract under some mistake or misapprehension. The DCFR/PECL therefore makes the rule certain that the contract can be avoided or partially avoided if it is concluded under this defective consent. Article II.-7:201(1) DCFR/4:103(1) PECL sets out that the mistake generally results from two aspects, which are the misapprehensions about the fact or misapprehensions about the existing law. In Europe, mistake is a traditional theory of will deficiencies, and since Roman law time, it has been a vital factor to render a contract void.[450] However, in order to ensure the certainty and security of business transactions, a party may not be allowed to escape frequently from contracts. The DCFR/PECL thus sets out several requirements for the constitution of mistake.

3.3.1.1.1. Mistake Must Make the Contract Fundamentally Different

'Fundamental' is a significant element to avoid a contract through mistake. The meaning of 'fundamental' is clearly defined in the DCFR/PECL as that the mistaken party would not have made the contract or would have done so only on fundamentally different terms, if they had known the truth. It is reasonable to say the misapprehension should be material or serious for a claim of remedy on the grounds of mistake. However, 'fundamental' is not the only element to render the contract void. The DCFR/PECL confines a circumstance that the other party knew or should have known this fundamental mistake.[451] So two aspects can be concluded for the term of being fundamentally different: (a) the mistake must be sufficiently serious so that the mistaken party will not enter into the contract if he knows the truth; (b) the requirement of causality and recognizability is demanded, which means the other party knows or should have known the matter was important to the innocent party.[452] It is worth mentioning that the interpretation of the contract shall be prior to the remedy based on the mistake, which means that if the disputes may be resolved through interpreting the provisions, the ground for invoking the mistake shall not be used.[453]

3.3.1.1.2. Causes for Mistake

The mistake could be generally induced in four ways by the party: (a) incorrect information: The incorrect information issued by a party to lead the other party into any misapprehension is the most likely ground for the mistake. Even if the party

449. Lando & Beale (2000b), *supra* n. 22, 230.
450. Borkowski (1997), *supra* n. 119, 206–262.
451. Von Bar & Clive (2009), *supra* n. 24, 460.
452. Hugh Beale & John Harrington, Fraud, Mistake and Misrepresentation, in Beale et al. (2002), *supra* n. 368, 346.
453. Von Bar & Clive (2009), *supra* n. 24, 458.

reasonably believes the information the other party gave was true, they cannot be relieved from the obligation if the misapprehension is seriously wrong enough;[454] (b) shared mistake: If both parties concluded the contract under a serious misapprehension as to the facts, then each party has the right to avoid the contract. As a case illustrated in the comments of DCFR/PECL, both parties concluded the contract to rent a cottage, but it was discovered that the cottage had been destroyed by fire the night before the contract was agreed upon, in which case, the contract may be avoided by either party;[455] (c) breach of pre-contractual information duty; (d) inaccuracy in communication. Article II.-7:202 DCFR/4:104 PECL states that the inaccuracy in communication can be regarded as an exception to the general rules of mistake. Since a requirement of knowing or expecting to know the mistake is required for remedial measures on the mistake, the inaccuracy in communication does not require this intention. But it is still treated as mistake if there is an inaccuracy in the expression or transmission of a statement. However, this inaccuracy must make the contract 'fundamentally different'. What is crucial to the inaccuracy in communication is that if the mistake occurs in the transmission of communication sent by a third party, without any fault on the part of the sender, then the sender still has to undertake the risk, which is still treated as a mistake made by the sender.

3.3.1.1.3. Remedies and Effects

Escaping from the contract is a remedy for mistake exercised by the mistaken party, through the way of adapting or avoiding the contract, in whole or in part. As a measure for avoidance, either restitution or damages can be claimed under the DCFR/PECL.[456] Regarding restitution, the party can claim damages for whatever it had supplied under the contract. If it is not reasonable, then a reasonable sum dependent on what has been received could be claimed. Another option to recover the loss is in the form of 'damages'. However, under the DCFR, the *loss* only refers to the negative loss, which puts the avoiding party into the same position if the contract had not been concluded.[457]

The other option is avoidance. If a contract is avoided, then the effect is retrospective to the beginning as if the contract had not been made, according to Article II.-7:212 DCFR. Whatever has been transferred or supplied under the contract shall be returned, and the rules on unjust enrichment governing this process will be implemented. If any property has been transferred, then the ownership shall be generally deemed as if it had not been passed to the transferor at all.[458] However, if the other party performs or indicates his willingness to perform the obligations as it was understood by the other party, then the contract cannot be

454. *Ibid.*, 459.
455. *Ibid.*, 461.
456. Article II.-7:212–7:214 DCFR; Art. 4:115–4:117 PECL.
457. Lando & Beale (2000b), *supra* n. 22, 280–284.
458. Von Bar & Clive (2009), *supra* n. 24, 524.

avoided, and it shall be regarded as having been adapted as the other party understood. However, after such indication or performance, the right to avoid is lost. But it is necessary to note the indication to perform or the performance shall be given in due time, after the notification of the right of avoidance.[459]

3.3.1.1.4. Relief

Two circumstances are regulated by the DCFR/PECL to limit the right to avoid the contract if a mistake happens such as: (1) the mistake is inexcusable in the circumstances: the inexcusable aspect is a core element for the party to get relief from the obligations, which should be made distinct from the careless or the fault. If it is easy for the party to detect the mistake, it shall be regarded as inexcusable; (2) the risk of mistake was assumed, or in the circumstances, it should be borne by the party itself: If it was easy for the party to assume the risk of mistake and the party did not assume it, then it should bear the risk itself.[460]

It is worth mentioning that regarding the issue of mistake, some provisions have been revised in the DCFR when compared with the PECL. In the DCFR, it draws on the circumstance in the PECL that a party could avoid the contract in the event of a mistake of fact or law. However, as to the facts causing the mistake, Article II.-7:201 DCFR also acknowledges the failure to comply with pre-contractual duty, which leads to the conclusion of contract as also being treated as mistake. However, it is necessary to distinguish pre-contractual liability and the remedy based on mistake. In the first, the contract should not have been concluded whereas in the latter, a contract has been made, and the failure to comply with the duty of information is in the pre-contractual stage.

3.3.1.2. Chinese Contract Law

The equivalent to the concept of a mistake in CLC is termed significant misunderstanding. In the practice of the People's Court, it is generally understood as what the parties make in cognizance of factual elements of the contract.[461] The provision on 'significant misunderstanding' in the CLC in fact draws from the GPCL, and the SPC interprets it as an act, which 'misapprehends the nature of the act, the other party, or the kind, quality, specification, quality and the like of the subject matter, so that the consequences of the act are contrary to its true intention, thereby resulting in substantial loss'.[462] Under the CLC, several requirements are set out for the constitution of significant misunderstanding.

459. *Ibid.*, 484.
460. Luisa Antoniolli & Anna Veneziano, *Principles of European Contract Law and Italian Law: A Commentary*, Kluwer Law International, 2005, 192.
461. Zhang (2006), *supra* n. 71, 185–187.
462. Article 71, Opinions of the Supreme People's Court on Several Issues Concerning the Implementation of the General Principles of the Civil Law of the People's Republic of China (For Trial Implementation), deliberated and adopted by the Judicial Committee of the Supreme People's Court on 26 Jan. 1988.

3.3.1.2.1. *Misunderstanding Must Be Significant*

A contract made under misunderstanding is avoidable as the contract fails to show the true intentions due to an erroneous understanding. But for the principle of business transaction fostering, which is to protect the certainty and stability of the market, only material misconception can be a ground for avoiding the contract. In addition to the concept of misunderstanding under the CLC, another word *significant* is usually used alongside this. As to the identity of significant, the consequence of the act that causes relatively serious losses is the major element to measure.[463] It is true to say there should be causation between the untrue intentions and their consequences. However, for the serious losses, some scholars argue that it should be determined by 'comparing between the benefit the mistaken party may have reasonably expected from a transaction based on its true intention and the benefit that it derives from the contract it has actually concluded'.[464] So although the consequences of misunderstanding which cause serious losses is the principal element in determining whether the contract can be avoided or not, it is still a vague concept in practice.

3.3.1.2.2. *Causes of Significant Misunderstanding*

From the definition issued by the SPC, misunderstandings can be derived from three options:

(a) Nature of the contract: A misunderstanding to the nature of the contract is a ground to lay claims for significant misunderstanding. However, it is argued that the misunderstanding in the CLC should only arise from fact, and the misapprehension of the existing law cannot be a ground for avoiding a contract.[465] But apparently, this opinion is not correct. Since the misunderstanding of the nature of the contract is a basis for the avoidance, it can be seen to arise from either the fact or the existing law, for instance, if a party believes a sale contract regulated by the law to be a loan contract, then the significant misunderstanding shall be placed. Hence, it is true to say the misunderstanding about the nature of the contract contains the misunderstanding of the fact and the existing law.

(b) The other party: In modern times, the transactions are frequently operated by the trustee or the agency, and if the party made any mistakes to the other contractual party, a ground for the significant misunderstanding can be claimed.

463. Article 71, Opinions of the Supreme People's Court on Several Issues Concerning the Implementation of the General Principles of the Civil Law of the People's Republic of China (For Trial Implementation), deliberated and adopted by the Judicial Committee of the Supreme People's Court on 26 Jan. 1988.

464. Ling (2002), *supra* n. 10, 190.

465. Zhang (2006), *supra* n. 71, 188.

(c) Subject matter: The subject matter refers to the goods, services or people that are dealt with under the contract. If any misunderstanding arises as to the kind, quality, specification, and quantity of the subject matter, then the significant misunderstanding may also be claimed. A case arising from the sale of a second-hand apartment is an obvious case to reveal how the significant misunderstanding is understood in the practice.

Facts

On 15 May 2006, a person with his family name *Liao* (hereinafter *Liao*) mandated an agent company to sell his apartment under the address of Room 601, No. 12, Wensha East 4th Street, Chancheng Area in Foshan. After the introduction by an agency, a person with his family name *Lu* (hereinafter *Lu*) signed the contract to buy this apartment on 24 May 2006, and *Lu* paid the deposit CNY 10,000 with CNY 50,000 which is the first part of the price. When the agency handed over the documents to the Housing Management Office of Chancheng Area for the transfer of the apartment, he found that under the policy of government, the governing office of the apartment changed to Nanhai Area. After this discovery, *Liao* did not agree to perform the contract, as the change of the name of area would result in various problems to his residence, the place of his children's education, the value of the apartment and so on.

After the case was brought to the court, the judge found the issue for this case, which was the area change of the apartment by the government. Since the seller did not have the intention of concealing the information about the apartment, and since the address he stated in the contract was the same as in his housing certificate, it was found that all the parties involved in the case were not at fault in this issue, and the contract was then decided to be made void because of significant misunderstanding, and the seller was asked to return CNY 60.000 to the buyer.

From the above case, it is obvious that under the CLC, if the misconception is not consistent with the common intention, and some serious losses result from misconception, then it shall be regarded as significant misunderstanding.

3.3.1.2.3. Remedies and Effects

The adaptation or the avoidance is the remedy for the mistaken party. Each of the means can be chosen by the party as remedies for the mistake. However, as Article 54 CLC regulated, 'where the party applies for adaptation, the People's Court or arbitral institution shall not rescind the contract'.[466] If the contract was avoided, then the contract did not have any retroactive effect, which means it did not take any effect from the time when the contract was concluded. Both parties therefore have to return what they get, and the effect shall be retroactive to the status as when there was no such contract originally. If the subjects cannot be returned, then the compensation for these subjects shall be paid.[467] Where any

466. Article 54 CLC.
467. Article 58 CLC.

party is at fault for the avoidance, then the damages can be claimed, and these can amount to the expectation loss.

3.3.1.3. Comparison

Although it is argued that the notion of mistake in European contract law is the same as the concept of significant misunderstanding under the Chinese contract law, and some Chinese scholars even use the word 'mistake' to replace 'misunderstanding' in academics,[468] the comparative description makes it seem that both concepts are slightly different from each other in the following aspects.

3.3.1.3.1. Coverage

'Mistake' in the DCFR/PECL refers to the misapprehension about a fact or the existing law, which is caused by incorrect information, mutual mistake, or an inaccuracy in communication. However, 'misunderstanding' under the CLC means the misconception about the nature of the contract, the other party or the subject matter, which is caused by the error in the expression or by negligence. It is true to say the coverage of 'misunderstanding' is broader than 'mistake', as the first includes any misconception about the fact, existing law and the contract itself, whereas the latter only covers the misconception about the fact and existing law.

3.3.1.3.2. Element

For 'mistake' under the DCFR/PECL, the concept of *fundamentally different* is required, which is interpreted as, the mistaken party should have known the truth, they would not have concluded the contract. Besides this, the requirement of knowing or expecting to know the truth is also demanded in constituting a 'mistake'. But in the CLC, except for the inconsistency in terms of true intentions, the misunderstanding merely requires the concept of *significant*, which will be judged by the consequence of the act because of which the serious losses occurred.

So it is reasonable to say that both the DCFR/PECL and the CLC require the misconception to be material. However, the CLC judges this material using the objective method through the losses suffered by the party, whereas the DCFR/PECL determines this from the subjective method, which states that a party must know or expect to have known that these acts would lead the other party to conclude the contract, and the other party would not have entered into the contract had they known the truth.

3.3.1.3.3. Remedies and Effects

Adaptation and avoidance are two effects seen for a contract in case of a mistake or misunderstanding. Under the DCFR and the CLC, if a contract is avoided, then it

468. Ling (2002), *supra* n. 10, 187.

shall be retroactively invalid. However, the difference between the DCFR and the CLC may be seen from the aspect of adaptation. Under the DCFR, if the party indicates or performs as the other party understands without undue delay, then the contract shall be considered as adapted. But in the CLC, adaptation is through the authority of the court. From this perspective, it is reasonable to say that the DCFR respects the parties' autonomy more than the CLC.

3.3.1.3.4. Relief

Under the DCFR, there are two circumstances, which may relieve the party from the remedy of the mistake. The first refers to the situation where the mistake is inexcusable under the circumstances, while the second regards the circumstances where the risk is afforded by the party itself. However, in the CLC, there is no provision concerning the relief of the mistake.

Therefore, the most striking difference evident from this comparison is that the individual's autonomy is more respected in the DCFR than in the CLC, which may be demonstrated from the requirements that constitute a mistake. In the DCFR it is mainly determined by the subjective method, which demands that a party should know or expect to have known the mistake because of which the other party would not enter into the contract if the other party knew the truth. But in the CLC, it is judged from the objective method, which states that serious losses are caused by the misunderstanding. So it may be reasonable to say the DCFR focuses more on the subjective minds whereas the CLC emphasizes more on the objective loss. The subjective method may be regarded as a way to respect party autonomy, as it tries to understand the individual's inner mind whereas the objective method favours market certainty since the actual loss can be measured, and which can be used to foresee the consequences of their conduct by the parties. This considerable difference maybe reasonably explained by the different roles and functions of party autonomy, since in traditional China, the subjective minds (party autonomy) had not been shown respect, and the achievement of an acceptable consequence was the purpose of law. So in Chinese legal history, civil matters were often resolved by the extra-legal mechanisms so as to achieve a result, which was acceptable to both parties. On the contrary, the classical will theory made the modern contract law of Europe more respectful of the subjective minds of the parties concerned. So it is reasonable to say that under the historical influence of party autonomy, the DCFR evaluates the mistake in a subjective way whereas the CLC determines it through the objective methods.

3.3.2. Fraud

Fraud is of a situation in which one party has been led into a mistake by a trickery committed by the other party. Almost all the legal systems allow avoiding the contract under this circumstance. But due to the different traditions and methods adopted by each system, the rules concerning fraud vary from country to country.

This subsection attempts to compare the differences in fraud between the DCFR/PECL and the CLC, and tries to find out whether these differences result from party autonomy.

3.3.2.1. European Contract Law

'Fraud is like a mistake in that anyone deceived into entering a contract does so under a mistake.'[469] But it is different from a mistake as the latter is 'to protect a mistaken party to a contract', while fraud is 'to punish the behaviour of a party who has fraudulently induced by the other to contract'.[470] Also, some scholars argue that a mistake is made by innocence or due to negligence, whereas fraud is made with knowledge of falsity.[471] However, it is reasonable to say that fraud is a kind of special mistake or fraudulent mistake or an intentionally caused mistake.

Like national laws within the EU, the DCFR/PECL recognizes that the contract could be avoided by a party's fraudulent representation or fraudulent non-disclosure of any information, which should be disclosed according to the principle of good faith and fair dealing.[472] In practice, there are several requirements for avoiding the contract by fraud.

3.3.2.1.1. Dishonesty

Fraud requires an intention to deceive the other party. This intention can be expressed either through words or in the form of conduct. But a mispresentation statement must exist for the constitution of fraud. There are two ways to mispresent a statement such as non-disclosure and providing incorrect information. Nowadays, keeping silent purposely on the matters about which the other party is ignorant can amount to fraud under most continental legal systems, which is in contrast to English law where only a false representation of fact amounts to fraud.[473] However, the DCFR still recognizes that a deliberate intention of deceiving the other party by the non-disclosure of information, which is of a significant situation influencing whether or not to conclude the contract, may be treated as fraud.[474] The other way is to provide the incorrect information, no matter if it was provided through words or in the form of conduct. However, the information with which the fraudulent party deceived the other party should be apparent in importance to the contractual party.

469. Kötz & Flessener (1997), *supra* n. 367, 196.
470. Ruth Sefton-Green, *Mistake, Fraud and Duties to Inform in European Contract Law, Cambridge University Press*, 2005, 11.
471. Kötz & Flessener (1997), *supra* n. 367, 196.
472. Article II.-7:205 DCFR; Art. 4:107 PECL.
473. Alain Verbeke & Yves-Henri Leleu, Harmonisation of the Law of Succession in Europe, in Hartkamp et al. (2004), *supra* n. 176, 337.
474. Von Bar & Clive (2009), *supra* n. 24, 494.

3.3.2.1.2. Reliance

The elements of fraud leading to avoidance of the contract require that the other party should have relied on the information, which was deceptive and issued by the fraudulent one. The reliance is also considered to be the basis for the party to claim remedies within some systems. However, a significant difference between mistake and fraud is demonstrated through the seriousness of the information. In terms of the mistake, it should be fundamental; otherwise, the avoiding party cannot avoid the contract. But in terms of the fraud, if the party has relied on the information when deciding to conclude the contract, then, the remedies can be claimed. It is worth a mention that both the continental and common laws allow avoidance of the whole contract just for a mere mistake.[475]

3.3.2.1.3. Remedies

In case of fraud, the misled party has the right to avoid the contract. If the fraud is only related to some individual terms of the contract, then, the contract may be avoided partially.[476] However, as required by Articles II.-7:209 and II.-7:210, a notice within a reasonable time should be given for the avoidance.

Although the DCFR draws the rules of fraud from the PECL, an additional rule defining the concept of misrepresentation is supplemented in the DCFR.[477] According to the definition, a fraudulent misrepresentation requires an intention to induce the recipient to make a mistake by providing him incorrect information, or by a non-disclosure of the information. It is true to say that, an intention to deceive is the principal element for the constitution of fraud under the DCFR.

3.3.2.2. Chinese Contract Law

In the GPCL, a civil activity under fraudulent practices employed by one party is invalid.[478] The CLC changes the effects of avoidance into avoidance or adaptation.[479] However, if the contract concluded under fraud with harming the interest of the state, then, it is invalid without any doubt.[480] It is worth mentioning that 'invalid' in the CLC means the contract does not have any effect since it was concluded. It is equivalent to the notion of avoid. The SPC interprets fraud as occurring where a party deliberately provides the other party with false information, or conceals the truth in order to induce the other party to make a mistaken

475. Brigitta Lurger, The 'Social' Side of Contract Law and the New Principle of Regard and Fairness, in Hartkamp et al. (2004), *supra* n. 176, 255.
476. Von Bar & Clive (2009), *supra* n. 24, 495.
477. Article II.-7:205(2) DCFR.
478. Article 58(3) GPCL.
479. Article 54 CLC.
480. Article 52(2) CLC.

expression of intent.[481] From this definition, generally speaking, there are five elements required to invalidate the contract.

3.3.2.2.1. Intent to Deceive

The intent to deceive means the deceiving party knows the falsity of the information that would induce the other to make a wrong decision. Two factors, which are the false information and the purpose to induce, should be placed from this definition. However, it frequently happens that a party would give the information that it is not certain, under which situation the statement may also amount to the intention to deceive, as the party will have assumed its statement is incorrect to induce the other to make a wrong decision, and this risk shall be afforded by the party concerned.

3.3.2.2.2. Conduct of Deceives

The conduct of deception requires the deceiving party to take action based on the intent to deceive. There are two ways in which this conduct can be exercised which are the false statement and the non-disclosure of information. For the first, there seems no distinction between the misrepresentation of fact and misstatement of opinion under the CLC.[482] If there is any misrepresentation in order to deceive the other party to enter into the contract, then, the requirement will be satisfied. Another way is through the non-disclosure of information. The non-disclosure in order to deceive the other party to make a false decision is also deemed as the conduct of deceives.

3.3.2.2.3. Reliance

Based on the false information, the deceived party should have made a false recognition of the facts. Normally it is required that the false information should be closely connected with the contents of the contract or the conduct of deceives, which means the false information is important to the party to make a decision as to whether to conclude the contract or not.

3.3.2.2.4. Mistaken Manifestation

Based on the false recognition induced by the deceiving party, the deceived party should make a mistaken manifestation, such as concluding the contract based on this false recognition. Concretely speaking, it means after relying on the false

481. Article 68, Opinions of the Supreme People's Court on Several Issues Concerning the Implementation of the General Principles of the Civil Law of the People's Republic of China (For Trial Implementation), deliberated and adopted by the Judicial Committee of the Supreme People's Court on 26 Jan. 1988.

482. Zhang (2006), *supra* n. 71, 173.

information, the party concludes the contract; otherwise it cannot be constituted as fraud.

3.3.2.2.5. Remedies

Under the GPCL, the court is endowed with a very broad power to invalidate the contract, which is argued as harmful to the security and stability of economic development. But it is vigorously argued that the purpose of contract law is to encourage business transactions.[483] The drafting committee of the CLC suggested making the contract voidable instead of invalid under the circumstances of fraud, which means the contract is not absolutely invalid it just needs to be claimed for avoidance by the party.[484] However, the national legislative body did not completely accept this suggestion, as it was believed that state ownership was of central importance in the national economy and that if the contract was harmful to the interests of the state, it should definitely be invalid. Therefore, it is true to say that with regard to the effects of the contract, in the case of fraud, three remedies can be applied. The first is applicable where the fraud is harmful to the interests of the state under which circumstance the contract is invalid. However, it should be noted that the interests of the state in Chinese law is a very vague concept, which may broadly include the public interest, the collective interest and even the interest of the Communist Party. The second remedy is to avoid the contract whereas the third one is adaptation. However, if the contract is to be avoided or adapted, then, the fraud should not entail any damages to the interests of the state.

3.3.2.3. Comparison

Both the DCFR/PECL and the CLC acknowledge that the contract could be avoided under the circumstances of fraud. As to the central constitutional elements of fraud, it is the intention to deceive and the fact of reliance on the deceiving party. Providing incorrect information and non-disclosure of information can amount to fraud in both the DCFR and the CLC. However, the information, which is incorrect or not disclosed, shall be important for both parties to conclude the contract, which means the party has relied on the information when entering into the contract. It is true to say fraud is one of the limitations to party autonomy, and both parties have to conclude the contract with a mutual intention. If the intention is made under some false information or influence, which is not disclosed, then, the contract can be avoided. From this perspective, it is reasonable to say that the constitution of fraud under contract law in Europe is similar to the contract law in China, because the CLC is transplanted from the West.

However, a remarkable difference between the DCFR and the CLC with regard to the fraud may be found from the remedies. Under the DCFR, the remedy

483. Wang (2002), *supra* n. 262, 640.

484. Huixing Liang, he tong fa de cheng gong yu bu zu [The Success and Deficiency of Contract Law], *zhong wai fa xue* [*Peking University Law Journal*], vol. 1, 2001, 92–100.

is to avoid the contract, whereas the CLC provides three options, which are invalidation, avoidance and adaptation. The parties may choose to adapt or avoid the contract if it was concluded under fraud. But if the fraud harms the interests of the state, then the contract is absolutely invalid. Starting from this point, it is true to say that in the CLC, if the fraud is not detrimental to the interests of the state, then the parties have the freedom to choose to adapt or avoid the contract, whereas on the other side, the parties do not have such freedom. This difference can be reasonably concluded after studying the historical and cultural reasons of the dominating role of state interests in China, which is a primary limitation to party autonomy.

3.3.3. Threats

Freedom of contract means a party should only be bound by the actions that are voluntarily exercised. The party must have some choices other than making the decision to conclude the contract. However, it happens frequently that a person can only simply move his hand to sign the contract if some other person has grabbed his arm and forced him to do so, under which circumstance, there would not be an enforced contract. 'All the systems recognise that a contract which is procured by one party making an illegitimate threat against the other may be avoided by the latter.'[485] Coercion or threats are an established rule in most continental countries to allow this avoidance. However, in common law, duress is a kind of parallel concept, which is 'established by showing that the agreement of the party seeking to have the contract set aside was induced by the threat to commit an unlawful act'.[486] This subsection thus describes the differences in threats for signing a contract in both the DCFR/PECL and the CLC and later answer whether these differences result from party autonomy.

3.3.3.1. European Contract Law

Although all legal systems acknowledge that, the contract could be avoided if the contractual party entering into the contract under a form of pressure, the elements of threats are diverse among the European national laws. The DCFR/PECL tries to bridge all these systems, and Article II.-7:206 DCFR/4:108 PECL endows the coerced party with the right to avoid the contract. There are four essential elements required by the DCFR/PECL for the avoidance of contract under the circumstance of threats.

3.3.3.1.1. Imminent and Serious

This is a principal element that constitutes threats under the DCFR/PECL. However, as to the evaluation of imminent and serious situation, the subjective

485. Lando & Beale (2000b), *supra* n. 22, 259.
486. Atiyah & Smit (2005), *supra* n. 290, 268.

and objective tests are divided. In English law, all the actual or threatened physical violence to the contractual parties and the victim's property could be considered as duress, provided that they are illegitimate and the coerced party has no other alternative options than to conclude the contract. It is true to say this is the subjective test, which is different from the objective test in French Law that the threats must have been considered as if a reasonable person of the same age, sex and condition would be influenced. However, the criteria and approach to determine the extent of what is imminent and serious situation under the DCFR/PECL is not clearly expressed.[487]

3.3.3.1.2. Wrongful by Itself or Should Be Wrongly Used

Not all warnings can be deemed threats. The act defined as a threat should be illegitimate or improper to obtain the conclusion of the contract. It should not only include the threats of physical violence or the damage to property, but should also contain economic loss, which has been wrongfully inflicted.[488] However, not all the warnings of non-performance can amount to threats. As illustrated by the drafting committee of DCFR, where one party cannot perform the contract unless the other party pays a higher price, and the first party informs the other of the fact, then the other party may not avoid its promise to pay a higher price.[489]

3.3.3.1.3. Lead to the Conclusion of the Contract

The right of avoidance will not be given if the threat has only influenced slightly the decision of entering into the contract instead of leading to the conclusion of the contract. It is reasonable to say that causation must exist between the threatened act and the conclusion of the contract.

3.3.3.1.4. Coerced Party Should Not Have Any Other Reasonable Alternatives

If there is another alternative solution, it should not show the threat is the real reason for the coerced party to enter into the contract. However, the burden of proving that the coerced party had a reasonable alternative solution is on the party, which made the threat.

It is worth mentioning that a notice within a reasonable time shall be given for the avoidance of the contract in case of a threat. The effect of threats is to avoid the contract, the remedy of which 'cannot be excluded or restricted by contrary agreement'.[490]

---

487. Antoniolli & Veneziano (2005), *supra* n. 461, 212–213.
488. Lando & Beale (2000b), *supra* n. 22, 257.
489. Von Bar & Clive (2009), *supra* n. 24, 501.
490. *Ibid.*, 503.

3.3.3.2. Chinese Contract Law

Based on the interpretation by the SPC, the threat to damage of life and health, honour, reputation, or property of the citizen or his relatives or friends, or to the honour, reputation or property of the person in order to force the other party to make a manifestation, which is against its true will could be regarded as 'threats'. From this interpretation, four elements clearly constitute threats under Chinese law. These are:

(1) Intent to coerce: The coercing party should know its conduct would create fear in the other party, and hope the other party will enter into the contract under this fear.
(2) Act of coercion: The action can be reflected in the threats to cause damage, which has not happened, or through threats that the coerced party is really facing. From the SPC's interpretation, threats cannot only cause damage to the coerced party itself, but also to that party's relatives or friends;
(3) Wrongfulness of the coercion: The coercion should have no legal basis and should not serve an illegitimate purpose, for example, it is not constituted as 'threat' if the coerced party threatens that he is going to the court to settle the dispute, if the other party does not conclude the contract. This coercion cannot be regarded as a threat that can lead to avoidance of the contract under the CLC.
(4) Causation: The threats should have a direct influence on concluding the contract, which means the coercion should be imminent and serious, which causes the coerced party to be fearful and under this fear, the coerced party has no other choice except to conclude the contract.

From these elements, threats in Chinese contract law seem quite different from the concept of significant misunderstanding as: (1) the first makes the coerced party conclude the contract under fear, while the latter deceives the party to the contract; (2) under the 'significant misunderstanding', the contents which are sought by the deceiving party should be a part of the contract, while the threats should not be seen in the contract; and (3) 'significant misunderstanding' can be made either by omission or action, while threats can only be conducted through the active act.

However, in the GPCL, the acts under the pressure of threats are invalid, and it is reasonable to say the concept of 'good faith' has been rooted into Chinese social life, and being honest to each other is a sort of morality. But like the doctrine of mistake, the CLC changed the effect due to the principle of 'business transaction fostering'. In the market economy, it is obviously seen that the rights of the contractual party and the business transaction itself cannot be protected if the contracts concluded through threats are frequently invalid. Two kinds of effects on contracts concluded by threats are mentioned in the CLC. The first refers to those effects that may damage the interests of the state in which circumstance, the contract is invalid. The other is avoidable or adapted if the contract is under threat without any damage to the interests of the state. It is worth noting that the word 'void' is different from the concept of avoidable, as the former is a parallel concept like 'invalid' while the second endows the coerced party with the right to avoid the contract. However, under the CLC, the avoiding party loses the right to avoid the contract if it fails to do so after one year, since he knows or ought to know the causes, or he explicitly expresses or conducts the acts to waive the rights.[491]

3.3.3.3. Comparison

In most legal systems, the contract is avoidable if concluded under threats. Both the DCFR/PECL and the CLC follow this approach and endow the coerced party with the rights to avoid the contract. It is true to say that in both contract laws, the coerced acts to make the other party have no other choice except to conclude the contract is a core element to constitute threats, and the wrongful use of or a wrongful act is another principal component. From the meaning and the constitution of elements that make up fraud, it can be said that the DCFR is quite similar to the CLC, as China transplants these provisions from the West. However, a sharp difference is observed in their effects. In the DCFR, avoidance is the only remedy for the contract concluded under threat. However, under the CLC, the contract can be avoided or adapted. But since the interests of the state, which have been highly appreciated in traditional China are still strongly influencing the CLC, it is clearly stated that if the threat is found to damage the interests of the state, then the contract is definitely invalid. This difference can also be reasonably explained by the dominating role of state interests in Chinese law, which are primary restrictions to party autonomy.

3.3.4. Imbalanced Bargaining

The principle of freedom of contract has traditionally been a fundamental rule in most of the European nations' contract laws. It has been assumed that individuals are the best judges for determining their values of exchange, and the law of contract facilitates this voluntary choice. But in modern contract law, contractual justice has been a new principle to reflect the development of justice in the society, which is not only limited to procedural fairness, but more concerned about substantive fairness.[492] It is of a significant restriction to limit the individuals' freedom to the contract. For the implementation of contractual justice, one of the most crucial ways is to protect a party against imbalanced bargaining. It can be said that the traditional theory of will deficiencies includes mistake, fraud, and threat, whereas in modern contract law, the weaker party protection reflecting from the remedies to imbalanced bargaining is seen as another restriction to the freedom of contract. This subsection compares the differences in the protection against imbalanced

491. Article 55 CLC.
492. Remiert Tjittes, Unfair Terms, in Beale et al. (2002), *supra* n. 368, 494.

bargaining as mentioned in the DCFR/PECL and the CLC, and notes whether the differences can be explained by party autonomy.

3.3.4.1. European Contract Law

In the DCFR, several provisions broadly deal with imbalanced bargaining. Article II.-1:110 concerns the definition of a term that is not individually negotiated, and the rule on the burden of proof has also been set up. According to this provision, if a party has not been able to influence the content of the contract, then, a term supplied by the other party shall be deemed as 'not individually negotiated'. It is true to say the criterion of a real and meaningful possibility to influence the content of the term is the principal assessment for the individually negotiated term.[493] However, if a term is merely selected from a menu supplied by the other party, then, it shall not be regarded as individually negotiated either, since the possibility of influencing the content of terms is only restricted to within the menu. The burden to prove the term, has been individually negotiated, is afforded by the party, which supplies the terms.

Another rule maybe found from Article II.-7:207 DCFR, which is about unfair exploitation. Under this Article, if a contract gives a party excessive advantage and unfair exploitation is involved, then, one can claim the remedy to avoid the contract. Generally speaking, there are three requirements, which constitute unfair exploitation:

(1) Weakness is an essential element. Relief is only given if an independent judgment cannot be exercised, which means the party was depending on or relying on the other party.
(2) The other party has the knowledge to exploit this weakness. The party gaining an advantage should know or should reasonably be expected to have known the other party's weak situation, and with this knowledge, it takes advantage of the weaker party.
(3) Excessive benefits exist. The remedy only applies if a considerable excessive exists in the contract. However, a shortage of supply, which leads to a high price, is not a basis for the remedy of unfair exploitation.

Worth noting is that for the effect of unfair exploitation, the contract can also be adapted by the court under two circumstances. The first refers to the situation where either party promptly requests the adaptation, which is before the party who has received a notice of avoidance has acted on it. The second refers to the appropriate situation if the court adapts the contract in accordance with what might have been agreed upon by the parties, which is consistent with good faith and fair dealing.

Besides the two Articles above, the provisions from Article II.-9:401 to Article II.-9:410 also deal with unfair terms, which refer to those that have not been individually negotiated. Article II.-9:401 regulates that the effects of

493. Von Bar & Clive (2009), *supra* n. 24, 161–162.

provisions in the section of unfair terms are mandatory and cannot be excluded by the parties. However, it is clearly stated that the mandatory effect is only 'in favour of the party who did not supply an unfair term, and not of the supplier of the unfair term'.[494] Article II.-9:402 states that the terms, which have not been individually negotiated, shall be drafted in plain and intelligible language. The concept of 'not individually negotiated' between a business and a consumer, and a standard of significant disadvantage that is contrary to good faith and fair dealing has been set up in Article II.-9:403.[495] Article II.-9:404 states the criteria for judicial control of terms in a contract between non-business parties as a significant disadvantage to the other party, contrary to good faith and fair dealing. Under Article II.-9:105, it defines the notion of unfair in contracts between businesses as gross deviation from good commercial practice, contrary to good faith and fair dealing, while the scope of application of the unfairness test from two situations is excluded in Article II.-9:406. The first situation refers to the contract terms based on the provisions of the applicable law, the applicable international conventions or the rules of DCFR. The second situation makes it certain that as to the definition of the main subject matter of the contract and the adequacy of the price to be paid, the unfairness test cannot be applied. Under Article II.-9:407, several factors are set out when assessing the unfairness test, which are the duty of transparency, the nature of what is to be provided under the contract, the circumstances prevailing during the conclusion of the contract, the other terms of the contract and the terms of any other contract on which the contract depends. However, for the contracts between a business and a consumer, the circumstance governing the extent to which the consumer was given a real opportunity to become acquainted with the term before the contract was concluded shall also be taken into account. The effects of unfair terms are regulated in Article II.-9:408 that states the unfair term shall not bind on the party, which did not supply it. But if the remaining terms can be isolated from the unfair term, then, those remaining terms will be binding. For the contract between a business and a consumer, if the exclusive jurisdiction for all disputes is conferred on the court located at the place where the business is domiciled, which is different from the consumer's domicile, then, it shall be regarded as an unfair term, as clearly expressed under Article II.-9:409. Article II.-9:410 contains a list of terms which constitute a serious disadvantage to a consumer.

From those concrete rules on unfair terms, it is thus reasonable to conclude that under the DCFR/PECL, there are three elements which are required to avoid the terms, which are: (1) the term is contrary to the principle of good faith and fair dealing; (2) the term will cause the significant imbalance between the parties; and (3) the significant imbalance will detriment the interest of the weaker party. It is worth mentioning that the PECL limits the unfair terms to the terms, which are not individually negotiated.[496] But the DCFR extends the unfairness test to the

494. *Ibid.*, 628.
495. *Ibid.*, 634.
496. Lando & Beale (2000b), *supra* n. 22, 266–271.

individually negotiated terms, which are revealed in Article II.-9:403 as words 'which has not been individually negotiated' are put in square brackets.[497]

Another difference between the DCFR and the PECL is that PECL does not contain any list of clauses, which can be deemed to be unfair. But in practice, the judges and arbitrators can find the inspiration from the EU Directives of 1993; the Council adopted the Directive on Unfair Terms in Consumer Contracts.[498] With high appreciation for substantive fairness, the usage of unfair clauses is not only to protect the consumers, but it also operates in favour of the whole contract, including government contracts and commercial contracts.[499] However, it has been criticized for the confused, unsystematic and sometimes even contradictory terms describing unfair terms in the PECL and the EU Directives.[500] And it is argued that the protective directives are called *minimum directive,* which means they only provide the minimum standards that are not strong enough to improve, and simply promote the cross-boards transactions.[501] However, the current DCFR seems to fully notice this issue, and Article II.-9:410 contains a list of unfair clauses. It is worth noting that currently a new Directive on Consumer Rights is being prepared.[502]

3.3.4.2. Chinese Contract Law

The protection against imbalanced bargaining in Chinese contract law is mainly reflected in the doctrine of obvious unfairness. The unfair contract can be held to be avoided or adapted in the CLC,[503] the provision for which is drawn from the GPCL that states that a civil activity can be avoided or adapted if it is made under the situation of obvious unfairness.[504] However, in the CLC, there is no further detailed explanation about the obvious unfairness except to state the effect of those terms. But the GPCL is supplementary to the CLC, and the interpretation by the SPC is considered to guide the lower courts. From the opinions to the implementation of the GPCL, the SPC defines the term *obvious fairness* as, if a party uses his superiority or dominant position or takes advantage of the other party's inexperience to make the unbalance of rights and obligations so obvious that the principles of fairness and equal bargain are clearly offended.[505] It is true to

497. Von Bar & Clive (2009), *supra* n. 24, 634.
498. Remiert Tjittes, Unfair Terms, in Beale et al. (2002), *supra* n. 368, 526.
499. Antoniolli & Veneziano (2005), *supra* n. 461, 220.
500. Brigitta Lurger, The 'Social' Side of Contract Law and the New Principle of Regard and Fairness, in Hartkamp et al. (2004), *supra* n. 176, 273–278.
501. *Ibid.*
502. Martijn Hesselink, The Consumer Rights Directive and the CFR: Two Worlds Apart?, *European Review of Contract Law*, vol. 5, 2009, 290–303.
503. Article 54(2) CLC.
504. Article 59(2) GPCL.
505. Article 72, Opinions of the Supreme People's Court on Several Issues Concerning the Implementation of the General Principles of the Civil Law of the People's Republic of China (for Trial Implementation), deliberated and adopted by the Judicial Committee of the Supreme People's Court on 26 Jan. 1988.

say there are two major characteristics of the contract, which are concluded under *obvious unfairness*:

(1) There is an apparent unfairness between the parties when the contract is established.[506] According to Chinese civil law, the civil activities, particularly the contract, should reflect the principle of fairness, equal price and equality for contractual justice. But in practice, if there is a clear imbalance in the rights and obligations of the contractual parties, then one of them has to afford considerably imbalanced obligations, while the other is overly benefited, which can be regarded as 'obvious unfairness' under Chinese civil law.
(2) The injured party is inexperienced or in a desperate situation when concluding the contract. It is necessary to note that 'obvious unfairness' is completely different from the doctrine of exploitation in the CLC as: (a) the imbalance needs to exist in the obligations and rights between the contractual parties under the circumstances of 'obvious unfairness', whereas the exploitation requires that the injured party has been taken advantage of when in a difficult situation; (b) in the first case the party may not necessarily be in a difficult situation while in the latter case, the difficulty faced by the injured party may be the essence.

However, as to the issue of 'obvious', it is argued that if the party profits by unfair means and if this exceeds the limit by the law, the unfairness could be considered as being obvious.[507] Except for the provision on 'obvious unfairness', another provision can be observed in the CLC regarding the unfair terms, which is the exploitation of another's distress.[508] Similar to the notion of 'significant misunderstanding', fraud, and threat, the concept of exploitation has not been defined in the CLC either. The definition has to be found out from the interpretation of the GPCL by the SPC. According to the SPC, exploitation of another's distress refers to an act whereby a party, for obtaining an unjust benefit, takes advantage of the other's distress to force the other party to make an untrue declaration of intention, thereby considerably damaging its interests.[509] It is true to say, generally, four requirements have to be satisfied to constitute exploitation:

(1) The innocent party is under a distress situation. However, the distress is not clearly stated under the CLC and the GPCL. But it is described as a situation where the interests such as the life, health, honour, reputation or

506. Wang (2002), *supra* n. 262, 692–693.
507. Ling (2002), *supra* n. 10, 189–190.
508. Article 54 CLC.
509. Article 70, Opinions of the Supreme People's Court on Several Issues Concerning the Implementation of the General Principles of the Civil Law of the People's Republic of China (for Trial Implementation), deliberated and adopted by the Judicial Committee of the Supreme People's Court on 26 Jan. 1988.

property of the innocent party or its relatives are in danger of serious damage.[510]

(2) An act of exploitation exists. When examining whether the exploitation is constituted or not, a conduct to acquire an unjust benefit and compel the other party to make an untrue intention has to exist.
(3) An untrue declaration of intention has been made. Under the act of exploitation, the innocent party should have no other alternative solution other than making the contract.
(4) Damages were caused by exploitation. It is required that the innocent party should suffer serious damages as a result of exploitation. Worth mentioning is that as to the effect of exploitation of another's distress, the contract can be claimed for avoidance or the adaptation.

3.3.4.3. Comparison

Protection against 'imbalanced bargaining' is becoming a principal reflection of revealing contractual justice in modern contract law. Both the DCFR and the CLC follow this tendency, and integrate it into their content. In the DCFR, the protection against 'unfair terms' may be demonstrated from three aspects, which are non-individually negotiated terms, unfair exploitation and unfair terms. But under the CLC, it can only be reflected through obvious unfairness and exploitation of another's distress. From the description, it would be correct to say that with regard to the exploitation, both contract laws require a distress situation, the act of exploitation and a grossly unfair advantage. And as for the unfair terms, both the DCFR and the CLC make it certain that the contract can be adapted or avoided.

However, a considerable difference may be found in the fact that under the DCFR, the rules are more systematic than in the CLC. Although both contract laws integrate the contractual fairness, which is a primary limitation to party autonomy, the DCFR has accepted it more widely. This considerable difference could be reasonably explained by the higher requirement of 'weaker party protection' in the DCFR, which primarily limits party autonomy under modern contract law.

3.3.5. Conclusion

This section compares the doctrine of mistake, fraud, threats and imbalanced bargaining between the DCFR/PECL and the CLC. The expression of 'significant misunderstanding' is adopted to elaborate the mistake in the CLC, for it has the same effect as mistake under the DCFR/PECL. However, the coverage of misunderstanding is broader than the scope of mistake, as the former not only includes the misconception with regard to the existing law and the fact, but also covers any

510. Jiafu Wang, *zhong guo min fa xue – min fa zhai quan* [*Chinese Civil Law – The Law of Obligations*], Law Press, 1991, 345–353.

misconception about the contract itself. In both contract laws, to constitute mistake and misunderstanding, the misrepresentation, which makes the contract fundamentally different, is required, but the approach differs. Under the DCFR/PECL, the requirement is to know or expect to have known the truth, whereas in the CLC, a serious loss as the consequence of the misrepresentation is of significant measure. It is thus true to conclude that the subjective method to determine the fundamental difference is regulated in the DCFR, whereas the objective method is adopted in the CLC. As to the comparison of fraud and threats, the constitutional elements are similar in the DCFR/PECL and the CLC. However, with regard to the effects, the CLC divides it into two types. The first type of effects refers to those fraud or threats that were harmful to the interests of the state, in which situation, the contract would certainly be void (invalid). The second category of effects concerns the fraud or threats that do not harm the interests of the state, in which case, the contract is avoidable or adapted. It is easy to see that in the latter case, the party is endowed with the freedom to either avoid or adapt the contract according to their wills, whereas in the first case, if the defects prove harmful for the interests of state, the individuals are not endowed with this freedom. However, under the DCFR/PECL, such a distinction to the effect has not been made, and the effect of those contracts, which are concluded under fraudulent misrepresentation or threats is stated as avoidance.

Concerning the doctrine of unbalanced bargaining, the DCFR integrates it from non-individually negotiated terms, unfair exploitation and unfair terms, whereas in the CLC, it only reveals the obvious unfairness and exploitation from another's distress. It is therefore obvious to see the DCFR protect against unbalanced bargaining in a more concrete and detailed manner than the CLC, and it is also reasonable to say that a higher standard of weaker party protection can be found in the DCFR.

Therefore, with regard to the doctrine of validity, the DCFR and the CLC differ with each other, and these differences can be explained through the different roles and functions of party autonomy. It can be said that party autonomy in the DCFR is more restricted to unfair bargaining, whereas in the CLC, it is more limited to the interests of the state, and it is even true to say that the history and culture of a region is the main reason that makes them different. From the comparison of fraud and threats, the constitutional elements between the DCFR and the CLC are seen to be obviously similar. But under the CLC, another provision is to supplement the maintenance of the interests of the state. This is drawn from the traditional history and culture that the personal interest is subject to the state interest. Also, from the comparison of imbalanced bargaining, it is clear that the rules in the DCFR are obviously more concrete than those in the CLC. As in modern times, party autonomy is not only about the freedom, but the limitations should be also connected, which are mainly derived from good faith and fair dealing, social justice and the protection of fundamental rights. It is thus reasonable to conclude that compared to the DCFR, China still lacks party autonomy in the modern sense.

3.4. ADAPTATION

Under the principle of *pacta sunt servanda*, a contract cannot be modified unilaterally since it may detrimentally affect the other party's rights and obligations. As pointed out by Hugh Collins, two obstacles were placed for the adaptation of the contract.[511] The first arose from the observation that debtors often tried to avoid the contract by claiming an appearance of some understanding or accommodation that helped them escape the obligations. The second referred to whether the creditor had been forced to consent to this modification through an exercising of pressure or some other means. So the classical law commonly required an express agreement for the adaptation of the contract.[512] However, as party autonomy has been widely recognized in most of the European countries, adjusting the contract in accordance with both parties' mutual consent is one of the most significant reflections of party autonomy in the law of contract. Also, modern contract law encourages the parties to cooperate with each other, which provides an incentive to renegotiate contracts and make some adaptation in order to mitigate losses arising from the breach of contract. Under this situation, the mutual modification of the contract can lead to maximize business opportunities, especially in a long-term contract. From this perspective, it is correct to say that respecting party autonomy will lead to the creation of social wealth.

Except for the mutual consent necessary to modify the provisions or the terms, although traditionally the adaptation has not been widely recognized, contract laws in most current systems allow the court to modify the contract in some situations if the contracts could still play a role in regulating the business transactions and satisfying the interests of the parties.[513] However, the court has to adapt the contract to both parties in an equal measure, which means the rights and obligations shall be justified by the adapted contract. It is true to say the modification of the contract by the court has to ultimately maintain the fairness between the parties. However, 'when adapting the contract, the court must always balance the parties' interests and try to minimize the intervention in the parties' contract'.[514] On the one hand, the intervention of the court may result in damaging the function of party autonomy, as the obligations would often not be the same as what the parties originally consented to. But on the other hand, it may encourage market transactions as the contract is not certainly avoided and it can still be enforced after the adaptation, which may lead to fostering business transactions. So it is reasonable to say the adaptation of the contract can play the function of balancing the encouragement of market transactions with party autonomy. This section therefore tries to compare the differences of the situations that can allow the adaptation of the

511. Collins (2008a), *supra* n. 5, 341–343.
512. *Ibid.*
513. Antoniolli & Veneziano (2005), *supra* n. 461, 199.
514. Christoph Brunner, *Force Majeure and Hardship under General Contract Principles: Exemption for Non-Performance in International Arbitration*, Kluwer Law International, 2008, 500.

contract in the DCFR/PECL and the CLC. Whether these differences can be explained by party autonomy will be analysed subsequently.

3.4.1. European Contract Law

Article III.-1:108 DCFR first of all, recognizes that the contract can be modified by agreement at any time. The right to modification does not need to be expressly written in the contract, as it is implied by the principle of party autonomy.[515] It is a default rule of contract law. Apart from the mutual consent to adapt the contract, the court has set aside three situations to consider modifying the contract under the DCFR. These are mistake, excessive benefit or unfair advantage, and change of circumstances.

3.4.1.1. Mistake

'Mistake' is one of the grounds for the non-mistaken party to avoid the contract because of the error in communication. However, sometimes if the non-mistaken party indicates that it is willing to or actually does perform what the mistaken party has understood then, the contract could be considered as modified.[516] Article II.-7:203 DCFR/4:105 PECL acknowledges that the contract could be treated as adjusted, if the non-mistaken party was willing to or actually did perform what the other party understood. After such indications, the non-mistaken party loses the right for avoidance. It should be noted that this adaptation is aimed at respecting self-determination as the contract is not modified by the court, but is modified according to the way the party understands it.

The same effect applies to the notion of 'shared mistake'. When both parties make the same mistake, at the request of either party, the court may modify the contract in accordance with what might have been agreed to reasonably if the mistake had not occurred. However, there are two situations which should be distinguished for the notion of 'shared mistake' to be considered: (1) if one party benefits from the mistake and the other is placed more disadvantageously, the former may indicate its willingness to perform in the way that the contract was originally understood; (2) if, which party stands to lose more than the other is not clear in some cases, then modification of the contract could be requested by either party.[517]

The difference between the unilateral and 'shared mistake' is that in the unilateral mistake, adaptation is referred to as the meaning intended by the mistaken party, whereas in the shared mistake, adaptation should refer to a hypothetical and

515. Von Bar & Clive (2009), *supra* n. 24, 701.
516. Lando & Beale (2000b), *supra* n. 22, 247–248.
517. M.M. van Rossum, Validity, in Busch, Hondius, van Kooten, Schelhaas & Schrama (2002), *supra* n. 389, 202.

reasonable agreement being drawn had the mistake not occurred. Also, the first adaptation is brought about through the initiatives of the parties, whereas the adaptation due to the shared mistake is undertaken by the court.

3.4.1.2. Excessive Benefit or Unfair Advantage

It is widely recognized that the parties are the best judges of the values to be exchanged. However, in some countries, the legal systems refuse to enforce contracts, which involve an obviously gross disparity in the performances, resulting from the weak bargaining by one party. Article II.-7:207 DCFR/4:109 PECL entitles the weaker party to avoid the contract if the other takes advantage of his economic distress or urgent needs at the time of contract conclusion. It is necessary to note that too much uncertainty can be created if a party can easily escape from a contract, which is contrary to the characteristic of certainty. The weakness should be apparent for the avoidance, which is an essential element that constitutes the doctrine. Two situations become clear here: (1) the value gained by one party should be demonstrably excessive when compared to the normal price; or (2) that grossly unfair advantage has been taken in other ways.

For the remedies of excessive benefits and unfair advantage, the disadvantaged parties are surely entitled to avoid the contract. However, in order to protect the security of business transactions, it is not appropriate to simply set aside the contract in some situations, which may result in unfairness towards the advantaged parties. Adaptation of the contract is thus another way to recover such damages. This remedy has been granted in most of the European countries such as France, the Netherlands (through the Dutch civil code). The second and third provisions of Article II.-7:207 DCFR/4:109 PECL permit the court to modify the contract. However, the requirements of good faith and fair dealing are the essential elements measuring whether the adaptation of the contract by the court is reasonable.

3.4.1.3. Change of Circumstances

It is frequently seen that an unforeseen event occurring after the conclusion of the contract renders the performance much more difficult. A majority of European countries adopt some mechanism to correct any injustice, which results from the supervening events. The clause of 'change of circumstances' is to supplement the general rules of law to maintain the justice between the contractual parties.

The notion of change of circumstances actually is the same as the concept of hardship, which has been recognized for more than a century. It refers to the situation where the performance of a contract becomes harder due to the occurrence of supervening events, which may not have been foreseen at the time of conclusion of the contract.[518] It is worth noting that hardship is different from the notion of *force majeure* since for the clause of hardship, the performance of the

518. Denis Tollon, Hardship, in Hartkamp et al. (2004), *supra* n. 176, 499.

contract is still possible but much more onerous,[519] whereas the latter prevents any performance.[520]

Although most of the European countries recognize the clause of hardship, they adopt different viewpoints to lead to the justice of the contract.[521] For example, with regard to the concept of hardship, German Law refers to it as the *Wegfall des Geschäftsgrundlage*, which means the disappearance of the basis of the contract, whereas the term *imprévision* is used in French Law. However, the DCFR/PECL adopts the term 'change of circumstances', and takes a broad and flexible approach in the pursuit of contractual justice. According to Article III.-1:110 DCFR/6:111 PECL, where the performance of the contract becomes excessively onerous because of the change of circumstances, the party can enter into negotiations to adapt the contract or terminate it. If the parties fail to do so within a reasonable time, then, the court may choose to adapt the contract for distribution of the losses between the parties. Accordingly, the change of circumstances shall satisfy the following conditions:

(1) Time factor: the change of circumstances that occurred after the conclusion of the contract.
(2) Performance excessively onerous: the first provision of Article III.-1:110 DCFR/6:111 PECL stipulates that the party is bound to fulfil its obligations even if the performance has become more onerous. However, if the performance becomes excessively onerous, then the clause of hardship may be satisfied. The concept of excessively onerous means 'the change in circumstances must have brought about a major imbalance in the contract'.[522]
(3) A reasonable man in the same situation cannot have foreseen the circumstances and the risk of the circumstances changing shall not be borne by one party.

The last provision of Article III.-1:110 DCFR/6:111 PECL gives the court wide power either to terminate the contract or to modify the terms. However, as is widely accepted that the contract shall be preserved in utmost order to ensure it can be used as a vehicle for business transactions. According to the provision, the court to distribute the losses and gains, resulting from the change of circumstances, could adapt the contract. The purpose of modification of the contract aims to maintain the justice between the contractual parties by ensuring the rule that the extra costs imposed by the unforeseen circumstances are shared equitably by the parties.

519. *Ibid.*, 500.
520. Denis Tallon, Supervening Events, in Beale et al. (2002), *supra* n. 368, 627.
521. Hannes Rosler, Hardship in German Codified Private Law – In Comparative Perspective to English, French and International Contract Law, *European Review of Private Law*, vol. 3, 2007.
522. Lando & Beale (2000b), *supra* n. 22, 324.

It is worth mentioning that compared with the PECL, the DCFR with regard to the adaptation of the contract due to the change of circumstances stipulates the court may 'vary the obligations in order to make it reasonable and equitable in the new circumstances'.[523] The revised rule in the DCFR appears more open and wide. It just adopted 'reasonable and equitable' as a measurement for the court to modify the clauses. However, for the open-text concept, it is obvious that in practice, on the one hand it is more flexible for the court to judge whether the case has satisfied the situations. But on the other hand, it is reasonable to say the open-text concept requires more judicial interpretation for the judges to unify their standards, which could possibly result unforeseen elements for the contractual parties.

In conclusion, with regard to the adaptation of the contract, the DCFR/PECL endows the contractual parties with freedom to modify the clauses according to their mutual consent, which reveals party autonomy is fully integrated. However, sometimes it is obvious that if the contract was to be terminated, the remedy would be even worse than the harm. This requires the court to be given a wide power to modify the contract. In the DCFR/PECL, if the situation happens in the mistake, excessive benefit or unfair advantage, and change of circumstances, then, the court may modify the clauses.

3.4.2. Chinese Contract Law

In Chinese contract law, some scholars argue that the adaptation of the contract has two levels of meanings.[524] In the broader sense, adaptation means 'alteration in any of the constituent elements of a contract, including the parties and the terms of a contract',[525] whereas in the narrower sense, adaptation means 'alteration of the terms of contract only'.[526] But in the CLC, the adaptation of the contract refers only to the narrower sense, which is the same as in the DCFR/PECL, and stated as the alteration of contractual parties is dealt with similar to the transfer of the contract.

According to the CLC, the mutual consent between the parties to adapt the contract is also recognized, which reveals party autonomy is acknowledged.[527] But the content of modification of a contract agreed to by the parties shall be definite.[528] If the modified contents are indefinite, then 'there will be a presumption in the law that the original contract has not been modified'.[529] As to the forms of modification, it could be any of the oral, written or other forms. However, for the consensus to modify the contract, the CLC also provides 'if laws or administrative

523. Von Bar & Clive (2008), *supra* n. 27, 184.
524. Zhang (2006), *supra* n. 71, 231.
525. Ling (2002), *supra* n. 10, 301.
526. *Ibid.*
527. Article 77 CLC: the parties may modify the contract upon reaching a consensus by consultation.
528. Article 78 CLC: a contract term is construed not to have been modified if the parties failed to clearly prescribe the terms of the modification.
529. Ling (2002), *supra* n. 10, 304.

regulations provide that procedures such as approval or registration shall be carried out when modifying a contract, such provisions shall govern'.[530] This means the modification of a contract can be void if such approval that is required by the law or administrative regulation has not been given.[531] According to the interpretation of the CLC by the SPC, the contract modification shall be effective as long as the necessary approval or registration procedure is completed before the conclusion of court debate at the trial of the first instance.[532] It is thus reasonable to say the mutual consent to modify the contract, a reflection of party autonomy, is recognized, but should be limited to the restrictions of laws or administrative regulations.

Except for the mutual consent to modify the contract, Article 54 states that a party may lay claim to the adaptation of the contract in the People's Court or the Arbitration Tribunal, if the contract was established under the following circumstances: (1) because of the significant misunderstanding; or (2) under the situation of obvious unfairness; or (3) by fraud, threats, or taking advantage of others. Among these situations, the GPCL states that a party can only claim modification of the contract under significant misunderstanding or obvious unfairness.[533] In the situations of fraud, threats or taking advantage of others, the contract can only be avoided under the GPCL.[534] However, due to the requirements of a market economy, the purpose of the CLC is to foster business transactions, and a wide situation to avoid the contract may prove harmful to the protection of certainty of transactions. Therefore the CLC broadens the scope of the situations for contract modification.

What is crucial to the modification of the contract is the doctrine of hardship in the CLC. It is worth noting that there was a fierce discussion on whether the doctrine of hardship should be incorporated into CLC when the CLC was being drafted.

It is widely accepted that *pacta servanda sunt*, a basic and universally accepted principle of contract law, reflects natural justice and the requirements

530. Article 77(2) CLC.
531. Zhou Xiaoyan, Provisions on Validity of Contracts in the Contract Law of China, Immanuel Gebhardt, Zhang Yuqing, Rainer Schroder, *Comparative Analysis on the Chinese Contract Law*, Berliner Wissenschafts-Verlag GmbH, 2003, 93–106.
532. Article 9(2), The Supreme People's Court issues an interpretation on the contract law of the People's Republic of China.
533. Article 59 GPCL: a party shall have the right to request a people's court or an arbitration agency to alter or rescind the following civil acts: (1) those performed by an actor who seriously misunderstood the contents of the acts, (2) those that are obviously unfair.
534. Article 58 GPCL: civil acts in the following categories shall be null and void: (1) those performed by a person without capacity for civil conduct; (2) those that according to law may not independently performed by a person with limited capacity for civil conduct; (3) those performed by a person against his true intentions as a result of cheating, coercion or exploitation of his unfavourable position by the other party; (4) those that performed through malicious collusion are detrimental to the interest of the state, a collective or a third party; (5) those that violate the law or the public interest; (6) economic contracts that violate the state's mandatory plans; and (7) those that performed under the guise of legitimate acts conceal illegitimate purposes. Civil acts that are null and void shall not be legally binding from the very beginning.

of economic development, as it binds a person to his promises and protects the interests of the promisee.[535] When the promisor cannot be held to perform the promise due to changed circumstances so fundamentally that a hardship would occur to him,[536] one party, in order to maintain the fairness, can be excused to have the contract modified or rescinded, if the change of circumstances beyond the contracting parties' expectation and control have frustrated the original basis of the contract so that the continuing performance would obviously render unfairness. Also, under the influence of Confucianism, Righteousness (*yi*) advocated to balance the interests of all the parties, it is held that any injustice which results from an imbalance of the contract caused by the supervening events that the parties cannot reasonably have foreseen when the contract was made, should be adjusted. So in order to pursue the ethics of fairness between the parties, the drafting committee of the CLC incorporated the 'doctrine of hardship' into the drafting proposal. This provision, however, was strongly criticized by the opponents. The reasons are:

(1) It was believed the provision of hardship endowed the judges with more discretionary power to modify or rescind the contract. While in China, the judicial system is not independent and the opponents insisted that the incorporation of hardship would endow the judges with more discretionary power, there was a huge risk that could result in more unfair judgments.[537]
(2) It is very difficult to distinguish the boundary between hardship and normal commercial risks. On the one hand, free market offers lots of good chances for the investors, but on the other hand, there also exist many risks that the investors cannot expect when concluding the contract. Since the boundary between those two concepts is so difficult to distinguish, it is possible for some commercial risks to be considered as hardship, which may be harmful to the development of a market economy and detrimental to the justice of law.

So the incorporation of hardship is criticized strongly by the society and even some drafting members who insisted on incorporating it into the CLC. Since the drafting proposal had to be approved by the National Committee to become an effective law in China as analysed by the members of the Legal Committee, it was impossible for the National Committee to approve the drafting if the notion of hardship was incorporated.[538] So before remitting the final drafting proposal to the National Committee Conference, the provision of hardship was deleted for the other drafting provisions to be approved. However, the background demonstrates that this principle actually has been widely accepted among the Chinese jurists, and has

535. Dietrich Maskow, Hardship and Force Majeure, *The American Journal of Comparative Law*, vol. 40, 1992, 657.
536. *Ibid.*
537. Liang (2000), *supra* n. 485.
538. *Ibid.*

emerged into practice by the opinions from the SPC through the letter of judicial instruction issued in 1992.[539] However, due to the non-independent Chinese judicial system, the provision has not been written in the CLC as it would endow the judges with a broad discretionary power to modify the contract, which could result in unfair judgments.

Although the notion of hardship has not been written in the CLC, on 9 February 2009, the SPC made some judicial interpretation of the CLC, and according to these, Article 26 recognized the doctrine of hardship, which has since been advocated in the Chinese academic circles for a long time. As expressed in the provision, the People's Court could either adapt or terminate the contract according to the principles of fairness if significant change occurred. The provision actually was to recognize the doctrine of hardship in Chinese law, so that in the event of any significant changes occurring when performing the contract, the court could adapt it in accordance with the principle of fairness. However, it expressly states that significant change shall differ from the commercial risks. As the judicial interpretation is considered a significant source for the court when deciding the case, it is reasonable to say the notion of hardship has finally been incorporated in Chinese law.

3.4.3. Comparison

Both the DCFR/PECL and the CLC recognized the contract could be adapted by the mutual consent of the parties, which reveals party autonomy is a fundamental principle in both contract laws. However, under the CLC, the mutual consent to modify the contract has to satisfy two requirements. The first is that the modification term shall be definite, while the second refers to the obtainment of the approval required by the laws or administrative regulations. Another difference in the mutual intentions to modify the contract can be found from the DCFR that under the notion of mistake, if one party indicates performance of what the other party has understood, then, the contract can be regarded as adapted. This rule in fact is to respect the self-determination of the individuals, which is a core essence of party autonomy.

Apart from the mutual consent for adaptation, most of the current legal systems also recognize some circumstances for the parties to lay a claim for adaptation, unilaterally. It is true to say, on the one hand, that the modification by the court is to maintain market certainty and fairness between the parties, but on the other hand, it may be detrimental to what the parties mutually agreed upon. It is to

539. The letter of judiciary instruction from Supreme Court is normally used to answer legal questions raised by a High Court concerning interpretation and application of specific law or regulation in a particular case. The Supreme people's Court endorsed the opinion of the High People's Court of Hubei Province on 6 Mar. 1992 to hold that, for purposes of the instant case, due to the change in circumstances that could not be foreseen and prevented by the parties during the performance of contract, it would be obviously unfair if asked to continue performing the obligations.

balance the principle of party autonomy with fairness. Under the DCFR/PECL, the contract is allowed to be adapted in the event of mistake, excessive benefits or unfair advantages, and a change of circumstances. However, in the CLC, generally speaking, the contractual parties could claim for adaptation in the event of significant misunderstanding, obvious fairness, fraud, threats and taking advantage of others if the defects of consent do not harm the interests of the state. The change of circumstances as an additional doctrine for the adaptation of the contract has been incorporated in the judicial interpretation by the SPC although in the CLC, it has not been officially recognized.

So a significant difference may be found in the adaptation of the contract under threats and fraud. In the CLC it is possible for the court to adapt those contracts, whereas the DCFR does not recognize these two situations. It should be noted that in the GPCL, in both these situations, the only effect is to avoid those contracts. However, since the 1990s it has been argued that simply avoidance will be detrimental to market transactions, which are inconsistent with the basic value of promoting business transactions of the contract law. Adaptation is thus allowed for the contract, which is concluded under threats and fraud. On the one hand, this change may contribute to promoting market certainty, but on the other hand it is reasonable to say that party autonomy may be impaired by adaptation, as fraud and threats are two serious, immoral acts, which shall be punished by law, and it is true to say there is even no mutual intention in the contract. If the contract is allowed to be adapted even if it is concluded under fraud or threats, then, it is true to say party autonomy will be somehow damaged. However, this difference is derived from the promotion of business transactions under the CLC.

3.5. TERMINATION

Termination is the significant vehicle, which balances the obligations and rights between the parties and maintains fairness of the contract. If one party does not perform the contract fundamentally, the aggrieved party shall be endowed with the right to terminate the contract as one of the remedies to safeguard its interests. However, 'whether the aggrieved party should have the right to terminate the contract in the case of a non-performance by the other party depends upon a weighing of conflicting considerations',[540] since the aggrieved party often requires a wide right of termination, while the non-performing party may desire to perform the contract as termination always proves to be a detriment. Therefore, a faithful intention to exercise the right of termination is often required, and the parties may not have such freedom to terminate the contract as they wished. It is true to say the termination of the contract is to balance the interests of the parties in accordance with good faith and fair dealing. So this section attempts to compare the doctrine of termination of the contract in the EU and China to show the differences, and examine whether these differences can be explained by party autonomy.

540. Lando & Beale (2000b), *supra* n. 22, 409.

3.5.1. European Contract Law

Since 'freedom of contract' not only includes the freedom to choose the counterparty and the freedom to conclude the contract, but also contains the freedom to agree upon the remedies, which will be followed when their rights are infringed;[541] it frequently agreed that an aggrieved party could terminate the contract when the other party does not perform any particular duties. The enforcement of this termination can reflect the respect of self-determination, which is the spirit of party autonomy in the law of contracts. The DCFR/PECL recognizes that the parties may have the freedom to determine the contents of the contract, which indirectly states that the mutual intention to the contents of the contract shall be respected.[542]

Apart from the agreement to terminate, some situations allow the unilateral termination. These are provided by the DCFR/PECL. Section V in Chapter III of Book III in DCFR/Section III in Chapter IX of PECL regulates the rules of termination of the contract. Generally speaking, three types of issues which include the grounds of termination, the loss of the right to terminate, and the effect of the termination are contained in this Chapter. This part gives a general description to the right of determination under the DCFR/PECL.

3.5.1.1. Grounds to Terminate the Contract

Articles III.-3:501 to III.-3:505 provide numerous situations for the parties to terminate the contract. Generally speaking, there are two main reasons to terminate the contract. These are the fundamental non-performance and the equivalents to non-performance, which includes the termination after notice, which fixes additional time for performance, anticipated fundamental non-performance and the failure to provide adequate assurance.[543] As widely accepted, termination is of a remedy for an aggrieved party to end the contract and secure its interests if the other party does not perform its duties. However, it can lead to the so considerable uncertainty in market transactions that the DCFR/PECL sets numerous requirements for termination.

3.5.1.1.1. Fundamental Non-performance

The requirement of fundamental non-performance has been laid down in Article III.-3:502 DCFR/8:103 PECL. Roughly speaking, two situations can be considered when judging the fundamental non-performance in DCFR. These are:

(a) Gravity of the consequences

According to Article III.-3:502(2)(a) DCFR, if the other's breach deprives the aggrieved party of its rights substantially, then, non-performance

541. Daniel Friedmann, Good faith and remedies for breach of contract, in Jack Beatson & Daniel Friedmann, *Good Faith and Fault in Contract Law*, Clarendon Press, 1995, 401–403.
542. Article II.-1:102 DCFR; Art. 1:102 PECL.
543. Von Bar & Clive (2009), *supra* n. 24, 851.

could be regarded as fundamental. But the non-performing party should foresee or know the consequences of its non-performance leading to the aggrieved party losing interest and benefit to perform the contract. As to the determination of whether the breaching party can foresee or should have known the consequences, it is pointed out by the drafting committee of the PECL that professional skill and knowledge shall be taken into account.[544] However, it is true to say that substantial deprivation of the rights, which depend on whether the aggrieved party lost interest in performing the contract if the other party did not perform its duties is essential to constitute fundamental non-performance. As described by the Study Group, three situations have to be considered when determining whether non-performance has substantially deprived the creditor of what the creditor was entitled to expect under the contract, which are the nature and terms of the contract, the usages and practices, and the qualifications and experience of the party concerned.[545]

(b) Intentional

In the event that the party committing the breach is doing it in bad faith, it can also be regarded as fundamental especially if the non-performance is intentional and the aggrieved party cannot rely on the other's future performance according to Article III.-3:502(2)(b) DCFR. It shall be noted that the concept of 'intentional' covers 'a series of situations ranging from the simple actual knowledge that a breach will be committed to the fraudulent or malicious behaviour on the part of the debtor.'[546] Also, this notion of 'intentional' gives the aggrieved party no reason to foresee the breaching party's future performance.

Therefore, the DCFR/PECL acknowledges fundamental non-performance as one of the reasons to terminate the contract. In this situation, 'fundamental' is of the essence to judge whether the termination is justifiable. However, when compared with the DCFR, the PECL states that the circumstance of strict compliance shall also be regarded as fundamental non-performance if it is essential for the contract. As described in Article 8:103(a) PECL, any deviation from the obligation that shall be strictly adhered to, can be regarded as fundamental non-performance, which can be reflected through either an express provision, or an implied rule in the contract.[547] Strict compliance with the non-performed obligation is essential for all parties should be clearly demonstrated by the nature or the language of the contract. Except for the express or implied provisions of the contract, under the PECL, the usage and the domestic law as well as other circumstances can also be taken into account when determining the requirement of 'essence'.[548] For instance,

544. Lando & Beale (2000b), *supra* n. 22, 364–365.
545. Von Bar & Clive (2009), *supra* n. 24, 853–854.
546. Antoniolli & Veneziano (2005), *supra* n. 461, 366.
547. J.M. Smits, Non-performance and Remedies in General, in Busch, Hondius, van Kooten, Schelhaas & Schrama (2002), *supra* n. 389, 330.
548. Antoniolli & Veneziano (2005), *supra* n. 461, 365.

in the case of commercial contracts, the time of delivery of goods is often essential to the contract. Under these contracts, the delayed delivery could be regarded as fundamental non-performance. So it is true to say the essence is a principal requirement for fundamental non-performance in the PECL. However, this circumstance has been excluded by the DCFR, due to the reason that '[this provision] left it open to a court to treat an obligation as "of essence" of the contract, so that any failure to perform it would give the other party the right to terminate the contractual relationship, even if the non-performance had no serious consequences for the other party'.[549] It is worth mentioning that the termination does not need to be brought to the notice of the court, and it is effective simply by dispatching a notice.

3.5.1.1.2. Delayed Performance

Except for fundamental non-performance, delayed performance can also be a cause for termination of the contract. Article III.-3:503 DCFR/9:301(2) PECL clearly states that in case of delayed performance, if the other party does not perform within the period fixed by the notice issued by the aggrieved party to provide an additional reasonable time-period for completing the performance, then, the right of termination shall also be issued even if the non-performance is not fundamental. However, the notice of a definite reasonable time to perform the delayed duties shall be provided. Two elements of definite period and reasonable time must be satisfied in the notice. A clear fixed time period determines the definite period. For instance, the notice may state that the performance shall be completed within a week, or before 1 January. As to the reasonable time, it shall be decided by the court after considering all the relevant circumstances. However, the creditor's quick performance is required. If the debtor does not perform the obligations after the period provided in the notice lapses, then, the contract is automatically terminated. The notice for delayed performance is ultimately consistent with the duty of caring for the other party's interests and fairness, and hence required. If the contract is terminated directly due to the other party's delayed performance, then, it is obviously unfair when the other party has already performed the principal obligations. So the DCFR/PECL sets the compulsory requirement of issuing a notice before the termination to balance this fairness between the parties. A notification to demand performance also ensures concern for the other party's interests, so that the other party may get some extra time to complete the performance in order to minimize the losses due to delays on its part.

3.5.1.1.3. Anticipatory Non-performance

Besides all the reasons to terminate the contract, Article III.-3:504 DCFR/9:304 PECL sets down anticipatory non-performance as another reason to terminate the contract. Based on the idea that a contractual party does not need to continue being bound by the contract once it has become clear that the other party will not or

549. Von Bar & Clive (2009), *supra* n. 24, 853.

cannot perform the contract as scheduled, it is clear that if there is an obvious unwillingness or inability to perform, which results in fundamental non-performance, the aggrieved party is entitled to terminate the contract. However, in the case of termination due to anticipatory non-performance, two elements need to be manifested.[550] The first is the inability or unwillingness to perform and that must be clear. Anticipatory non-performance only applies if it has become clear that the other party will not perform the contract. If it is not certain that the other party will perform the contract at the scheduled time, the aggrieved party can demand an adequate assurance of due performance, or withhold the performance of its obligations. The second element requires that anticipatory non-performance must be fundamental. Only if the pending non-performance meets the requirement of 'fundamental' as regulated in the DCFR/PECL, could the aggrieved party be entitled to terminate the contract. This provision is finally to balance the fairness between the parties. Where the creditor is insecure about his interests, he may demand that the other party provide the assurance for the performance. If the other party does not provide this assurance, then he may terminate the contract. Otherwise, he has to wait until the other party does not perform the obligation at the scheduled time, which will lead to an unfair outcome for the creditor. However, the creditor may not terminate the contract directly once his interests are rendered insecure, as it may be detrimental to the debtor's interests. So the requirement of assurance is provided by the DCFR/PECL to balance the fairness between the parties.

3.5.1.1.4. Inadequate Assurance of Performance

The ground for inadequate assurance of performance differs from anticipatory non-performance, although the right to terminate based on the above two grounds is exercised prior to the time of performance. In the first case, the creditor has the feeling that the creditor will be unable or unwilling to perform the contract on the due date. But the debtor may still perform the contract afterwards. Therefore, the creditor is reluctant to terminate the contract based on anticipated non-performance. In contrast, under anticipatory non-performance, the creditor may reasonably feel that the debtor will not perform the contract fundamentally, so he may exercise the right of termination to secure his own interests. However, it shall be noted that after receiving the purported assurances, the demanding party must determine if the assurance is adequate or not. If the assurance received is adequate, then, the obligations under the contract must be performed. If the demanding party suspends the performance as it believes the assurance is inadequate, but later the court finds the assurance is adequate, the demanding party will be considered the breaching party.[551] As described by the DCFR drafting committee, the general rule on adequate assurance of performance is drawn from the American Uniform

550. Antoniolli & Veneziano (2005), *supra* n. 461, 374–375.
551. John R. Trentacosta & Steven R. Fox, Demand for Adequate Assurance of Performance under the UCC, *The Michigan Business Law Journal*, Spring, 2003, 13.

Commercial Code, and it may not be widely found in the law of EU Member States.[552]

It is worth mentioning that in the DCFR/PECL, the notions of excused and non-excused non-performance are treated the same way, which is contrary to many European systems where the termination of contract occurs due to the reason of impossibility, which differs from the termination due to a breach of contract.[553] In most continental legal systems, the termination of contract due to the notion of impossibility is separately dealt with by the theory of risks, while in common law systems, frustration is used as a replacement.[554] But under the DCFR, obligations get extinguished if excused non-performance occurs due to impediments, such as force majeure and frustration.[555]

It could thus be reasonable to say, for the termination of the contract, if the breaching party's non-performance is fundamental, the aggrieved party can terminate the contract simply by providing a notice. If the non-performance or delay is not fundamental, the aggrieved party may also be entitled to terminate the contract. However, the notice of a reasonable time period to perform the contract shall be given to the breaching party. Also, prior to the performance of the contract, if the creditor faces reasonable insecurity, then, the assurance of performance can be demanded.

3.5.1.2. Notice

The notion of fair dealing demands that an aggrieved party should give a notice to the non-performing party if it wishes to terminate the contract. Uncertainty on whether the aggrieved party will accept the late performance will always be a serious detriment to the non-performing party. If the aggrieved party can give a notice that it will not accept the late performance within a reasonable time, or it will accept the performance if it is performed within a reasonable time period, then, the non-performing party can make some arrangements regarding its services and goods. Article III.-3:507 DCFR/9:303 PECL therefore, lays down the requirements for the aggrieved party to provide the notice in order to maintain fair dealing between the contractual parties, and attempt to decrease the losses caused by uncertainty as to whether the aggrieved party will accept late performance.

However, the aggrieved party loses its right to terminate the contract unless it gives notice within a reasonable time period after it knows or expects to have known of the non-performance, as stated in Article III.-3:508 DCFR/9:303(3) PECL. As to the concept of reasonable time period, the aggrieved party must be allowed ample time to check whether the performance achieves the requirement,

552. Von Bar & Clive (2009), *supra* n. 24, 871.
553. Lando & Beale (2000b), *supra* n. 22, 411.
554. Daniel Friedmann, Good Faith and Remedies for Breach of Contract, in Beatson & Friedmann (1995), *supra* n. 542, 399–426.
555. Article III.-3:104 DCFR.

and it shall depend upon the circumstances.[556] 'It is preferable to leave this decision to the judges and arbitrators.'[557] If the delay in making a decision is due to his fault or wastage of time, then, the reasonable time period will be shorter. If the defaulting party tries to conceal the defects, then a longer time shall be given to the aggrieved party.

It is worth mentioning that there are two exceptions to the rule about issuing a notice of termination. The first is according to Article III.-3:508(3) DCFR/8:106(3) PECL which states that in case of a delay in performance, which is not fundamental, if the aggrieved party has given a notice fixing an additional reasonable time period, it may terminate the contract at the end of the period stated in the notice if the defaulting party does not perform within that time period. In this case, the notice of termination does not have to be given to the defaulting party. However, it shall be noted that the time period fixed in the notice should be reasonable. Under the DCFR, in the event of anticipated non-performance and inadequate assurance of performance, the right to terminate is also lost after the reasonable time period has lapsed. The second exception is regulated in Article III.-3:104(4) DCFR/9:303(4) PECL which states that if the non-performance is due to a permanent impediment, then, the obligation can be extinguished automatically without notice. However, in the case of excused non-performance, the impediment needs to be completely permanent. If it is a partial or temporary impediment, the aggrieved party still needs to provide a notice of termination.

3.5.1.3. Effects of Termination

Articles III.-3:509 to III.-3:713 of DCFR/9:305 to 9:308 of PECL regulate the nature and effects of termination. Generally speaking, under the DCFR/PECL, termination releases the parties from their obligations to perform and receive the performance, which is the perspective of the notion of forward-looking. It has been stated clearly that termination does not have a retroactive effect, which means in general, termination cannot 'undo' what has taken place before the date of termination.[558] According to the comments of the drafting committee of the PECL, the reasons why termination does not have retroactive effects under the DCFR are[559] first, the claim for damages for the loss of expectation may be precluded if the contract indicates it had never been made, which is in contrast to the rule that a party does not lose its right to damages by exercising another remedy. Secondly, some clauses, such as dispute settlement clauses, may be prevented from application if the contract like it had never been made. Another reason provided by some other scholars is that inappropriate results could arise from undoing what has

556. Lando & Beale (2000b), *supra* n. 22, 414–415.
557. Hans Henrik Edlund, Termination of commercial contracts by giving notice, *European Review of Contract Law*, February 2008, 15–30.
558. Lando & Beale (2000b), *supra* n. 22, 419.
559. *Ibid.*, 420.

already taken place in some contracts.[560] However, an exception is made in the form of the provision in the contract for the settlement of disputes that are not affected by the termination. Besides this, the DCFR extends this effect to certain rights, which are to operate after the termination, such as the 'preservation of the ancillary relationship'.[561] Another development in the DCFR is the rule on the right to damages. As clearly stated in the DCFR, a creditor not only retains rights to damages for actual non-performance, 'but also has the same right to damages or stipulated payment for non-performance as the creditor would have had if there had been actual non-performance of the now extinguished obligations of the debtor'.[562] This additional rule seems to give the penalties to the breaching party, or it can be considered to maintain the expectation interests for the creditors. However, in the long-term contracts, the creditor may only be allowed to recover damages for loss in relation to that part of the contract in which the non-performance occurs.

3.5.2. Chinese Contract Law

Under the CLC, the contract can end in several different ways. The first is dissolution of a contract, the second refers to the termination of a contract, and set-off, lodgement, release as well as the merger can also lead to the extinguishing of the rights and obligations. All the five ways mentioned above mean, a contractual relationship is winding up and that the rights and obligations arising under the contract cease to be enforceable at law.[563] It is worth noting that dissolution is slightly different from termination in the following aspects: (1) the effect of the contract: the dissolution only extinguishes the future rights and obligations, whereas termination may not only affect the future rights and obligations, but can also retroactively affect the past rights and obligations; (2) in case of termination, restitution may be followed to avoid any unjust enrichment while in case of dissolution, the contract may only end up; (3) the scope of application: termination is always used in the case of breach of contract as a method to punish the party in breach, but on the contrary, the dissolution is mostly applied to cases where there is no breach of contract.[564]

According to the CLC, termination of the contract is a legal act whereby the contractual relationship ends by a declaration of intention of the contractual parties. Roughly speaking, terminating the contract may be based on two points: One is termination on the basis of agreement between the contractual parties and the other is according to the statutory provisions. This subsection intends to analyse the doctrine of termination of contract in the CLC.

---

560. Antoniolli & Veneziano (2005), *supra* n. 461, 425.
561. Von Bar & Clive (2009), *supra* n. 24, 888.
562. *Ibid.*
563. Ling (2002), *supra* n. 10, 331.
564. Wang Jiafu, *min fa zhai quan* [obligatory rights in civil law], fa lv chu ban she [Law Press], 2004, 362.

3.5.2.1. Termination by Agreement

Article 93 of the CLC states that a contract may be terminated upon the consent of both parties through their negotiations. The termination through negotiation is advocated in China, since it is not only suitable to the principle of the freedom of contract, but also, it saves the unnecessary costs of bringing the case to the Court.[565] There are two ways to exercise the right of termination: one is through the termination agreement and the other is by the agreed conditions. 'Termination agreement' refers to a consensual conduct, which is achieved through negotiation to end the contractual relationship. There are three distinctions made for the termination agreement: (1) the agreement is made after the conclusion of the contract but before the completion of the performance; (2) the agreement intends to discharge the existing contractual relationship; and (3) the agreement reflects the consent of both parties. The termination by agreement is inherent in the freedom of the contract.[566] However, the exercise of the freedom cannot violate the mandatory rules of law nor may it injure the rights of a third party.

The second method of exercising the right of termination by agreement is through the agreed conditions by which the terms of the agreement permit the contractual party to terminate the contract when the conditions are met. Article 93(2) stipulates that the parties may agree upon the condition under which a party may terminate the contract. In this case, the contract can be terminated merely through a unilateral notice. However, if in the contract, the parties agree that the contract may be terminated by performing an act other than giving notice to the other party, then, this term shall prevail over the requirement of issuing a notice.

It is worth noting a question arising from the circumstance that after termination by agreement, if both parties have not reached the agreement about the damages and compensation, then, whether the contractual party can claim the damages and compensation. There are three different views to this question. Some scholars argue the parties may still have the right to claim the damages and compensation. Since the parties agree on the term to terminate the contract, this will not affect the rights to demand damages and compensation. The termination does not relate to the abandonment of rights. On the contrary, some other scholars believe the rights to claim damages and compensation shall be extinguished based on the termination of the contract. They insist that if the parties do not reach the agreement on the damages and compensation, they cannot agree to termination of the contract. It is logical to say if the problem of damages and compensation has not been solved in the agreement of termination; the party can be regarded as having abandoned the rights to claim damages and compensation. Furthermore, the purpose of termination by agreement is to solve the disputes, which shall lead to a reduction of other costs incurred in bringing the case to the

565. Zhou Linbin, *bi jiao he tong fa* [*Comparative Contract Law*], Lanzhou University Press, 1989, 320–331.

566. Huixing Liang, *min fa zong lun* [General Introduction to Civil law], Law Press, 1996c, 42–109.

court. Apart from these two different views, there is a moderate approach that advocates a focus on the intention of the parties. Under this approach, if both parties have not discussed the damages and compensation, then, the rights can be deemed as abandoned. If both parties have discussed this question but have not reached the agreement on this aspect, then, the rights shall not be deemed as abandoned. As to these three approaches, in the practice of Chinese contract law, it still remains as a vacuum.

3.5.2.2. Statutory Rights of Termination

Apart from the termination by agreement, the CLC also provides several statutory bases for the party to terminate the contract unilaterally. According to Article 94 CLC, there are five statutory basis for the termination of the contract which are (a) the purpose of the Contract cannot be realized due to force majeure; (b) a contractual party, before the expiration of the time of performance, expresses explicitly or indicates through its conduct that it will not perform the principal obligations; (c) a contractual party delays the performance of its main obligations and fails to perform them within a reasonable time period after being demanded; (d) a contractual party delays the performance of an obligation or commits another breach of contract which makes it impossible to realize the purpose of the contract; (e) other situation provided by the law.[567] However, in fact there are only three types of statutory bases for the termination of the contract, which shall be: force majeure, breach of contract, and other statutory reasons.

3.5.2.2.1. Force Majeure

As defined in Article 117 CLC, force majeure refers to the objective circumstances, which are unforeseeable, unavoidable and insurmountable.[568] Not only does it include the natural disasters, but also the social or political changes as well as the change of law, which should be within its scope.[569] However, the CLC does not define the specific instance of force majeure. It is argued by some scholars that there are several tests for the constitution of force majeure in the CLC: (a) the event should be beyond the control of the non-performing party; (b) the event cannot be foreseen when concluding the contract; (c) the event and its consequence cannot be avoided in advance; (d) the event and its consequence cannot be overcome after the occurrence; (d) the event must have led to the impossibility of performance of a contractual obligation.[570]

However, force majeure may also affect the three different ways of the performance of a contract: (i) performance of the whole contract may be impossible;

567. Article 94 CLC.
568. Article 117 CLC.
569. Li Guoguang, *zhong guo he tong fa tiao wen jie shi* [*Interpretation to the Provisions of Chinese Contract Law*], Xinhua Publisher, 1999, 255–258.
570. Ling (2002), 406–409.

(ii) performance of the partial contract may be impossible; (iii) performance may be delayed. But not all of these three results can lead to the termination of the contract. According to the CLC, only if force majeure makes it impossible to realize the purpose of the contract, can the contract be terminated. It is reasonable therefore, to say the termination may occur in all the circumstances above, if the purpose of the contract cannot be realized by force majeure. For instance, if the time period of performance is essential to the contract, the delayed performance resulting from force majeure could be within the circumstances for the termination. Also, if the partial performance occurring due to force majeure is the essence of the contractual obligation, then, termination will surely be allowed.

3.5.2.2.2. Anticipatory Repudiation

Anticipatory repudiation is another statutory basis for the termination of the contract according to the CLC. It is one of the remedies for the contractual party in cases where the other party denies performing the obligation before the performance is due. There are three grounds to determine if the anticipatory repudiation is constituted or not: (a) as it is argued that 'repudiation is a party's wrongful declaration that it will not perform the contract',[571] so the manifestation of the intention to not perform shall be made. However, the manifestation cannot only be made through the explicit expression, but also can be made through the implied conduct. Basically, the aggrieved party should have reason to believe the other party will not perform the obligation; (b) the manifestation should be made before the performance of the contract. The essence of anticipatory repudiation in fact aims to protect the interests of the aggrieved party. It often happens that the other party's non-performance is obvious before the expiration of the performance. Under this situation, the aggrieved party shall be endowed with some remedies to try to reduce its loss incurred because of the other's non-performance. Anticipatory repudiation is therefore one of the remedies to protect its interests. However, for the constitution of anticipatory repudiation, it is clear that the manifestation of non-performance shall be obvious before the expiration of the performance, which will reasonably lead the aggrieved party to believe that the other party will not perform; (c) the non-performance obligation shall be principal. The question then arises from the definition of principal obligation that since in the CLC, the principal obligation is not explicitly defined, should the content of particular contracts be referred to for their determination? However, it is reasonable to say if the purpose of the contract cannot be realized due to the non-performing obligation, then, the obligation should be deemed as principal.

3.5.2.2.3. Unreasonable Delay

The CLC also sets the case that if a party delays the performance of its main obligations and still fails to perform them within a reasonable time period after

571. *Ibid.*, 388.

being demanded, the other party shall have the right to terminate the contract.[572] The situation of unreasonable delay is different from anticipatory repudiation, since in the first situation, the delay happens during the performance period whereas in the latter case, the non-performance is manifested before the time of performance. Also, unreasonable delay is different from force majeure, since in the situation of unreasonable delay, the obligor is able to perform but without a justifiable reason to fail the performance, whereas in force majeure, the obligor cannot perform due to the objective reasons.

In case of a delay in performance, the obligee is required to make a demand. Under the CLC, after the obligee has made a demand, if the obligor does not perform within a reasonable time period, the party can terminate the contract. It is obvious to say the demand is a key element for unreasonable delay. As to the means of making the demand, it can be exercised orally or may be written. However, it should be noted that the obligation the obligor delays to perform is the principal obligation.[573]

3.5.2.2.4. Frustration of Contract Purpose

In some situations, if the delayed performance or other breach conduct leads to the frustration of the contract purpose, the obligee can terminate the contract without making any demand. In this situation, the frustration of the contract purpose as a result of delay or other breach conduct shall be required. In some specific contracts, if the time of performance is the essence of the contract, then, the delayed performance may lead to the frustration of the contract purpose. In this case, the obligee can terminate the contract without any demand made to the obligor.

Apart from the four statutory grounds for termination, the CLC permits termination also for other reasons provided by law. Therefore, it is concluded in the CLC that there are two ways for the party to terminate the contract. The first one is to terminate by agreement, which is rooted into the principle of the freedom of contract. The other is to allow the party to terminate unilaterally based on statutory grounds. For statutory grounds, there are five reasons provided by the CLC, which are force majeure, anticipatory repudiation, delay in performance within a reasonable time period after performance has been demanded, delay in performance or other breach conduct, which leads to the frustration of the contract purpose, and other reasons provided by law.

3.5.2.3. Notice

Under the CLC, the right of termination is to be exercised through issuance of a notice, no matter if the contract is terminated through the agreement or on statutory grounds.[574] This rule in fact is consistent with the CISG. Giving notice could be

572. Article 94(3) CLC.
573. Wang (2002), *supra* n. 262, 290–292.
574. Article 96(1) CLC.

deemed as a compulsory procedure to terminate the contract in the CLC. If the party fails to give notice within a reasonable or prescribed time, then, the right of termination will be lost.[575] As to the effect of this notice, the CLC stipulates the notice of termination becomes effective when the other party receives it. After receiving the notice, if the other party objects to it, the former may apply to the People's Court or an arbitral institution for the determination of the validity of the termination. Therefore, it can be concluded that there are three elements governing the procedures of termination under the CLC:

(a) The reason of termination shall be consistent with the law. As analysed above, the contract can be terminated through the agreement between the parties, or it can be terminated unilaterally within the scope of statutory reasons. However, it shall be noted in the unilateral termination, that the reasons for termination are often disputed in fact. So if the other party objects to the termination, then the People's Court or an arbitral institution can be applied to for purposes of resolution.
(b) The termination shall be notified by the other party. In any of the reasons set by the CLC, the procedure of issuing a notice is compulsory. Principally, the notice can be issued orally or in the written form or other forms. However, it becomes effective when it is received by the other party.
(c) The notice shall be given within a reasonable or prescribed time. It is clearly stated in the CLC that the contractual party shall lose the right of termination if the right is not exercised within a reasonable or prescribed time period. Since the aggrieved party can choose to terminate the contract or demand that the other party performs in the case of the other party's non-performance, the right to terminate the contract then is required to be given within a reasonable time period.
(d) If approval or registration is required by the law or administrative regulation, the approval or registration shall be followed. It is commonly known that in China, for the transfer of real property, such as a house, car, boat, etc., registration is a compulsory procedure for the transaction. Even under the CLC in some particular contracts, the contract is effective only upon its registration or approval. Therefore, if the contract is terminated, the approval or registration shall be recovered to its original status.

3.5.2.4. Effect of Termination

'After a contract is terminated, the unperformed party ceases to be performed. As to the performed party, a party may demand restoration to its original status, resort to other remedial measures and have the right to claim damages depending on the amount of performance and the nature of the contract.'[576] From this provision, it is

575. Article 95 CLC.
576. Article 97 CLC.

reasonable to say the effect of termination consists of three parts, which are release from performance, restitution, and damages.

3.5.2.4.1. *Release from Performance*

For a contract that has not been performed, termination simply results in the extinguishment of the contractual relationship. It is obvious to say that after termination, both parties shall be released from future obligations without any regard to the question whether the obligation is due or not. However, it is noted that if a contract involves several parts or instalments and the defaulting party only conducts the breach on one part or instalment, then the contract can only be terminated for the defective part or instalment.[577] In this case, termination cannot release the parties from their obligations to other parts or instalments.

Another aspect to be noted is that the terms on settlement of dispute resolution in the contract are however, not released upon the termination.

3.5.2.4.2. *Restitution*

Apart from the future consequences of release from performance, the termination can also have retroactive effects. Like many other civil law jurisdictions, the CLC provides for the duty of restoration to the original status of the performed obligations. However, it has been debated that some scholars argue that the termination only reverts the title in the subject matter to the performing party, and the right to reclaim the subject is based on the right of ownership, which shall be returned through the doctrine of unjust enrichment.[578] It is generally held that the subject matter passes to the other party upon delivery or registration instead of the conclusion of the contract. The rule shall be deducted similarly in case of the termination of the contract. When the contract is terminated, the subject matter can only be returned through the delivery or the registration. On the contrary, some commentators suggest the retroactive effect of termination could be better in protecting the interests of the aggrieved party. The CLC finally adopted the latter viewpoint to allow for restitution upon termination. Article 97 CLC sets forth that if performance has been rendered, a party may require the other party to restore the subject matter to its original condition or otherwise remedy the situation. However, the remedies are not specified in the CLC itself, and it is analysed by some scholars that several situations could thus be used to explain the other remedies in this article:[579]

(a) If the performance of the contract involves the supply of service or the use of a thing that cannot be restored by its nature, the party, which supplied the service or the thing could demand its value.

577. Ling (2002), *supra* n. 10, 356–357.
578. *Ibid.*
579. Ping Jiang, *A Detailed Explanation of the Contract Law*, China University of Political Science and Law Press, 1999b, 78–85.

(b) If the thing delivered for the performance has been destroyed, damaged or lost, the party, which benefits from the thing shall compensate its value.
(c) If the thing delivered for the performance has been transferred to a third party in good faith, the third party shall not be asked to return the thing, but the party, which transfers the thing to the third party shall compensate for its value.

Therefore, it is concluded that the termination of the contract cannot only lead to the release of future obligations of the contract, but can also have retroactive effects. Briefly put, the termination aims to restore all the situations to the position where they parties will stand if the contract has not been performed.

3.5.2.4.3. Damages

Besides the restitution permitted by the CLC, Article 97 also allows the parties to claim damages if they have losses resulting from the termination. This rule is basically rooted into the principle of fairness. It is widely accepted in the Chinese academic circles that under the situation if a party's breach leads the other party to bear the loss of benefits or interests, it is fair to claim damages from the breaching party. A question then arises as to what kind of damages does the breaching party have to bear? Generally speaking, the damage in the CLC refers not only to interests of reliance, but also to expectation interests. Some authors have particularly illustrated the damages as including: (a) necessary expenses spent on the formation of the contract; (b) costs for the performance of the contract; (c) the costs of losing other opportunities when concluding the contract; (d) costs incurred by restoring the situation to its original status; and (e) other costs resulting from the termination.[580]

However, it is necessary to note that if the termination is caused by force majeure, then, the non-performing party shall be excused from the liability for breaching.

Therefore, it is concluded that the CLC allows both the termination by agreement and unilateral termination based on statutory reasons. As to the statutory reasons, there are five reasons based on which the party can terminate the contract unilaterally, which are force majeure, anticipatory repudiation, unreasonable delay, frustration of purpose, and other reasons set forth in other laws or regulations. However, for termination to take place, the party shall give a notice within a reasonable time period. If the notice is not given within the reasonable time, then, the right of termination is lost. The notice takes effect when the other party receives it. After the contract is terminated, both parties are released from all the future performances and the performed obligations are restored to the original status as if the contract has not been performed at all. If any of the parties have damages resulting from the non-performance, then, the claims for this can also be allowed.

580. Li (1999), *supra* n. 570, 379–384.

3.5.3. Comparison

Both the DCFR/PECL and the CLC set forth the rules regulating the termination of a contract. The first way to terminate is through the agreement, which in fact has been recognized in both contract laws. In the DCFR/PECL, the parties have been clearly endowed with the freedom to determine the contents of the contract, and it is true to say the termination by mutual agreement is permitted. Similarly, in the CLC, parties are also allowed to reach an agreement to terminate the contract. For a specific way of termination, not only can the parties reach an agreement to terminate, but also set forth in their contract some conditions for the termination, and when the conditions are met, the contract is terminated. It is reasonable to say that for termination by agreement; both contract laws are consistent with the principle of the freedom of contract.

Another way to terminate the contract is based on statutory reasons. The DCFR has clearly stated four bases, which are fundamental non-performance, anticipatory non-performance, delayed performance and inadequate assurance of performance. In this aspect, the CLC states clearly that there are five bases for termination such as (i) force majeure, (ii) anticipatory repudiation, (iii) unreasonable delay, (iv) frustration of the contract purpose and (v) other reasons regulated by other laws or regulations. However, as to the force majeure and frustration, under the DCFR the obligations are extinguished if the impediment is permanent. Therefore, in the case of the statutory reasons for termination, both contract laws have to regulate similar reasons. A difference is only with regard to the permanent impediment that in the DCFR the obligations are extinguished, whereas in the CLC the contract is terminated.

Another difference is found in the effects of termination. Although both contract laws allow the parties a release from future obligations, the DCFR/PECL does not permit the termination to have retroactive effects, which in contrast with the CLC means that termination indicates that all the obligations, which have been performed shall be undone. But both the DCFR/PECL and the CLC regulate clearly that the dispute settlement clauses shall not be affected by the termination, and the expectation interests can be claimed for non-performance.

However, the considerable difference shall be taken to an additional rule in the CLC that the reasons regulated by other laws or regulations could also be the basis for the termination. It is difficult to conclude what other grounds are stated in other laws or regulations for the termination, as this provision is rather vague and broad. This difference is mainly derived from the dominant role of the administrative organs, which significantly impact civil society.

3.6. MANDATORY RULES

As revealed from the merits of party autonomy, parties are free to determine the contents of their contract and most of the legal rules do not interfere with this freedom. However, contract law in every country tries to contain some detailed provisions on every possible aspect of contractual rights and obligations. These provisions consist of mandatory rules and default rules. The distinction between mandatory and default rules lies in whether parties can deviate from them when concluding the contract. In the case of the default rules, the contractual parties can deviate from them in the contract, whereas for the mandatory rules, the parties can only be bound by them. The purpose of providing default rules is to make it easier and less costly for the parties to enter into a well-regulated legal relationship, as the parties cannot draft all the rules of their contract,[581] while the mandatory rules are mostly to protect the interests of the other parties and the State. However, the mandatory rules are mostly regarded as one of the primary limitations to the freedom of contract, which is a sort of the expression of party autonomy. This section therefore attempts to compare the differences in mandatory rules in the contract laws of the EU and China, and answer whether those differences can be explained by party autonomy.

3.6.1. European Contract Law

As pointed out by some scholars, the reasons for legislators to enact non-mandatory rules in fact are aimed at promoting the welfare and justice in society.[582] Similarly, there are two fundamental aims that make legislators enact mandatory rules in general. These are to forbid actions that are against the interests of one of the parties, and prohibit terms that are harmful to a third party's lawful interests.[583] The mandatory rules undertake the functions of protecting the weaker parties, public order, third parties and some underlying social values, such as the fundamental rights, social justice, etc. With regard to the effects of violating these rules, it must be understood that the terms or contracts cannot be enforceable by law, because the exercise of personal freedom cannot harm other parties, the state, and the society.

Like most of the national laws, the DCFR/PECL also adopts both mandatory and non-mandatory laws. As to the mandatory rules, they are divided into substantive rules and procedural rules. The former forbids certain contractual terms, while the latter merely requires certain actions to be taken either before or during the contractual relationship.[584] For instance, the DCFR/PECL requires the disclosure to be consistent with good faith and fair dealing as a compulsory obligation for the parties, the provision of which is to be regarded as a procedural mandatory rule. By contrast, other mandatory rules that prohibit the use of any of the terms, such as

581. Von Bar & Clive (2009), *supra* n. 24, 38.
582. Martijn W. Hesselink, Non-mandatory rules in European Contract Law, *European Review of Contract Law*, vol. 1, 2005, 45–65.
583. Attila Menyhard, Karoly Mike & Ako Szalai, Mandatory rules in contract law, German Working Papers in Law and Economics, vol. 2007, paper 18, 3–4.
584. *Ibid.*

unfair terms, are the substantive ones. This subsection describes the sources of mandatory rules in the DCFR and their effects.

3.6.1.1. Sources of Mandatory Rules

Generally speaking, mandatory rules in the DCFR may be derived from either European or national laws. 'If they are European, they can either be included in the DCFR itself or in any other European enactment.'[585] The DCFR divides the mandatory rules into two categories that are fundamental principles and mandatory laws.[586]

3.6.1.1.1. Fundamental Principles

The DCFR clearly states in Article II.-7:301 that a contract is void if it infringes a principle recognized as fundamental in the law of the EU Member States. It is true to say those rules are often described as illegality, immorality, public policy, public order or good faith.[587] Although the Europeanization of private law is to promote the aim of a single market, the convergence at the EU level cannot impair the underlying values of its Member States. So the DCFR does not touch the issue of the illegality, the immorality or the incapacity. However, if a contract infringes the fundamental principle of a Member State, then the contract is rendered void as provided in the DCFR:

> The DCFR does not spell out when a contract is contrary to public policy in this sense, because that is a matter of law outside the scope of the DCFR – the law of competition or the criminal law of the Member State where the relevant performance takes place. However, the fact that a contract might harm particular third persons or society at large is clearly a ground on which the legislator should consider invalidating it.[588]

Besides the national underlying values, the fundamental principles at the EU level shall also be included here.[589] At the EU level, generally speaking, the fundamental rules may be derived from the free movement of goods, services and persons, and the protection of market competition regulated in the EC Treaty, and the fundamental human rights provided by the European Convention on Human Rights and European Union Charter on Fundamental Rights. Also, the underlying principles of DCFR itself shall be taken into account. Freedom, protection of human rights, economic welfare, solidarity and social responsibility, promotion of internal

585. Jacobien W. Rutgers, The Draft Common Frame of Reference, Public Policy, Mandatory Rules and the Welfare State, in Alessandro Somma, *The Politics of the Draft Common Frame of Reference*, Kluwer, 2008, 117.
586. Von Bar & Clive (2009), *supra* n. 24, 551–547.
587. Jacobien W. Rutgers, The Draft Common Frame of Reference, Public Policy, Mandatory Rules and the Welfare State, in Somma (2008), *supra* n. 586, 117–119.
588. Von Bar & Clive (2009), *supra* n. 24, 40.
589. *Ibid.*, p. 536.

market, preservation of cultural and linguistic plurality, rationality, legal certainty, predictability, and efficiency are provided as fundamental principles of DCFR.[590] However, since a mere national concept may not be invoked directly, the notion concerning those principles should be recognized in the EU at large.[591]

Therefore, it is true to say the fundamental principles have been derived from the laws of the EU Member States, the EU enactment and the DCFR itself.

3.6.1.1.2. Mandatory Rules

Similarly the mandatory rules can also be derived from the national laws, EU law and the DCFR/PECL itself. It is true to say there exist a large number of mandatory rules in the applicable laws of the EU Member States, which often undertake a strong public policy that the parties cannot violate. However, compared with the fundamental principles, it is true to say Article II.-7:302 'deals with less important violations of the law',[592] and the statutory regulation is often contained. Apart from the mandatory rules from the applicable national law, the rules which have a mandatory nature in the EU laws and the DCFR/PECL itself, need also to be obeyed by the parties. As to the EU law, it is true to say the EU mandatory rules are mainly derived from the EC Treaty, EC Directives and ECJ judgments.

However, with regard to the DCFR itself, the mandatory rules are specifically reflected in the following aspects:

(1) Non-discrimination: Article II.-2:101 DCFR provides a general prohibition of any discrimination on the grounds of sex, ethnicity or racial origins, which are mandatory. These provisions in fact make equality, an underlying value of the EU, a more specific expression.
(2) Information duty: For the consumer contracts in particular, the DCFR provides a number of concrete rules on disclosing duty, which may not be violated by the parties.
(3) Unfair terms: As social justice is a fundamental value of the DCFR, a contract shall be negotiated and concluded according an equal status to the parties. The DCFR provides various rules that the contract should be avoided or adapted if it is concluded under 'unfair bargaining' power.
(4) Validity of the contract: The DCFR requires the contract to be concluded through mutual intentions. If anything is concealed or if there is any deliberate intention existing in the contract, then the contract can be avoided or adapted.

Worth mentioning is that a possibility may exist for conflicts between the mandatory rules of the national laws and EU laws. But it is still unclear whether the DCFR or a part of it will be endowed with any legal effects, whereas the PECL

590. *Ibid.*, 8–10.
591. Jacobien W. Rutgers, The Draft Common Frame of Reference, Public Policy, Mandatory Rules and the Welfare State, in Somma (2008), *supra* n. 586, 118–119.
592. Von Bar & Clive (2009), *supra* n. 24, 539.

is an optional instrument that the parties may choose to apply in their contracts. So the DCFR does not deal with the issue of the conflicts between the DCFR itself and other laws, such as national laws or the EU law. However, the PECL makes some rules on this issue. Article 1.:103(1) PECL clearly states that if the applicable law allows them, then, the parties can choose the PECL to govern their contracts, with the effect that national mandatory rules are not applicable. According to this provision, there are two elements to be noted. Firstly, the conflict of law rules should permit the parties to choose their contracts to be governed by the PECL. It is indicated by Article 8(1) of the Rome Convention that the existence and validity of a contract or a contractual term shall be determined by the law, which is applicable if the contract or the term is valid.[593] Also, the New York Convention (1958) on the Recognition and Enforcement of Foreign Arbitral Awards recognizes and enforces foreign arbitral award in more than 190 countries. It is revealed from the comments written by the Lando Commission that the proceedings in national courts shall differ from the arbitral proceedings,[594] as the national judges are bound by the choice of law rules, whereas the arbitrators are freer to adopt the governing law which they believe is the most appropriate rule to solve disputes. So it is safe to say in the arbitral proceedings, the choice of the PECL as a governing law is much easier, particularly if the parties expressly choose it in the contract.

Secondly, if the contract is governed by the PECL, then, both the mandatory and non-mandatory rules of the PECL govern all the issues it covers and the national mandatory laws do not apply. It shall be noted that the mandatory rules of the PECL cannot be excluded by the parties if they choose their contract to be governed by it.[595] However, if the parties choose to incorporate the PECL in their contract, which is governed by a national law, then, it will depend on the circumstances whether the mandatory rules of the PECL should be excluded.[596] So it is true to say where the parties choose the PECL to govern their contract, as permitted by the choice of law rules, the mandatory rules of the PECL cannot be avoided by the parties, and all the matters covered by the PECL shall be governed by it.

However, this issue has been regulated in the PECL but has not been incorporated in the DCFR.

3.6.1.2. Effects of Contracts Infringing Fundamental Principles or Mandatory Rules

The effects of contracts infringing mandatory rules have been set in Section III in Chapter VII of Book II of the DCFR, under which two categories of effects are provided. With regard to the contracts infringing the fundamental principles, then, nullity is provided, whereas in case of the infringement of mandatory rules, the

593. Antoniolli & Veneziano (2005), *supra* n. 461, 37.
594. Lando & Beale (2000b), *supra* n. 22, 101.
595. *Ibid.*, 102.
596. F.W. Grosheide, Scope of the Principles, in Busch, Hondius, van Kooten, Schelhaas & Schrama (2002), *supra* n. 389, 35–36.

effects of that infringement prescribed by that mandatory rule shall be adopted, as when 'determining the effects of an illegality upon a contract, regard is to be had first to what the mandatory rule in question provides upon the matter.'[597] However, the DCFR/PECL makes distinctions in two cases with regard to the effect of mandatory rules. Firstly, if the provisions of law, whose mandatory rules make the effects of the contract null, void, voidable, annullable, or unenforceable, then, the effect shall be followed. According to the example given by drafting committee, Article 81 of the EC Treaty prohibits all the agreements that have the object of preventing, restricting or distorting of competition within the common market, and declares such agreements to be automatically void.[598] So if there is an agreement infringing this mandatory rule, then the effect of 'automatically void' provided by the EC Treaty shall be followed. Secondly, if those laws do not expressly prescribe the effects of the infringement, then, the question can be left to the judges or arbitrators. In fact, in some EU Directives, the prohibition rules have been set without any provisions regarding their effects. In such a case, the DCFR/PECL gives the judge or arbitrator some discretionary powers to deal with this matter. The DCFR/PECL offers the judges or arbitrators four choices when determining the effect, which are full effect, some effect, no effect, or to be subject to the modification. However, the decision must be 'an appropriate and proportional response to the infringement'.[599]

When determining the effect of infringements, several relevant circumstances have been set for the judges or arbitrators to consider. Although the circumstances provided by the DCFR/PECL are not the only situations to be considered by the judges, the expressed circumstances may well overlap in the application.

3.6.1.2.1. Purpose of the Rule

If there is no express provision about the effect on the violation of mandatory rules, the legislative intent of those mandatory rules shall be considered. Particularly, whether the purpose of those rules is merely to prohibit the activities domestically, or whether the rules are attempting to be applied to trans-national transactions. This is an important element to determine the effects. 'The usual rules on the interpretation of the law' may be considered for understanding this legislative purpose.[600]

3.6.1.2.2. Category of Persons for Whose Protection the Rule Exists

The category of persons for whose protection the rules exist is closely related to the purpose of the rule. There are some rules attempting to protect the interests of particular persons, such as some EC directives, which try to protect the weaker parties, like consumers, workers, etc. In this case, only those parties, which are

597. Lando & Beale (2000b), *supra* n. 22, 215.
598. Lando et al. (2003), *supra* n. 304, 215.
599. Article 15:102(3) PECL.
600. Lando et al. (2003), *supra* n. 304, 216.

protected by the rules can plead illegality to prevent the contract from taking effect, and the other party may not plead it. This is consistent with the purpose of the rule that the weaker parties are protected.

3.6.1.2.3. Any Sanction that May Be Imposed under the Rule Infringed

When determining the effects of infringement, the sanctions imposed by other laws shall also be considered. As to the effect of illegality, some national laws often set a criminal or administrative sanction against the wrongdoer, in this situation, those sanctions imposed shall be taken into account. It is widely held that the sanction through criminal or administrative law is better to achieve the goal of deterrence rather than the way of private law.[601]

3.6.1.2.4. Seriousness of the Infringement

Since the effect of the contract is closely related to business transactions, if too many contracts are invalidated due to any infringement of the mandatory rules, then, it will be harmful to the development of a common market. Hence, when the judges decide the effect of the infringements, the seriousness of the infringement shall be taken into account. If the infringement is minor, then, the contract may be subject to some modifications. Only when the infringement incurs some serious consequences, does the contract have no effect or a partial effect.

3.6.1.2.5. Where the Infringement was Intentional

Intention to committing an infringement is an important factor for the judges to determine the effect of the contract. If both parties are aware of the illegality of their contract, then, the contract should be rendered ineffective. Where the parties are innocent of the infringement, then, the judges should take note of this innocence for determining the next step. With regard to the question of whether it was 'intentional', the knowledge and profession of both parties may be considered.

3.6.1.2.6. Relationship between the Infringement and the Contract

If the infringed performance is consequential to the contract, then the contract may have no effect. Where the infringing performance is not essential to the contract, the contract may be modified. When determining the effect of the contract, the relationship between the infringement and the contract shall also be taken into account.

Therefore, as to the effect of the infringement on mandatory rules, if those laws express the effect of the infringement, then, those effects shall be followed.

601. Danny Busch & Ewoud Hondius & Hugo van Kooten & Harriët Schelhaas, *The Principles of European Contract Law (Part III) and Dutch Law: A Commentary II*, Kluwer Law International, 2006, 244–258.

Where there is no express provision of the effect, the question will be left to the judges or arbitrators for the decision. Concretely speaking, four effects can be chosen by the judges. These are full effect, partial effect, no effect or modification. However, the decision shall be appropriate with regard to the infringement, and the circumstances of the purpose of the rule, the category of persons the rules protected, the sanction imposed by other rules, the seriousness of the infringement, whether the infringement was intentional, and the relationship between the infringement and the contract shall be taken into account for the determination.

3.6.2. Chinese Contract Law

The CLC, like all other national contract laws, also consists of default rules and mandatory rules. The default rules are aimed at filling the gap in the contracts for economizing the parties' interests. However, it also sets forth that the contract shall abide by law and administrative regulations, and respect social ethics, and may not disrupt the socioeconomic order nor impair social and public interests, which make up the mandatory effects, through Article 7.[602]

3.6.2.1. Sources of Mandatory Rules

Accordingly, in China, the mandatory rules exist in the laws, administrative regulations, authoritative interpretations, and state policies.

3.6.2.1.1. Laws

In China, the term *law* actually has two different meanings. As to the wider interpretation, it includes all binding instruments of the State, like Constitutional Law, laws enacted by the national legislative organs, administrative regulations by the state council, ministerial rules, local regulations and rules, as well as other authoritative interpretations of these instruments.[603] In contrast, the narrow interpretation only refers to the laws enacted by the national legislative organs that include National People's Congress (NPC) and the Standing Committee of the National People's Congress (SCNPC).

The NPC and SCNPC are the most important legislative organs in China. According to the Legislation Law, the difference in the powers of the NPC and the SCNPC is that the 'basic law' can only be enacted by the NPC, while other laws except for the basic law can be adopted by the SCNPC. Whether the laws within civil affairs constitutes 'basic' or not depends on whether the law is about 'basic systems on civil affairs' and 'basic economic systems'.[604] For instance, the Law of

602. Article 7 CLC.
603. Zhang Wenxian, *fa li xue* [Jurisprudence], Higher Education Publishing House, 2007, 4–17.
604. Article 8, Legislation Law of the People's Republic of China, Adopted at the third session of the Ninth National People's Congress on 15 Mar. 2000.

Real Rights, the CLC and the GPCL are within the category of basic laws, while others like Arbitration Law, Consumer Rights Protection Law, etc., belong to the other laws. The NPC actually meets once a year while the SCNPC meets once every two months. It is interesting to know that when the tort law was passed by SCNPC at end of 2009, many criticized it because the tort law could only be passed by the NPC, for it to be considered a '*basic law*', and the same as contract law, property law, etc.

Like most Western countries that are ruled by law, in China too, all other laws are inferior to the Constitutional Law. However, with regard to the conflict between the other laws excluding the Constitutional Law, the regulation that special provisions takes precedence over general provisions and new laws take precedence over old laws, is accepted in the Chinese academic circles. So if there is any provision in the CLC which conflicts with the GPCL, then, the CLC shall take precedence, due to the reason that the CLC is a more special law, which particularly regulates the contracts and also a newer law adopted only in 1999, compared with the GPCL which is of a higher degree of generality and adopted in 1986. Similarly, if there are any inconsistencies between the CLC and other specific contract laws, like labour contract law, or civil laws relevant to the contracts, like marriage law, then, other specific contract laws or civil laws relevant to the contracts shall prevail over the CLC.

Therefore, it is reasonable to say the mandatory rules limited to the freedom of contract in China could arise from the laws. As to the definition of *law*, a narrow interpretation is chosen that the laws enacted by the NPC and the SCNPC are referred to. If there is any consistency in the mandatory rules between these laws, it is certain that Constitutional Law plays the supreme role to which all the other laws are subject. For the conflicts between all other laws, the rule prescribes that special provisions takes precedence over general provisions and new laws take precedence over old laws.

3.6.2.1.2. Administrative Regulations

The administrative regulations refer to all the instruments, which are consistent with the laws, enacted by the state council or ministries with the approval of the state council. During the development of the Chinese market economy, the administrative regulations play an important role in regulating economic orders. They are used to regulate the matters for carrying out laws, or for exercising the administrative power that endows them and is derived from the Constitutional Law. As to the conflicts between laws and administrative regulations, the laws shall take precedence over the regulations. Hence, both the mandatory rules from the laws and administrative regulations shall be abided in the CLC. Roughly speaking, there are about five aspects by which the laws and administrative regulations could influence the contract:

(a) Establishment of contracts: Party autonomy endows the individuals and legal persons with the freedom to choose the forms to establish the contract. The private law shall respect the consensus of parties to choose any form for the establishment of their contract. Nowadays, both the oral and written means are widely recognized in most national legal systems. In China too, the CLC permits oral, written and other forms of establishment of the contract. However, the CLC also prescribes that if the laws or administrative regulations provide for the use of the written form, then, the written form shall be followed. There are several specific contracts which are required by the laws or administrative regulations to maintain that the contracts shall be in writing: Contracts for the assignment of land-use rights, contracts for the transfer of housing, security contracts, insurance contracts, partnership contracts, labour contracts, advertisement contracts, contracts for the transfer, mortgage or lease of ships or aircraft and contracts for authorization of auction.[605] The CLC itself and not just other laws and regulations require some contracts to be in the written form through its specific provisions: Loan contracts, lease contracts with the term of lease of over six months, contracts of financial leasing, construction project contracts, contracts for the supervision of construction projects, contracts for technological development, and contracts for the transfer of technology.[606]

However, it is interesting to note that Article 36 CLC provides that if the parties have not followed the rule to write their contracts as is prescribed by the law or regulations, and if one party has performed the main obligations and the other party has accepted, then, the contract shall be considered established. It is thus reasonable to say as to the mandatory rule of written form regulated by the laws or regulations that if the party has not performed the main obligations, then the contract shall not be considered established.

(b) Effectiveness of contracts: Not only do the mandatory rules of laws or regulations influence the establishment of contracts, but the effect of the contracts is also subject to them. Article 44 CLC provides that if laws or regulations prescribe the effectiveness of contracts and are subject to their approval or registration, then, those rules shall be followed. The approval could be regarded as a condition for the formation or effectiveness of the contract in those contracts. If the formation is subject to the approval, then, no contract is concluded before the approval is provided. Similarly, if the contracts require approval for effectiveness, the contract shall not be effective if the parties fail to do so and pre-contractual liability may be adopted for those contracts. In fact, there are some contracts where approval is required, such as Chinese-foreign joint venture contracts, contracts for the import of technology, etc. It is worth mentioning that the function of approval is usually to maintain the economic order and public interest.

605. Ling (2002), *supra* n. 10, 97.
606. *Ibid.*

With regard to registration, primarily, it applies to the contracts affecting real rights and intellectual property rights. It is used to issue public notice or maintain governmental record of these contracts. Some laws and regulations require the contract be effective subject to registration, while other require that only if the contract is registered, can it be invoked against a third party.

The requirement of approval and registration is also often necessary for the modification and transfer of contracts.[607] For those contracts, which are effective upon registration or approval, in case they are modified or transferred, then too, they will need registration and approval.

(c) Validity of contracts: As analysed in the section on illegality, the violation of laws or administrative regulations is one of the reasons judges and arbitrators may use to invalidate the contract. This provision has been accepted in most national contract laws. However, for the principle of fostering business transactions in China today, it is advocated that only if the violation is serious, should the contract could be invalidated. If the violation is minor, then, the judges or arbitrators should try to modify the contracts. For example, the transfer of weapons in China is prohibited for non-authorized persons or organizations, if the natural persons reach an agreement for transferring or making the weapons, then, the contract shall certainly be invalidated as the object of the contract will violate the mandatory rules. Whether the violation of mandatory rules invalidates the contract or not is subject to the seriousness of violation.

So it is logical to conclude that the mandatory rules in Chinese contract law arise from the laws and administrative regulations, and those rules can influence the formation, effectiveness and validity of a contract.

3.6.2.1.3. Authoritative Interpretation

The interpretation of laws and regulations plays a significant role in Chinese civil law. Those authoritative interpretations shall be abided by the judges or arbitrators when determining cases. Three categories of authoritative interpretation can be clearly seen. These are legislative interpretation, judicial interpretation, and administrative interpretation. These interpretations in fact explain the rules enacted by the NPC and SCNPC as well as the State Council. Some mandatory rules can be also contained in these interpretations:

(1) Legislative interpretation: The SCNPC has in fact been conferred the power of interpretation of laws by the Constitutional Law. However, due to the members of the SCNPC only meeting once every two months, it is difficult for them to interpret all the problems accruing from the laws. So until now, the SCNPC has not interpreted too many laws, but have instead interpreted the issues which relate to the unity of the territory, like

607. Articles 77 and 87 CLC.

Interpretation on Several Questions Concerning the Implementation of the People's Republic of China Nationality Law in Hong Kong Special Administrative Region (1996), Interpretation on Several Questions Concerning the Implementation of the People's Republic of China Nationality Law in Macao Special Administrative Region (1998), etc. With regard to the procedures, legislative interpretation may be requested by the State Council, the Central Military Commission, the Supreme People's Court, the Supreme People's Procuratorate, Special committees of the NPC, and Standing Committees of provincial People's Congresses.[608] However, the legislative interpretation in fact has not greatly influenced the aspect of contracts.

(2) Judicial interpretation: Judicial interpretation constitutes an important part of Chinese contract law. Within the area of civil law, this primarily arises from the interpretation of the SPC. Conferred by the SCNPC through the Resolution of the Strengthening of the Work of Interpretation of Law (1981) (hereinafter Resolution), the SPC, and the Supreme People's Procuratorate (SPP) are endowed with the rights to interpret the laws connecting the concrete application of laws and their adjudication or procuration work.[609] But for civil issues, the interpretation from the SPC makes a significant impact.

Roughly speaking, the forms of judicial interpretation can be divided into three categories, which are interpretation, regulations, and reply. The *interpretation* refers to the rules regarding the application of law concerning a particular law or issue. Under the file of contract law, the SPC has issued two pieces of interpretation in the year of 1999 and 2009, respectively, through the Interpretation on Certain Questions Concerning the Application of Contract Law of PRC. All these provisions issued may be adopted by the court or arbitration tribunal directly in the judgments. They have the same effects as the law enacted by the NPC or SCNPC in practice. The second category of judicial interpretation that is 'regulation' refers to the guidelines or provisions on judicial administration, while the last category 'reply' is the response to the high people's courts or military courts on the question of specific application of law during practical judgments.

(3) Administrative interpretation: The State Council and its subsidiary organs are also conferred the rights to interpret the laws through the Resolution in 1981. Also, laws enacted by the NPC or the SCNPC authorize the State Council or its subsidiary organs to make specific regulations for the implementation of such laws. All these regulations may be regarded as the administrative interpretation of the law. However, the difference

608. Article 43, Legislation Law of the People's Republic of China, Adopted at the third session of the Ninth National People's Congress on 15 Mar. 2000.

609. Liu Jingwei, History and Perspective of China Civil Law, People's Court Publishing House, 2004, 227–261.

between the judicial interpretation and the administrative interpretation are firstly, to interpret the concrete application of the law, and secondly to make specific regulations for the implementation of the law.

All the three categories of interpretation play an important role in Chinese law, but within the area of civil law, the judicial and administrative interpretations are enacted and these in practice will be adopted by the judges when determining cases. They constitute a significant part of Chinese law.

3.6.2.1.4. State Plan

The mandatory rules are not only contained in the laws, regulations and interpretation, but also included in the state plans. Under Article 38 CLC, the parties' contracts may be subject to the state mandatory task or state purchasing order. The types of state mandatory task and state purchasing order are deemed as 'state plan' in China. Those individuals or organizations, which receive the state mandatory task or purchasing order are required to follow those plans to make their contracts, and the task or order cannot be avoided by the parties. So it is reasonable to say that the state plan in fact is a mandatory rule for the parties to make their contract. Questions often arise about the definition of 'state plan', since the term is so vague that it is difficult to distinguish between the 'state plan' and the 'plan of Communist Party'. Sometimes it happens that the court applies the policies or plans in their judgment although the plans or policies are not legal documents.[610]

3.6.2.1.5. International Treaties

Since China signed numerous international treaties that impacted the parties concluding the contract, the mandatory rules in those international treaties cannot be violated by the individuals. It is true to say the effect of the international treaties is given higher priority over national law, except for the provisions, which have been reserved. So the signed international treaties are also within the sources of mandatory rules in China.

Therefore, in China the mandatory rules may be interpreted in a wide sense to contain the laws enacted by the NPC and SCNPC, administrative regulations enacted by the state council, authoritative interpretations, state plans, and international treaties. All the mandatory rules cannot be avoided by the parties, and they are effected through the formation, effectiveness and validity of contracts.

3.6.2.2. Effects of Contracts Infringing Mandatory Rules

For the contracts that infringe mandatory rules, the CLC sets the effect of the contract as invalid, which means the contract shall be retrospective to the time when there was no such contract. As the mandatory rules often maintain the

610. Ling (2002), *supra* n. 10, 37.

socioeconomic values and the interests of the state, the infringements are considered serious problems, which shall be penalized. As for those, which require approval or registration, the effect shall be in accordance with the law or the regulation which sets the requirement of approval or registration.

3.6.3. Comparison

The law of contracts consists of default rules and mandatory rules. The first one can be excluded by the parties in the contracts, whereas mandatory rules are widely accepted to be a limitation to the freedom of contract, since contractual parties cannot avoid them in the agreement. In fact, all legal systems more or less adopt some mandatory rules, as these rules are mostly used to maintain the social values and public interests. The DCFR/PECL and the CLC, both contain some mandatory provisions that parties can only choose to be bound by. For the mandatory rules in the DCFR/PECL, they may arise from the national laws, EC laws and the DCFR/PECL itself. As to the mandatory rules in the CLC, they arise from the law, administrative regulations, authoritative interpretation, state plans, and international treaties.

However, it is difficult to make the comparison with regard to mandatory rules between the DCFR/PECL and the CLC, because the DCFR/PECL is at the EU level, which can be regarded as super-national law and the issue of public policy is left to its Member State, while the CLC is a national law, in which the public policy and the interest of the state are strongly rooted. But this section provides a general view of mandatory laws in the EU and China, which may stimulate further discussions in the legal comparisons. However, it is worth mentioning that the role of administrative organs in China has a significant impact on limiting the private autonomy, since the administrative regulations and state plans can also be considered sources of mandatory rules.

3.7. CONSTITUTIONALIZATION OF CONTRACT LAW

Traditionally, contract law has been immune to the effect of constitutional rights due to the historical distinction between the private law and public law.[611] However, the constitutional rights, which are regarded as being opposed to the power of the state in order to protect the individual's rights, have recently been interacting with private law, which has drawn many scholars' attention.[612] It is of significance in private law, since the question arises as to how far private law should be shaped autonomously. Also, 'party autonomy as one of the fundamental

611. Olha Cherednychenko, The Constitutionalization of Contract Law: Something New Under the Sun?, *Journal of Comparative Law*, vol. 8.1, 2004, 1–3.
612. Chantal Mak, The Constitution of a Common Frame of Reference for European Contract Law, Centre for the Study of European Contract Law Working Paper Series No. 2008/6, 1.

rights in the process of weighing the conflicting fundamental rights in the concrete cases',[613] from the description, the balance between party autonomy and fundamental rights protection may be demonstrated. This section therefore analyses the differences in Constitutionalization of contract law in the EU and China, and whether these differences can be explained by party autonomy.

3.7.1. European Contract Law

It is well known that the political and legal rights of citizens had suffered serious infringements during the Second World War, after which concerns about human rights accelerated. Within a short time, several international treaties such as the Universal Declaration of Human Rights in 1948, The European Convention for the Protection of Human Rights and Fundamental Rights in 1950, the European Social Charter in 1961, the International Covenant on Civil and Political Rights in 1966, the International Covenant on Economic, Social and Cultural Rights in 1966, Chapter of Fundamental Rights of the European Union in 2009, etc. tried to secure the fundamental rights of citizens. The influence of these constitutional rights regulated in the international treaties or national constitutional law is moving towards the aspect of private law.[614] Some scholars therefore argue that there are two tendencies in modern contract law, which are geared towards a constitutionalization of contract law and a more society-oriented contract law.[615] However, the society-oriented contract law in fact refers to the integration of social justice, which aims to promote the social solidarity that is also regulated in the constitutional documents. It is true to say 'the process of socialisation had a constitutional dimension as well'.[616] So this section describes the Constitutionalization from the perspective of fundamental rights and social justice.

3.7.1.1. Fundamental Rights

Fundamental rights refer to the constitutional rights or the human rights embodied in national constitutions and international human rights treaties. Some authors distinguish the definition of fundamental rights from a formal and substantive perspective. Under the formal standard, the fundamental rights are defined as a

613. Stefan Grundmann, Constitutional Values and European Contract Law: An Overview, in Stefan Grundmann, *Constitutional Values and European Contract Law*, Kluwer Law International, 2008, 7.

614. Hugh Collins, Utility and Rights in Common Law Reasoning: Rebalancing Private Law Through Constitutionalization, ISE Law, Society and Economy Working Papers 6/2007, 1.

615. Olha O. Cherednychenko, *Fundamental Rights, Contract Law and the Protection of the Weaker Party: A Comparative Analysis of the Constitutionalisation of Contract Law, with Emphasis on Risky Financial Transactions*, European Law Publishers, 2007b, 8–11.

616. Martijn W. Hesselink, Chantal Mak, Jocobien W. Rutgers, Constitutional Aspects of European Private Law: Freedoms, Rights and Social Justice in the Draft Common Frame of Reference, Centre for the Study of European Contract Law Working Paper Series No. 2009/05, 7.

codification of a constitutional category of human rights, whereas according to the substantive standard, they are interpreted in more concrete terms, such as the norms aimed at guaranteeing human dignity or rights that are fundamental for the protection of personal autonomy.[617] It has been also concluded that there are three features of the fundamental rights, which are: (a) fundamental rights are an expression of legal rules regarding human dignity and personal freedom; (b) they have been widely formulated in a rule; and (c) the rights have been recognized as constitutional rules by the legislators or the courts.[618] Traditionally, these rights have rarely been applied in private law due to the sharp differences between private law and public Law, which are based on the Roman scholar Ulpian's writings. 'Justinian's Digest opens with Ulpian's description of the distinction between a law pertaining to the Roman state and a law pertaining to the interests of individuals.'[619] As pointed out by Maine, the Roman model regards the law as a series of relationships or chains.[620] The first relationship arises from the actions in personam while the second is from the actions in rem, both of which in fact are under the category of 'private law'. It is distinguished from the third relationship that is 'public law,' which regulates the relationship between the individual and the state.[621] However, the Roman lawyers mainly focused on the private law, and left the public law to be filled in by those legal philosophers who came later.[622] This historical distinction has rendered an important impact on the continental legal systems. However, in the Middle Ages, due to the increased influence of feudalism, the distinction between private Law and public Law became vague. Only in the sixteenth century, did it again become separate. Being a section of public Law, fundamental rights, as an instrument for the protection of individuals against the state, therefore does not make too great an impact in the area of private law, and its reasoning, which 'was quite distinct from questions of politics and of distributive justice'.[623]

After the Second World War, the protection of human rights was immediately advocated by the society and contractual relationships, which had also been losing their immunity from the constitutional rights. The application of fundamental rights to contract law can be traced back to Germany's *Lüth* case[624] in the 1950s. In that case, the Germany Federal Courts held that the constitutional rights should be applied to all areas of the legal systems, including private law. It opened the era for the application of fundamental rights between private parties. Besides

617. Chantal Mak, *Fundamental Rights in European Contract Law: A Comparison of the Impact of Fundamental Rights on Contractual Relationships in Germany, the Netherlands, Italy and England*, Kluwer Law International, 2008, 6–9.
618. *Ibid.*
619. J.W.F. Allison, *A Continental Distinction in the Common Law: A Historical and Comparative Perspective on English Public Law*, Oxford University Press, 2004., 1.
620. Sir Henry Maine, *Dissertations on Early Law and Custom*, 1883, 391–382.
621. Cherednychenko (2007b), *supra* n. 616, 23–24.
622. *Ibid.*
623. Collins (2007), *supra* n. 615, 4.
624. BVerfG 15 Jan. 1958, BVerfGE 7, 198 (Lüth).

the German law, the application of fundamental rights in contract law can be founded also in Dutch law, Italian Law, etc.[625] Even in English Law, the enactment of the Human Rights Act 1998 sparked the discussion whether fundamental rights could be directly applied to private relationships.[626]

Not only did the fundamental rights get applied to the national private laws, but also at the EU level, this trend became very clear. The *Pla* case[627] was an obvious example, where the ECJ held:

> The court is not in theory required to settle disputes of a purely private nature. That being said, in exercising the European supervision incumbent on it, it cannot remain passive where a national court's interpretation of a legal act, be it a testamentary disposition, a private contract, a public document, a statutory provision or an administrative practice appears unreasonable, arbitrary or, as in the present case, blatantly inconsistent with the prohibition of discrimination established by Article 14, and more broadly with the principles underlying the Convention.[628]

This case was determined by the ECJ and it asked for direct application of the fundamental rights to private law issues. As the application of fundamental rights appeared in some judicial judgment both at the national and EU levels, it was argued by some scholars that the real issue today was not whether but how fundamental rights and private law could relate to each other.[629]

Some scholars even consider the movement of the application of fundamental rights to contract law as a process of inter-textuality or inter-legality. As expressed by Hugh Collins, '[I]t is suggested that a method must be found to translate public law ideas of rights into a form and content suitable for reasoning in private law. This method may be better described by the terms inter-textuality or inter-legality.'[630]

However, with regard to the application of fundamental rights to contract law, there are two theories to determine their effect on relationships between private parties, which are direct and indirect horizontal application. Direct horizontal effect refers to the fundamental rights being directly applied to contractual relations and private parties being bound by it, which is the same as the state-citizen relationship.[631] It was described by the German scholar Hans Nipperdey in 1950 with regard to the equal pay for men and women where he stated that the basic rights should be bound not only by the legislator, the executive powers and the

625. Stefan Grundmann, Constitutional Values and European Contract Law: An Overview, in Grundmann (2008), *supra* n. 614, 3–18.
626. Collins (2007), *supra* n. 615, 1–21.
627. *Pla and Puncernan v. Andorra*, EHRM 13 Jul. 2004.
628. *Ibid.*, para. 59.
629. Olha O. Cherednychenko, Fundamental Rights and Private Law: A Relationship of Subordination or Complementarity?, *Utrecht Law Review*, vol. 3, 2007a, 2.
630. Collins (2007), *supra* n. 615, 3.
631. Olha O. Cherednychenko, Subordinating Contract Law to Fundamental Rights, in Grundmann (2008), *supra* n. 614, 55.

judges, but also by the citizens and all fields of law should be finally based on the constitutional values, to which all the law shall give effect.[632] Through the application of the direct horizontal effect, private parties may invoke fundamental rights in their relations, and the court in contract law disputes may directly apply fundamental rights which are recognized on a constitutional level without further considerations to the norms of contract law for embedding 'the outcome of striking a balance between fundamental rights into the existing norms of contract law'.[633] Take the validity of contracts, for instance, under the application of the direct horizontal effect the court could invalidate the contract directly upon the fundamental rights even if it had not been provided in the contract law. Under this situation, the role of contract law is just to provide the effect of this invalidity. The German approach by the Irish Supreme Court in the case of *Educational Company of Ireland Ltd. v. Fitzpatrick*[634] is an obvious example, the Justice Budd pointed out: 'if one citizen has a right under the Constitution there exists a correlative duty on the party of other citizens to respect that right and not to interfere with it'.[635] And examples of direct application of fundamental rights can be found from the freedom of association,[636] the right to earn a livelihood,[637] the freedom from sex discrimination,[638] and the right to due process[639] under Irish Law. In those cases, the court has to protect the fundamental rights on a constitutional level to achieve the well-being of society, and consideration of how this outcome may finally be implemented by the court and whether it is in accordance with the contract law have not been taken into account.[640] To put it briefly, the proponents of direct horizontal effect are ultimately based on the implication that all areas of law are founded on the constitutional human values, which shall have effects and be accepted by all fields of law, including private law.

Indirect application is opposite in view to the direct horizontal effect for it holds that fundamental rights can only affect private law by guiding the judicial interpretation of its existing civil norms, such as good faith, good morals and fairness, etc., instead of directly influencing the substantive private law. This argument is based on the assumption that the distinction between private law and public law should be preserved, and the fundamental values of private law should not be imposed on by other values, no matter how much we respect those values.[641] This approach in fact has been adopted in several cases in German such

632. Mak (2008), *supra* n. 618, 47.
633. Olha O. Cherednychenko (2008), *supra* n. 63255.
634. *Educational Co. Ltd, v. Fitapatrick (No 2)*, 1961, IR 345.
635. Maria Vittoria Onufrio, The Constitutionalization of Contract Law in the Irish, the German and the Italian Systems: Is Horizontal Indirect Effect like Direct Effect?, *InDret*, vol. 4, 2007, 3.
636. *Meskell v. CIE*, 1973, IR 121.
637. *Lovell v. Gogan*, 1995 (1), I.L.R.M. 12.
638. *Murtagh Props., Ltd v. Cleary*, 1972, IR 330.
639. *Glover v. B.N.L., Ltd*, 1973 (1), IR 388.
640. Cherednychenko (2008), *supra* n. 632, 55.
641. Collins (2007), *supra* n. 615, 17.

as in the *Lüth* case[642] and *Bürgschaft* case,[643] etc. In those cases, the fundamental rights rendered a dominant impact on the judgments. However, the value of autonomy of private law has been respected in the outcomes, while the balance for the constitutional rights has also been considered through the judicial interpretation of private law norms.

It is therefore reasonable to say the direct horizontal effect of fundamental rights implies that the court may derive its opinion for the solution of private law disputes directly from the constitutional rights without consideration to finding grounds for justifying its decisions in private law, whereas the indirect horizontal effect indicates that fundamental rights may be applied as a principle or the highest value instead of a norm, and the grounds for effecting these principles or values shall be found within the spheres of private law.[644]

It is worth mentioning that under the approach of indirect horizontal effect, some scholars divide it even further into strong indirect horizontal effect and weak indirect horizontal effect.[645] The former refers to the implication that the courts guarantee the constitutional values by interpreting the rules of contract in the light of these values in order to achieve absolute consistency between fundamental rights and contract law, and the role of judges is to firstly resolve the case of the level of constitutional rights and then, see how to transpose this outcome into contract law.[646] On the contrary, the weaker indirect horizontal effect means that fundamental rights serve as inspiration to solve the private law disputes and the role of judges is to find the solution to the disputes at the level of the contract law and to consider any possible impact of fundamental values.

All the three approaches above imply the subordination of fundamental rights in contract law, which is a tendency of modern private law. Therefore, the Lando Commission has recognized this tendency through Article 15:101 where it maintains that a contract is of no effect to the extent that it is contrary to the fundamental principle, which is recognized in the laws of the EU states. It is also pointed out that not only may these fundamental principles be obtained from either the documents at the EC level, like the inspiration of single market regulated by the EC Treaty and the fundamental rights set down by the European Convention on Human Rights and the European Union Charter on Fundamental Rights, but they can also be derived from the laws of the Member States.[647] This argument implies to the contrary that the fundamental rights are a ground to make the contract ineffective. However, due to the deeper integration of constitutional rights with private law in recent years, it has become central importance in the DCFR, as expressed by the

642. BverfG 15-1-1958 BverfG 7, 198 (Lüth).
643. BverfG 19-10-1993, BVerfG 89, 214 (Bürgschaft).
644. Stefan Leible, Fundamental Freedoms and European Contract Law, in Grundmann (2008), *supra* n. 614, 72–82.
645. Stephen Gardbaum, *Where the (State) Action Is, International Journal of Constitutional Law*, vol. 4, 2006, 760–764.
646. *Ibid.*, 388–459.
647. Lando & Beale (2000b), *supra* n. 22, 211–213.

drafting committee: 'The DCFR itself recognises the overriding nature of this principle. One of the very first Articles provides that the model rules are to be read in the light of any applicable instruments guaranteeing human rights and fundamental freedoms.'[648] However, generally speaking, the DCFR lays down the integration of fundamental rights through three aspects, which are interpretation, non-discrimination and validity of the contract.[649]

3.7.1.1.1. Interpretation of Rules

Article I.-1:102 regards the interpretation of the rules in the DCFR. Paragraph (1) of that Article stipulates that the rules of the DCFR shall be interpreted autonomously, which is consistent with the underlying objectives and principles. The underlying values can be derived from the introduction of the DCFR and the later content. As expressed by the drafting committee, 'the protection of human rights, the promotion of solidarity and social responsibility, the preservation of cultural and linguistic diversity, the protection and promotion of welfare and the promotion of the internal market' are the overriding principles.[650] It is clear that the protection of human rights in fact is one of the overriding principles for the interpretation of DCFR rules. Paragraph (2), then, makes it certain that the applicable instruments addressing human rights and fundamental freedoms shall be met for the interpretation. It is true to say the DCFR adopts a broad formula because the relevant instrument in the future is impossible to foresee at this time. However, '[h]uman rights requirements may, of course, have a direct and powerful effect of their own right in relation to legislation or contracts which use the rules'.[651]

It is worth mentioning that human rights are merely one of the underlying values regulated in the DCFR, and there are several other values, like the protection of solidarity, welfare, diversity, etc., whose interpretation shall be taken into account. So the question arises to what extent shall the fundamental rights be considered, and how to deal with the problem if the protection of fundamental rights conflicts with other values. It is widely accepted that the application of fundamental rights is one of the limitations to party autonomy, and paragraph (3) also indicates the interpretation shall be consistent with the promotion of good faith, fair dealing, etc. Therefore, it is reasonable to say the question of the extent of the application of fundamental rights has not been clearly indicated in the DCFR. However, the fundamental rights are integrated into the interpretation of the DCFR rules.

---

648. Von Bar & Clive (2009), *supra* n. 24, 16.
649. Chantal Mak, Fundamental Rights in the DCFR, Centre for the Study of European Contract Law Working Paper Series No. 2009/01, 1–7.
650. Von Bar & Clive (2009), *supra* n. 24, 8.
651. *Ibid.*, 88.

3.7.1.1.2. Non-discrimination

Articles II.-2:101 to II.-2:105 DCFR concern the right 'not to be discriminated against on the grounds of sex or ethnic or racial origin in relation to a contract or other juridical act the object of which is to provide access to, or supply, goods, other assets or services which are available to public'.[652] Among these rules, Article II.-2:102 contains a definition of discrimination, while Article II.-2:103 is with regard to the exceptions to such discrimination if the aim of the means is appropriate and necessary. Article II.-2:104 explains the remedies for the infringement of the right, which should not be discriminated, and Article II.-2:105 provides that the burden of proof shall be imposed on the other party to prove there has been no such discrimination.

The provisions on the anti-discrimination rules provided in the DCFR imply that the constitutional values have shifted from the public sphere to the area of private law. These rules are in fact derived from the general rules of the EC Treaty, Article 12 of which prohibits discrimination on the basis of nationality and Article 141 states the prohibition of sexual discrimination regarding payment. Also, Article 13 EC Treaty ensures that any discrimination based on sex, racial or ethnic origin, religion or belief, disability, age or sexual orientation shall be prohibited. However, although the words of these provisions are remarkably authoritative in public law,[653] the ECJ in the *Defrene* case ruled that 'the prohibition on discrimination between men and women applies not only to the action of public authorities, but also extends to all agreements which are intended to regulate paid labour collectively, as well as to contracts between individuals'.[654] In recent years, with the implementation of numerous directives concerning the question of non-discrimination[655] and the European Convention for the Protection of Human Rights and Fundamental Rights as well as the EU Charter of Fundamental Rights, the anti-discrimination rules have been greatly interpreted into the aspect of private law. The DCFR has followed this tendency to integrate this value, and Article III.-1:105 extends the application even further into the law of obligations.

---

652. *Ibid.*, 165.
653. Arthur S. Hartkamp, Fundamental Rights, Fundamental Freedoms and Contract Law, in Grundmann (2008), *supra* n. 614, 89.
654. Case 43/75 *Defrenne v. Sabena (I)* [1976] ECR 455 (ECJ).
655. Council Directive 2000/43 of 29 Jun. 2000 implementing the principle of equal treatment between persons irrespective of racial or ethnic origin; Council Directive 2000/78 of 27 Nov. 2000 establishing a general framework for equal treatment in employment and occupation; Directive 2002/73 of the European Parliament and of the Council of 23 Sep. 2002 on the implementation of the principle of equal treatment for men and women as regards access to employment, vocational training and promotion, and working conditions; Council Directive 2004/113 of 13 Dec. 2004 implementing the principle of equal treatment between men and women in the access to and supply of goods and services; Directive 2006/54 of the European Parliament and of the Council of 5 Jul. 2006 on the implementation of the principle of equal opportunities and equal treatment of men and women in matters of employment and occupation.

3.7.1.1.3. *Validity of Contract*

Article II.-7:301 DCFR is inspired by the rule from the PECL that provides that a contract is void if it infringes a fundamental principle in the laws of the EU Member States. The formulation of this rule is in fact to avoid the varying national concepts of immorality, illegality and public policy, etc., through invoking a broader concept of fundamental principles. It has been pointed out by the drafting committee that the fundamental principles can be derived from the EU Treaty, the European Convention on Human Rights, and the European Union Charter on Fundamental Rights as well as the national laws of the Member States.[656] So it is reasonable to say the concept of fundamental rights should be included in the notion of 'fundamental principles'. And it is logical to deduce a contract is void if it infringes the fundamental rights recognized in the laws of the EU Member States. However, it is worth mentioning that as the application of fundamental rights is a significant limitation to party autonomy, the extent of the application shall be clearly expressed by the DCFR for the protection of party autonomy.

Therefore, the application of fundamental rights has been rapidly developing in recent years, and there are three methods to recognize the relationship between the constitutional rights and private law, which are directly horizontal effect, strong indirect horizontal effect, and weak indirect horizontal effect. The PECL has regulated the rule that a contract is void if it infringes the fundamental principles in the laws of the EU Member States, which is drawn upon by the DCFR, and the scope of fundamental principles in fact contains the concept of fundamental rights. However, it is not certain as to what extent shall these fundamental rights be applied. Apart from this rule, the anti-discrimination rule and the interpretation provided by the DCFR also indicate that fundamental rights are strongly protected, and the application of constitutional rights into private law has been gradually recognized.

3.7.1.2. Social Justice

Since the late nineteenth century, contract law has undergone a gradual transformation from classical to modern model. In the classical contract law, party autonomy was expressed in the idea of 'freedom of contract' which rendered a dominant impact, whereas during the process of transformation into modern contract law, the demands for social solidarity reflected from the protection of weaker parties played a more profound role. It is reasonable to say that modern contract law in fact balances the individual interests with social solidarity.

But the integration of social justice into private law is still being debated today. Opponents doubt the regulatory legitimacy to bring social justice into private law, as private law is mostly concerned with the aim of maximizing social wealth, which should not take any distributive function. In contrast, the role of social justice is to suggest 'a fair distribution of shares or goods in society

656. Von Bar & Clive (2009), *supra* n. 24, 536.

according to merit and desert'.[657] Therefore, the integration of social justice with private law has been doubtful because of opposite aims. However, in 2006 a Manifesto raised the issue of social justice and argued that the EU should be 'based on common fundamental values regarding social and economic relationships between citizens'.[658] And a model of distributive justice that is in alignment with constitutional principles has been suggested. Also, the relationship of social justice and European cultural identity was described for the promotion of social justice in European contract law.[659]

However, it is true to say that consumer protection embarks on the convergence of private law in Europe since the 1980s. Although the PECL reflects the common principles that have been widely accepted in most European countries, it has been criticized that the weaker party protection, a new tendency of modern contract law, has not been widely integrated. Starting from the aspect of weaker party protection, the PECL merely constructs the doctrine of 'excessive profit and unfair advantage',[660] but the scope of social justice should be drawn with more attention. From this perspective, it is argued that the PECL cannot be considered a common core of the European contract law because of the marked lack of weaker party protection. Furthermore, the political process of European private law, which has focused mainly on the internal market has also been criticized, arising from the fact that the fundamental value of social justice has been ignored.[661] The Manifesto is a reaction to the political CFR process announced by the EC in the Action Plan. In the Manifesto, the importance of the basic scheme of social justice has been described through provision of rules of just conduct among citizens.[662] The DCFR seems to have paid attention to this issue, and seems to have regarded the 'promotion of solidarity and social responsibility' as a core value it pursues.[663]

Although social justice is argued to be a very vague concept and it is difficult to describe what it looks like in substance,[664] the protection of the weaker party is a typical category reflecting its ideology. The DCFR is partly prepared by the *Acquis* Group, which aims to make the existing EC private laws coherent and consistent. And in fact, a number of existing EC private laws hold consumer protection in high regard.[665] So the coherence of the existing private law to some extent can be reasonably considered as making the existing consumer laws more consistent.

---

657. Ruth Sefton-Green, Social Justice and European Identity in European Contract Law, *European Review of Contract Law*, vol. 2, 2002, 278.
658. Marisa Meli, Social Justice, Constitutional Principles and Protection of the Weaker Contractual Party, *European Review of Contract Law*, vol. 2, 2006, 159.
659. Sefton-Green (2002), *supra* n. 658, 278–286.
660. Article 4:109 PECL.
661. Study Group (2004), *supra* n. 2, 654–657.
662. *Ibid.*
663. Von Bar & Clive (2009), *supra* n. 24, 16.
664. Ole Lando, Liberal, Social and 'Ethical' Justice in European Contract Law, *Common Market Law Review*, vol. 43, 2006, 817–833.
665. The consumer directives are Doorstep Selling Directive; Package Travel Directive; Unfair Terms Directive; Timeshare Directive; Distance Contracts Directive; Consumer Price Directive; Injunction Directive; Consumer Sales Directive.

The integration of the *Acquis* Group into the drafting of the DCFR is more or less to make the DCFR concerned with consumer protection.[666] However, generally speaking, the social justice reflected in the DCFR can be analysed from the following aspects:

3.7.1.2.1. Definition of Consumer

Article I.-1:105(1) defines *consumer* as 'any natural person who is acting primarily for purposes which are not related to his or her trade, business or profession'.[667] From this definition, two components need be satisfied for a consumer: (1) a natural person; (2) acting for purposes that are outside his business, commercial and trade activities. This definition in fact is derived from Directives 93/13/EC, 97/7/EC, 1999/44/EC and 2002/65/EC, which are unlike the national laws in terms of extending the scope of the consumer to certain legal persons.[668] However, it is argued that this definition makes the scope of protection very limited. Under the value of social justice, if a party negotiates with a monopolist, or an oligopolist, or with the purchaser in industrial supply relationship, then, the party should be protected. Similarly in the definition of 'consumer', if a party is acting for purposes outside his business, then, it should be considered as the 'consumer' who can acquire more protections. Particularly in modern times, the SMEs shall be included in the scope of 'consumer'.

3.7.1.2.2. Extension of Weak Party Protections

While the DCFR has integrated the existing EU consumer laws, the protection of weak parties has also been highlighted. Articles II.-3:101 to II.-3:109 concern with the information duties for imposing the obligation to disclose information on business when the subject matter of the contract to be concluded is regarding the supply of goods, other assets or services.[669] This expressed duty makes it more concrete to the concept of social justice, a fundamental value the DCFR pursues. Also, Article II.-7:207 drawn from Article 4:109 PECL to protect the parties under an obvious bargaining weakness,[670] and Articles II.-9:401 to II.-9:408 concerning the unfair terms make it certain that the rules of the DCFR are in favour of consumers and other weak parties. Besides, the protection of consumers has also been integrated into the specific contracts, like in the sale of contract, Articles IV.A-6:101 to IV.A-6:108 are also regarding consumer goods guarantees. All the rules above regarding the weak party protection are in fact trying to promote the value of social justice within the EU countries.

666. Horst Eidenmuller et al., The Common Frame of Reference for European Private Law – Policy Choices and Codification Problems, *Oxford Journal of Legal Studies*, vol. 4, 2008, 667–668.
667. Von Bar & Clive (2009), *supra* n. 24, 91.
668. *Ibid.*, 92–94.
669. *Ibid.*, 200–202.
670. *Ibid.*, 507–515.

Therefore, it is concluded that in the transformation of contract law from classical into modern model, social solidarity plays a significant role. However, due to the traditional theory that contract is a vehicle for the exchange justice, the integration of social justice, which aims at distributive justice lacks legitimacy. The Manifesto in 2006 contributes to promoting the value of social justice in European contract law, and the DCFR has paid full attention to this issue to make this value a fundamental principle it pursues. As reflected from the DCFR, social justice can be described as the protection of consumers and other weak parties. Although the narrow scope of weak party protection in the DCFR is still under criticism, it is representative of the fact that social justice in modern contract law is a profoundly important value to achieve the social solidarity, and to protect the fundamental human right of citizens, which constitutes a part of constitutionalization of European contract law.

3.7.2. Chinese Contract Law

The function of constitutional law in China is to regulate the structure of the state governing organizations and fundamental rights of the citizens. However, it is not litigable, which means the citizens cannot bring a case to the court based on the provisions of Constitutional Law. The role of Constitutional Law is to provide the basic principles for other laws to make them more specific. However, in 2001 the judgment of *Qi Yuling* case opens an era in China to apply the Constitutional Law directly in the private law cases.[671]

Facts

In 1990, Chen Xiaoqi and Qi Yuling took an entrance examination for higher education. Chen Xiaoqi failed the exam and Qi Yuling passed. Chen Xiaoqi's father, a local leading cadre, knew the examination result before it was published to the public, and lied to Qi Yuling that she did not pass the exam. At the same time, he arranged for his daughter Chen Xiaoqi to take Qi Yuling's school entrance place under Qi Yuling's name after colluding with the school and local educational committee. Chen Xiaoqi in the name of Qi Yuling then entered college. After her graduation, she got a good job in a local bank, but still using the name of Qi Yuling. In contrast, Qi Yuling's family could not support her desire to retake the exam after she was told she had failed the exam in 1990, and she had since been living in poverty. In 1998, Qi Yuling discovered the truth and later brought a suit to the Shandong Intermediate Court for the infringement upon the right to her name and the right of receiving education. However, the defendant argued that the right of education was not provided by the law in force and the plaintiff should not have the cause of action. An intermediate court in Shandong then held that Chen Xiaoqi had

671. Wang Weiguo, qi yu ling an pi fu zhi si [The Death of the Written Reply of Qi Yuling Case], *fa zhi yu she hui fa* zhan [*Law and Social Development Review*], vol. 3, 2009, 73–79.

> infringed the plaintiff's right of name and had to compensate the plaintiff about almost CNY 70,000. Both the plaintiff and the defendant later appealed to the Shandong High Court. The court then could not find a legal basis in positive laws in force to uphold the claim of educational right. So the High Court requested the Supreme Court's instruction for the decision in this case. In 2001, the Supreme Court gave an official reply to the Shandong High Court concerning the issue of the application of the educational right, and said: 'According to the facts of this case, Chen Xiaoqi and the others through the means of infringing the right of personal name, violated the basic rights of receiving education that Qi Yuling should enjoy according to the relevant provisions of the Constitutional Law, and caused concrete damages, shall bear the relevant civil responsibility for all the losses arising therefrom.' After receiving this judicial interpretation, Shandong High Court held Chen Xiaoqi as having infringed Qi Yuling's right of education on the basis of Constitutional Law and that she should compensate for the damages. However, in 2008, the judicial interpretation regarding the case of Qi Yuling by the Supreme Court was rescinded.

The above case is described as the first case that directly applied the Constitutional Law to a private case in China. This case led to a hot debate on the legitimacy of the application of Constitutional Law to private issues. Some supporters argue the judicial interpretation of this case is a cornerstone in Chinese law, since the direct application of Constitutional Law into a private case reveals that the fundamental rights are moving towards a new era for greater protection. In China, the Constitutional Law can only be applied and interpreted by the highest legislative organ that is the NPC, so some fundamental rights that have not been conveyed in other specific laws in force cannot be guaranteed. But the judicial interpretation of *Qi Yuling* case makes it possible that in order to protect the fundamental rights the court can determine the case by the means of direct application of the Constitutional Law. So it is argued that the effect of *Qi Yuling* case to the whole Chinese legal system is unquestionable. In sharp contrast to this viewpoint, opponents are worried about the judicial interpretation of *Qi Yuling* case since it is against the traditional legal theory that the Constitutional Law cannot be directly applied by the judges otherwise it will lead to a corruption of the Chinese legal system. They even insist that the direct application of Constitutional Law as the foundation of judgment disobeys the legal theory that Constitutional Law is different from other laws in force and it only constitutes the basic values that all other laws and the whole society needs to respect. But it cannot be applied directly in the case as a foundation for the judgment.[672] But the application of Constitutional Law as a discourse of legal reasoning has been highly advocated by all the academics, because the application of Constitutional Law as a discourse of legal reasoning could, on the one hand, help the society respect Constitutional Law,

---

672. Tong Zhiwei, xian fa shi yong ru he zou chu 'si fa hua' de qi tu [Out of the Way in Judicature of Constitution], *Political Science and Law*, vol. 1, 2009, 10–13.

and on the other hand it would not impair the construction of the legal system. Also, it is believed that in the judgment, the citation of Constitutional Law can help the judges clearly interpret the private law. But nevertheless, the official judicial interpretation for the judgment of *Qi Yuling* case by the SPC reveals the direct application of Constitutional Law by the judges had been doubted. However, in 2008 this judicial interpretation was rescinded. It is interesting to note the SPC has not given any reasons for this rescission. In academic circles, it is argued the rescission of the official judicial interpretation demonstrates two facts:[673]

(1) In a broad sense, it means the application of Constitutional Law by the judges is not allowed since in China, the average level of the judges' knowledge is still rather low as compared to the Western countries and many problems it is felt may arise from the interpretation or application of Constitutional Law by the judges. So the rescission of the judicial interpretation can mean the direct application and interpretation of Constitutional Law by the judges is not allowed.
(2) In a narrow sense, it is analysed that the judicial interpretation of *Qi Yuling* case in fact is wrongly applied Constitutional Law. In this case, it is not necessary to adopt the provisions from Constitutional Law, and the application of civil law can still achieve a positive outcome. Some scholars argued the right of education, which is only recognized in Constitutional Law, but not in the laws in force, does not have to be applied by the judges. A contract could have been assumed between *Qi Yuling*, the education committee and the school, which admitted her, from the fact that *Qi Yuling* registered in the entrance examination for higher education.[674] The school and the education committee colluded with *Chen Xiaoqi*'s father to replace *Qi Yuling* for the education and this could have been regarded as a breach of the contract between *Qi Yuling*, the education committee and the school. Through this analysis, it is argued both the school and the education committee should compensate for the breach of contract. Also, *Chen Xiaoqi* used *Qi Yuling*'s name and infringed the right of name regulated in the GPCL. So *Chen Xiaoqi* should also have to compensate for this infringement. Therefore, in this case it is not necessary to apply the right of education from the Constitutional Law for the mere application of civil law can achieve the same result that requires *Chen Xiaoqi*, the education committee, and the school to forward

673. Chen Hongyi, qi yuling an 'pi fu' de fei zhi yu 'xian fa si fa hua' he fa yuan yuan yin xian fa wen ti [Recission of the reply regarding the case of Qi Yuling, Judicature of Constitution and the question of application of constitution by the judges], from the website: <www.law-thinker.com> (last accessed in March 2010).

674. Huixing Liang, zui gao fa yuan guan yu qin fan shou jian yu quan an de fa shi No. [2001]25 pi fu ping xi [Comments on the Judicial Interpretation by the Supreme Court of No. [2001] 25 Regarding the Case of Infringment upon the Right of Education], *min shang fa lun cong* [*Civil and Commercial Law Review*], vol. 23, 2002.

> the compensation. So the rescission of the judicial interpretation may also reveal the correction of the wrong application of Constitutional Law.

From the above case, it is true to say the direct application of Constitutional Law by the judges as a foundation of their determination in fact was not allowed, or at least is still being debated upon. But the application of Constitutional Law by the judges as a discourse of legal reasoning to interpret the laws in force has been widely accepted. However, some fundamental rights regulated in the Constitutional Law have not been conveyed to the laws in force and if Constitutional Law cannot be directly applied, the question then arises as to how to protect those constitutional rights, which have not been conveyed.

Another aspect of reviewing the constitutionalization of contract Law in China is the topic of social justice. As ancient China was more focused on social justice and personal freedom had been ignored for a long time, the adoption of social justice in contract law in fact is drawn from Chinese legal history. In fact two aspects of reviewing the protection of social justice in Chinese contract law would be: (1) obvious unfairness. Under the CLC, the contract is voidable if it is obviously unfair at the time of conclusion. From the judicial interpretation, a contract is obviously unfair if a party uses his superiority or dominant position, or takes advantages of the other's experience to make the rights and obligations so obviously unbalanced that the fairness and equal bargain are infringed.[675] This provision in fact is to protect the weaker party, which is a reflection of the achievement of justice among the society; (2) consumer protection. Although the Consumer Protection Law has been adopted since 1993, there is no single Consumer Contract Law in China until now. For the protection of consumers, the strict liability regulated in the GPCL has been widely applied, which serves for the basis of the consumer law. Also, the Product Quality Law, which was adopted in 1993 and amended in 2000 is to protect the interests of consumers. However, it is true to say within the scope of contract law, the consumer protection is still lacking in China.

Therefore, it can be easily seen that the constitutionalization of contract law still meets many problems in China. The first problem refers to the legitimacy of the application of constitutional law into private law issues, while the second one concerns with the conveyance of the traditional value of social justice into modern contract law.

3.7.3. Comparison

Constitutionalization of private law is a tendency for the development of modern contract law. It could be reviewed from two perspectives, which are the application of fundamental rights and the protection of social justice. In Europe, the

675. Article 72, Supreme People's Court, Opinions on Implementation and Application of the General Principles of Civil Law of the People's Republic of China, 1988.

constitutional rights have been applied into some private law cases both at the national and at EU levels. The DCFR has fully integrated the value of human rights protection through the interpretation, non-discrimination and the validity of contract. The protection of human rights has been stated as an overriding principle in the DCFR. On the contrary, in China, the direct application of constitutional rights has only applied in the *Qi Yuling* case, the judgment of which is based on the official reply by the SPC. Various debates and doubts have subsequently been voiced over this decision. Some supporters believed the direct application of constitutional rights revealed the development of human rights protection in modern society and that it should be advocated, whereas the opponents insisted that the direct application of Constitutional Law would lead to the corruption of the Chinese legal system since in today's China it is not feasible. However, later, the official reply by the SPC was rescinded, which could signify that the direct application of constitutional rights in private law was not allowed. As to the development of social justice, in Europe, it is clear from the consumer and other weaker party protections which have come about. Although the traditional European private law had not widely recognized the value of social justice, which was a restriction to party autonomy, in modern society, particularly in recent years, social justice has been highly promoted by the legal society, and the DCFR has integrated it through the consumer and weaker party protection norms. In contrast, the traditional Chinese law was in pursuit of social justice, and it is true to say that the value of social solidarity had been deeply rooted in Chinese society. However, this value has not been widely conveyed into modern Chinese contract law. The rules regulating the consumer and weaker party protection in the area of contract law are still very lax. Therefore, the scope of constitutionalization of contract law is broader in Europe than in China, and it would be correct to say party autonomy in modern Europe is more restricted to the protection of fundamental rights and social justice than in modern China.

Conclusion

This dissertation is the first extensive comparative research on the law of contract between Europe and China. However, as China is not a case law country, it is difficult to know how legal concepts are really understood by the practicing judges. Also, when referring to the DCFR, there is no case law regarding it at this moment. So this comparative study is mostly limited to the academic level, but it is of significant interest and may stimulate further comparative legal researches between the EU and China in future. Also it is hoped that some researchers may go beyond this academic work to see how contract law is really understood and adopted in practice.

Although it is often argued that the CLC is mostly transplanted from the Western countries and the international treaties so that they are quite similar, the striking point observed from this comparison is that the CLC still differs considerably from the laws in Europe.

The most dramatic difference lies in the notion of party autonomy, as reflected in the freedom of contract. It is correct to say the law of contracts in fact is constructed around party autonomy – to recognize the freedom and to make some limitations to restrict the freedom. Under the DCFR/PECL, the principle of freedom of contract has been clearly stated, and it is an underlying principle of the DCFR, where freedom is 'protected by not laying down mandatory rules or other controls and by not imposing unnecessary restrictions of a formal or procedural natural on peoples' legal transactions', based on the assumption that 'party autonomy should be respected unless there is a good reason to intervene'.[676] However, in China, this principle has been changed to contract voluntariness, which can somehow reveal the obstacles to recognizing party autonomy in present day China. The obstacles in fact are mainly derived from Chinese culture and

676. Von Bar & Clive (2009), *supra* n. 24, 38.

history, since the dominant philosophy of Confucianism advocates loyalty to others and abeyance to your superiors (including the youngers to the elders, the wife to the husband and the citizens to the kings, etc.), and these traits had been significant in maintaining the hierarchy and sovereignty of traditional society. It is correct to say traditional Chinese society lacked private autonomy, under the influence of which the current Chinese contract law can hardly accept freedom of contract as unequivocally as Europe. The other obstacle is derived from the concept of Socialism, which can be argued to be either a political reason or a historical reason. Since China has been a socialist country since 1949, traditionally socialism refers to the society, which is exclusively in pursuit of collective interests, and before the 1980s China had implemented this traditional regime. So in modern China, although the market economy has been established since 1990s, it is difficult for the CLC to integrate the freedom of contract, a reflection of party autonomy as seen in Capitalist countries based on this historical and cultural ideology. So the concept of contract voluntariness was adopted instead.

However, party autonomy must be associated with its limitations, as absolute freedom cannot exist in fact because it will easily lead to the intervention of the other's interests. Hence, every legal system sets out numerous limitations so that the individual's freedom does not interfere with that of the others. In modern times particularly, party autonomy has been frequently understood together with its limitations. A significant difference between the DCFR and the CLC with regard to the limitations to party autonomy is that in the former, contractual (substantive) fairness is a primary restriction whereas in the latter, the interests of the state are of the most significant limitations. The obvious example can be found in the *contra proferentem* rule in the DCFR when the application is extended to the negotiated contract, if a party can influence it predominantly. As party autonomy allows the individual to freely negotiate and conclude the contract according to his will, the strict enforcement of that will has been considered to be contractual fairness for a long time. However, since the late nineteenth century, stringency of performance has often impaired the weaker parties' interest as the contract has frequently been concluded under the 'unfair bargaining' clause. So substantive fairness has impacted significantly on attempts to achieve social justice. In the recent decades, the protection of the weaker party has become a hotly discussed issue in Europe, and it would be correct to say Europeanization of private law started with consumer protection. Following this tendency, the *contra proferentem* rule in the DCFR, was extended to the negotiated contract so that if a party could dominantly influence the contract, the purpose of the rule would be to maintain substantive fairness between the parties. Besides this, the rule regarding unfair terms also present in the DCFR is another obvious example. It is easy to see when compared with the CLC, although both laws integrate the protection against the unfair terms, the rules under the DCFR are more detailed and concrete, which makes it easy for the party to predict the consequence of their legal acts. However, in the CLC, the interests of the state are a significant limitation to party autonomy. The validity of the contract is a telling example. Two major categories of effects are provided for the effects of the contract concluded under threats and mistake. The first refers to those contracts where fraud and mistake do not harm the interests of the state, the parties can then, choose to adapt or avoid the contract. The second concerns those contracts where fraud and mistake can harm the interests of the state, in which case, the contract is certainly invalid. However, it should always be kept in mind that the interests of the state, public interest, socioeconomic order, collective interest and morality are often converged with each other. When referring to the interests of the state, the concept often includes public interest, market order, collective interests, and even the interest of Communist Party. It is a very vague concept that in the practice can be broadly used to invalidate the contract directly. That is one of the reasons why public interest in the CLC is considered a fundamental principle limiting the freedom of contract.

Another striking point found from this comparison is that although the CLC has been transplanted from the West, some rules in the CLC are much more modern than the DCFR. The possibility of adapting the contract under threats and fraud is a good example. In most of the legal systems in Europe, the adaptation of the contract started in recent decades, and the contract nowadays can be allowed to modify under mistake, change of circumstances, etc. The only remedy for fraud and threats is to avoid the contract. On the one hand, it may reveal the deliberate intention to mislead the other party to conclude the contract, which is a serious immorality for which the law must accord some punishment, which may in turn lead to a moral and secured civil society. However, on the other hand, simple avoidance may sometimes lead to uncertainty in business transactions. In order to promote the market economy, the CLC allows the court to adapt the contract according to the principles of fairness, reasonableness and good faith, even if the contract is concluded under threats and fraud. To some extent, it is reasonable to say that this rule in the CLC is quite modern compared to the DCFR as it gives more discretionary power to the judges for deciding the case according to the principle of fairness. Also, the 'information duty' under the pre-contractual liability is another telling example. In the DCFR, the information duty is only imposed on the businesses engaged in the supply of goods, other assets and services, whereas in the CLC it can be integrated into the general principle of contract law. The reason for this difference may be found in the obstacles in Europe because of which continental law systems and common law systems differ dramatically. It is hard for the DCFR to currently promote the information duty as the general principle of contract law. However, in China, there are no obstacles presented by the country's history and culture, which may prevent the adoption of 'information duty', so those rules may be easily adopted in the CLC.

A third considerable point can be found in that the DCFR gives more attention to the intention of the parties, which can be seen from the interpretation and 'mistake'. With regard to the interpretation, the preliminary negotiation and subsequent conduct are within the relevant circumstances that the judges have to consider when interpreting the contracts. It is correct to say the preliminary negotiation and subsequent conduct are the individual means of communication, which may reveal the intentions better. Although both the DCFR and the CLC mainly adopt the subjective approach to discern both parties' mutual intentions for the interpretation, the DCFR pays more attention to the communication between the parties. This observation may also be proved by the notion of mistake. Except for the inconsistency in mutual intentions, which is a requirement for the notion of mistake to be apparent, both contract laws set out the requirement of seriousness. However, the DCFR determines the extent of seriousness through a subjective method that the party should know or expect to have known that the other party would not enter into the contract if he knew the truth. On the contrary, the CLC judges the extent of seriousness through the objective method that the consequence of serious loss is demanded. Besides these two examples, the same observation may also be proved through the process of adaptation. In the DCFR, for the contract concluded under mistake, if the party indicates the performance of what the other party has understood, then, the contract shall be considered adapted, whereas under the CLC there is no such provision. This rule in fact tries to respect the self-determination of the parties, which is of an expression of party autonomy.

The fourth point deals with the role of the administrative organs in the CLC. Since the establishment of the People's Republic of China until the 1980s, the policy had had a crucial impact on society, and the administrative organs had predominantly influenced peoples' lives and work. Even for the contract laws in 1980s, the administrative organs had strongly influenced the contract. For instance, the AIC could invalidate the contract directly if it found some elements, which were inconsistent with the socioeconomic order involved in the contract. However, the wide powers of the administrative department would certainly lead to the detriment of the interests of contractual parties. So during the drafting of the CLC it was argued that the administrative organs should not be allowed to interfere in the contracts, which will be inconsistent with the market economy. However, mainly influenced by the traditional role of the administration and for maintaining the interests of the state, there are numerous provisions in the CLC, which can still be found to legitimize the influence of the administrative organs. The termination of the contract is an obvious example. With regard to the statutory grounds of termination, a provision provides that the other grounds regulated by other laws or administrative regulations can also be the basis for the termination. As administrative regulation is enacted by the state council or ministries with the approval of the state council, it is true to say that this open provision makes the administrative regulations have the same effect as law, which allows the intervention by the administrative organs on the completion of the contracts. So the expression of 'except regulated by other laws or administrative regulations' can be frequently found in the CLC. The pre-contractual liability is another example. The rule regulating the situations provided by other laws or administrative regulations can be the statutory grounds for the party to claim liability. In brief, this sort of provision in fact is to legitimize the intervention of administrative organs in the contracts, the role of which is ultimately to maintain the interests of the state or the collective interests.

The last but not the least striking difference can be found in the constitutionalization of contract law. With the integration of human rights regulated in the international treaties and constitutional laws, the application of fundamental rights into the private law cases has existed in both the EU and national judgments. The DCFR has followed this tendency to consider the protection of human rights as an overriding principle, and which has now been integrated into the provisions on anti-discrimination, validity of contract and interpretation of contracts. In contrast, under Chinese law the constitutional Law is not litigable. But in 2001 the judgment of the *Qi Yuling* case based on the official reply by the SPC opened an era of directly applying the Constitutional Law into the private law cases. After the judgment was passed on this case, the legal society was entrenched in a hot discussion. Some supporters believed this case would lead China towards a more fundamental rights-protected country. But the opponents doubted the legitimacy and necessity of applying Constitutional Law as was done by the judges. In 2008 the official reply by the SPC in the *Qi Yuling* case was rescinded, which somehow reveals the direct application of Constitutional Law in China was not allowed. Therefore, it is easy to see that in Europe, the fundamental rights have made an enormous impact on private law whereas in China, the constitutional rights cannot be the basis for judgments if they have not been conveyed into specific laws in force. The other perspective with which to look at the constitutionalization of contract law is through the development of social justice, since the function of social justice is to promote social solidarity, which is a fundamental value provided by the international treaties and constitutional documents. However, it is difficult to give a concrete description of the substantive meaning of social justice. But it is correct to say the value is mostly revealed through the protection of weaker parties, such as the consumers. In Europe, it is correct to say the consumer protection aspect leads the process of Europeanization of private law development. Since the 1980s, some directives regarding consumer protection have been adopted by the EU Commission, and it is reasonable to say consumer protection constitutes the central part of *acquis communautaire*. As one of the purposes of DCFR is to integrate and highlight the *acquis communautaire,* consumer protection in the existing EC contract law seems to have genuinely emerged in the DCFR. Concretely, in the DCFR the integration of social justice is evident from the rules on the consumer contract law, information duty and unfair bargaining power. However, in contrast, although the value of social justice has been rooted in Chinese society, it has not been widely conveyed in modern Chinese contract law. In China, the rules on consumer contract law are still lacking, and from the CLC, social justice is merely reflected by the unfairness and also the information duty. It is worth mentioning that from the pre-contractual liability, it can be found that the standard of information duty in the CLC is more stringent than in the DCFR. Under the former, a deliberate intention to conceal or provide false information is demanded, whereas in the DCFR, the requirement of what the other party can reasonably expect is required. Till now it may be concluded that the protection of human rights and social justice is much broader in the DCFR than the CLC.

From the abovementioned, five considerable differences between the DCFR and the CLC, it is clear that Chinese contract law differs dramatically from Western contract law, although the CLC implemented in 1999 was mostly transplanted from the West. Strong Chinese characteristics from the country's history and culture still influence it, and it is even true to say the same concepts are often interpreted and understood differently by the Chinese legal society. However, as described in the beginning, since China is not a case law country and until now there has been no judgment regarding the DCFR either, it is difficult to see how these rules are really understood by the judges in practice. But on the academic level, until now, it can be said that the hypothesis of this dissertation that contract law in China differs considerably from contract law in Europe owing to historical and cultural differences in roles and functions as well as in the substance of party autonomy cannot be falsified or disproved. This can be clearly revealed from the fundamental principle of public interest, the role of administrative organs, the concept of contract voluntariness, the protection of human rights and the promotion of social justice.

Bibliography

J.W.F. Allison, *A Continental Distinction in the Common Law: A Historical and Comparative Perspective on English Public Law*, Oxford University Press, 2004.

Luisa Antoniolli & Anna Veneziano, *Principles of European Contract Law and Italian Law: A Commentary*, Kluwer Law International, 2005.

P.S. Atiyah, *The Rise and Fall of Freedom of Contract*, Clarendon Press, 1979.

P.S. Atiyah & Stephen A. Smith, *Atiyah's Introduction to the Law of Contract*, Clarendon Press, 2005.

Randy E. Barnett, A Consent Theory of Contract, *Columbia Law Review*, 1986.

Hugh Beale, The European Commission's Common Frame of Reference Project: A Progress Report, *European Review of Contract Law*, vol. 2, 2006.

Hugh Beale et al., *Cases, Materials and Text on Contract Law*, Hart Publishing, 2002.

Jack Beatson & Daniel Friedmann, *Good Faith and Fault in Contract Law*, Clarendon Press, 1995.

Harold J. Berman, *Law and Revolution: The Formation of Western Legal Tradition*, Harvard University Press, 1983.

George A. Bermann, *Party Autonomy: Constitutional and International Law Limits in Comparative Perspective*, Juris Publishing, 2002.

Nik J. de Boer, The Theoretical Foundations of the Common Core of European Private Law Project: A Critical Appraisal, *European Review of Private Law*, vol. 5, 2009.

Andrew Borkowski, *Textbook on Roman Law*, Blackstone Press, 1997.

Christoph Brunner, *Force Majeure and Hardship under General Contract Principles: Exemption for Non-Performance in International Arbitration*, Kluwer Law International, 2008.

John William Burgess, *The Foundations of Political Science*, Transaction Publishers, 1994.

Steven J. Burton, *Elements of Contract Interpretation*, Oxford University Press, 2008.

Danny Busch et al., *The Principles of European Contract Law and Dutch Law: A Commentary*, Kluwer Law International, 2002.

Danny Busch et al., *The Principles of European Contract Law (Part III) and Dutch Law: A Commentary II*, Kluwer Law International, 2006.

Carlo Castronovo, Information Duties and Precontractual Good Faith, *European Review of Private Law*, vol. 4, 2009.

David Charny, Hypothetical Bargains: The Normative Structure of Contract Interpretation, *Michigan Law Review*, Vol. 89, 1991, pp.1823–1828.

J. Chen, *Chinese Law: Towards an Understanding of Chinese Law, Its Nature and Development*, Kluwer Law International, 1999.

Feng Chen, The New Era of Chinese Contract Law: History, Development and A Comparative Analysis, *Brooklyn Journal of International Law*, vol. 27, 2001.

Yin-Ching Chen, Civil Law Development: China and Taiwan, *Stanford Journal of East Asian Affairs*, vol. 2, Spring 2002.

Chen Hongyi, qi yuling an 'pi fu' de fei zhi yu 'xian fa si fa hua' he fa yuan yuan yin xian fa wen ti [Recission of the reply regarding the case of Qi Yuling, Judicature of Constitution and the question of application of constitution by the judges], from the website: <www.law-thinker.com> (last accessed in March, 2010).

Lucie Cheng & Arthur Rosett, Contract with a Chinese Face: Socially Embedded Factors in the Transformation from Hierarchy to Market, 1978–1989, *Journal of Chinese Law*, 1991.

Olha Cherednychenko, The Constitutionalization of Contract Law: Something New Under the Sun?, *Journal of Comparative Law*, Vol. 8.1, 2004.

Olha Cherednychenko, Fundamental Rights and Contract Law, *European Review of Contract Law*, vol. 4, 2006.

Olha O. Cherednychenko, Fundamental Rights and Private Law: A Relationship of Subordination or Complementarity?, *Utrecht Law Review*, vol. 3, 2007a.

Olha O. Cherednychenko, *Fundamental Rights, Contract Law and the Protection of the Weaker Party: A Comparative Analysis of the Constitutionalisation of Contract Law, with Emphasis on Risky Financial Transactions*, European Law Publishers, 2007b.

Hugh Collins, Utility and Rights in Common Law Reasoning: Rebalancing Private Law Through Constitutionalization, ISE Law, Society and Economy Working Papers 6/2007.

Hugh Collins, *The Law of Contract*, Cambridge University Press, 2008a.

Hugh Collins, *The European Civil Code: The Way Forward*, Cambridge University Press, 2008b.

A More Coherent European Contract Law – An Action Plan, COM (2003) 68 final, 12 Feb. 2003.

Communication from the Commission to the European Parliament and the Council of 10 November 2004 – European Contract Law and the Revision of the *Acquis*: The Way Forward, COM (2004) 651 final.

Antonio, S. Cua (ed.), *Encyclopedia of Chinese Philosophy*, Routledge, 2003.

R. David & J. E. C. Brierley, *Major Legal Systems in the World Today*, Stevens & Sons, 1985.

Martin J. Doris, *Dispute Avoidance and European Contract Law Dealing with Divergence*, European Law Publishing, 2008.

Sam Dragga, Ethical Intercultural Technical Communication: Looking through the Lens of Confucian Ethics, *Technical Communication Quarterly*, vol. 8, 1999.

Hans Henrik Edlund, Termination of commercial contracts by giving notice, *European Review of Contract Law*, February 2008.

Horst Eidenmuller et al., The Common Frame of Reference for European Private Law – Policy Choices and Codification Problems, *Oxford Journal of Legal Studies*, vol. 4, 2008, 659–708.

E. Allan Farnsworth, Duties of Good Faith and Fair Dealing under the Unidroit Principles, Relevant International Conventions, and National Laws, the text is available at: <http://tldb.uni-koeln.de/php/pub_show_document.php?pubdocid=122100> (last accessed in May 2010).

Florian Faust & Gregor Thusing, *Beyond Borders: Perspectives on International and Comparative Law*, Carl Heymanns Verlag, 2006.

G.P. Fletcher, Comparative Law as A Subversive Discipline, *American Journal of Comparative law*, 1998.

Marilyn Friedman, *Autonomy, Gender, Politics*, Oxford University Press, 2008.

M.P. Furmston, *Law of Contract*, Oxford University Press, 2006.

Xiantian Gong, yi bu wei bei xian fa he bei li she hui zhu yi ji ben yuan ze de wu quan fa cao an [A Drafted Law of Real Rights Deviating from the Basis Principle of Socialism], 2005.

Roy Goode, *Contract and Commercial Law: The Logic and Limits of Harmonisation*, 2003 METRO, Institute for Transnational Legal Research.

James Gordley, *The Philosophical Origins of Modern Contract Doctrine*, Oxford Press, 1992.

James Gordley, *The Enforceability of Promise in European Contract Law*, Cambridge University Press, 2001.

James Gordley, *Foundations of Private Law: Property, Tort, Contract, Unjust Enrichment*, Oxford University Press, 2006.

Benjamin Gregg, The Modernization of Contemporary Chinese law, *The Review of Politics*, vol. 55, 1993.

Stefan Grundmann (ed.), *An Academic Green Paper on European Contract Law*, Kluwer Law International, 2002.

Stephen Gardbaum, *Where the (State) Action Is, International Journal of Constitutional Law*, vol. 4, 2006.

Stefan Grundmann, *Constitutional Values and European Contract Law*, Kluwer Law International, 2008.

Stephan Grundmann, Wolfgang Kerber & Stephen Weatherill, *Party Autonomy and the Role of Information in the Internal Market*, Walter de Gruyter, 2001.
Axel Hagedorn, Cultural Characteristics in the Chinese Contract Law: A Multidisciplinary Approach, thesis, VU University Amsterdam, 1996.
Chaibong Hahm, Confucianism and the Concept of Liberty, *Asia Europe Journal*, Springer-Verlag, 2006.
Arthur Hartkamp, Perspectives for the development of a European Civil Law, Paper presented to the Trento Conference of July 15, 1999.
Arthur Hartkamp et al. (eds), *Towards a European Civil Code*, Kluwer Law International, 2004.
Martijn W. Hesselink, Non-mandatory Rules in European Contract Law, *European Review of Contract Law*, vol. 1, 2005.
Martijn W. Hesselink (ed.), *The Politics of a European Civil Code*, Kluwer Law International, 2006.
Martijn W. Hesselink, A Spontaneous Order for Europe? Why Hayek's Libertarianism Is Not the Right Way forward for European Private Law, Centre for the Study of European Contract Law Working Paper Series No. 2008/07.
Martijn Hesselink, The Consumer Rights Directive and the CFR: two worlds apart?, *European Review of Contract Law*, vol. 5, 2009.
Martijn W. Hesselink, Chantal Mak, Jacobien W. Rutgers, Constitutional Aspects of European Private Law: Freedoms, Rights and Social Justice in the Draft Common Frame of Reference, Centre for the Study of European Contract Law Working Paper Series No. 2009/05.
Martijn W. Hesselink & Gerard J. P. de Vries, *Principles of European Contract Law*, Kluwer, 2001.
Marjorie Hoch, Is Fair Dealing A Workable Concept for European Contract Law, *Global Jurist Topics*, vol. 5, 2005.
Ewoud Hondius, European Private Law – Survey 2000–2002, *European Review of Private Law*, vol. 10, 2002.
Ewoud Hondius, The Draft Common Frame of Reference: Building Block or Stumbling Block for a European Civil Code?, *European Review of Private Law*, vol. 4, 2009.
Morton J. Horwitz, The Historical Foundations of Modern Contract Law, *Harvard Law Review*, vol. 87, 1974.
Philip C. Huang, *Code, Custom, and Legal Practice in China*, Stanford University Press, 2001.
Quanyu Huang, Richard S. Andrulis & Tong Chen, *A Guide to Successful Business Relations with the Chinese: Opening the Great Wall's Gate*, International Business, 1994.
The Introduction to the Contract of Law of China and its Major Drafts, edited by the Civil Law Office, the Legal Affairs Committee of the Standing Committee of the National People's Congress, China Law Press, 2000.
Nils Jansen & Ralf Michaels, Beyond the State? Rethinking Private Law: Introduction to the Issue, American *Journal of Comparative Law*, vol. 56, 2008, 527–540.

Nils Jansen & Reinhard Zimmermann, Restating the *Acquis Communautaire*? A Critical Examination of the 'Principles of the Existing EC Contract Law', *The Modern Law Review*, vol. 71, 2008.

Ping Jiang, Drafting the Uniform Contract Law in China, *Columbia Journal of Asian Law*, 1996a.

Ping Jiang, *A Detailed Explanation of the Contract Law*, China University of Political Science and Law Press, 1999b.

Ping Jiang, lun xin he tong fa zhong de he tong zi you yuan ze yu cheng shi xing yong yuan ze [The Principles of Freedom of Contract and Good faith in New Contract Law], *zheng fa lun tan* [Politics and Law Forum], vol. 1, 1999c.

Ping Jiang, *zhong hua ren min gong he guo he tong fa jing jie* [*A Detailed Explanation of Contract Law*], China University of Political Science and Law Press, 1999d.

Ping Jiang, *zhong guo xing he tong fa quan shu* [*Encyclopedia of Contract Law of China*], zhong guo ren ming gong an da xue chu ban she [People's Public Security University Press], 1999e.

William C. Jones, *The Great Qing Code*, Oxford University Press, 1994.

Avery Wiener Katz, Contract Formation and Interpretation, *New Palgrave Dictionary of Economics and the Law,* 1998.

Jens Karsten & Gosta Petri, Towards a Handbook on European Contract Law and Beyond: The Commission's 2004 Communication European Contract Law and the Revision of the *Acquis*: The Way Forward, *Journal of Consumer Policy*, vol. 28, 2005.

Jens Karsten & Ali R. Sinai, The Action Plan on European Contract Law: Perspectives for the Future of European Contract Law and EC Consumer Law, *Journal of Consumer Policy*, vol. 26, 2003.

Masanobu Kato, Civil and Economic Law in People's Republic of China, *The American Journal of Comparative Law*, vol. 30, 1982.

Nicole Kornet, *Contract Interpretation and Gap Filling: Comparative and Theoretical Perspectives*, Intersentia, 2006.

Hein Kötz & Axel Flessener, *European Contract Law, Vol. 1: Formation, Validity, and Content of Contracts; Contract and Third Parties*, Clarendon Press, 1997.

Jody S. Kraus, Reconciling Autonomy and Efficiency in Contract Law: The Vertical Integration Strategy, *Social, Political, and Legal Philosophy*, 2001.

Dori Kimel, Neutrality, Autonomy, and Freedom of Contract, *Oxford Journal of Legal Studies*, vol. 21, 2001.

Alyona N. Kucher, Pre-contractual Liability: Protecting the Rights of the Parties Engaged in Negotiations, the text is available at: <http://centers.law.nyu.edu/jeanmonnet/fellowsforum/Kucher-paper.rtf> (last accessed in May 2010).

Ole Lando, Liberal, Social and 'Ethical' Justice in European Contract Law, *Common Market Law Review*, vol. 43, 2006.

Ole Lando, The Structure and the Legal Values of the Common Frame of Reference (CFR), *European Review of Contract Law*, vol. 3, 2007a.

Ole Lando, Is Good Faith an Over-arching General Clause in the Principles of European Contract Law?, *European Review of Private Law*, vol. 6, 2007b.

Ole Lando & Hugh Beale (eds), *Principles of European Contract Law: Parts I and II*, Kluwer Law International, 2000.

Ole Lando et al., *Principles of European Contract Law: Part III*, Kluwer Law International, 2003.

Haflidi K. Larusson & David J. Sharp, West Meets East: The New Chinese Contract Law, *Ivey Business Journal*, November 1999.

Pierre Legrand, European Legal Systems Are Not Converging, *The International and Comparative Law Quarterly*, vol. 45, 1996.

Kim Lewison, *The Interpretation of Contracts*, London: Sweet & Maxwell, 2004.

Li Guoguang, *zhong guo he tong fa tiao wen jie shi* [*Interpretation to the Provisions of Chinese Contract Law*], Xinhua Publisher, 1999.

Huixing Liang in the book of *min shang fa lun cong* [*Civil and Commercial Law Review*], vol. 6, 1996a.

Huixing Liang, zhong guo he tong fa qi cao guo cheng zhong de zheng lun dian [Debates on the Drafting of Chinese Contract Law], *fa xue* [*Journal of Law*], vol. 2, 1996b.

Huixing Liang, *min fa zong lun* [*General Introduction to Civil law*], Law Press, 1996c.

Huixing Liang, zhong guo he tong fa qi cao guo cheng zhong zheng lun de jiao dian [The Debates in the Drafting Process of the Contract Law of China], 1996d.

Huixing Liang, guan yu zhong guo tong yi he tong fa cao an di san gao [The Third Draft of Chinese Contract Law], *jin ji fa zhi* [*Economics and Law*], vol. 2, 1997.

Huixing Liang, he tong de jie shi gui ze [The Interpretation Rule of Contracts], *min shang fa lun cong* [*Civil and Commercial Law Review*], vol. 6, 1997, 539–545.

Huixing Liang, shi chang jing ji yu gong xu liang shu yuan ze [Market Economy and the Principles of Public Order and Good Morals], *min shang fa lun cong* [*Civil and Commercial Law Review*], vol. 1, 1999.

Huixing Liang, he tong fa de cheng gong yu bu zu [The Success and Deficiency of Contract Law], *zhong wai fa xue* [*Peking University Law Journal*], vol. 1, 2001, 92–100.

Huixing Liang, zui gao fa yuan guan yu qin fan shou jian yu quan an de fa shi No. [2001]25 pi fu ping xi [Comments on the Judicial Interpretation by the Supreme Court of No. [2001] 25 Regarding the Case of Infringment upon the Right of Education], *min shang fa lun cong* [*Civil and Commercial Law Review*], vol. 23, 2002.

Huixing Liang, zhong guo dui wai guo min fa de ji shou [The Reception of Foreign Civil Laws in China], *yue dan min shang fa* [*Journal of Yuefan Civil and Commercial Law*], vol. 3, 2003.

Huixing Liang, Some Opinions and Suggestions on the Draft of Real Property Law, *Front Law China*, vol. 2, 2007.

Bing Ling, *Contract Law in China*, Sweet & Maxwell, 2002.

Liu Jingwei, History and Perspective of China Civil Law, People's Court Publishing House, 2004.

Brigitta Lurger, The Future of European Contract Law between Freedom of Contract, Social Justice, and Market Rationality, *European Review of Contract Law*, vol. 5, 2005.

Herbert H. P. Ma, The Chinese Concept of the Individual and the Reception of Foreign Law, *Journal of Chinese Law*, Fall 1995.

Chantal Mak, The Constitution of a Common Frame of Reference for European Contract Law, Centre for the Study of European Contract Law Working Paper Series No. 2008/6.

Chantal Mak, *Fundamental Rights in European Contract Law: A Comparison of the Impact of Fundamental Rights on Contractual Relationships in Germany, the Netherlands, Italy and England*, Kluwer Law International, 2008.

Chantal Mak, Fundamental Rights in the DCFR, Centre for the Study of European Contract Law Working Paper Series No. 2009/01.

Vanessa Mak, Review of the Consumer *Acquis*: Towards Maximum Harmonization?, *European Review of Private Law*, vol. 1, 2009.

Sir Henry Maine, *Dissertations on Early Law and Custom*, 1883.

Maria Rosaria Marella, The Old and the New Limits to Freedom of Contract in Europe, *European Review of Contract Law*, vol. 2, 2006.

Dietrich Maskow, Hardship and Force Majeure, *The American Journal of Comparative Law*, vol. 40, 1992.

Ewan McKendrick, *The Creation of A European Law of Contracts*, Kluwer, 2004.

Marisa Meli, Social Justice, Constitutional Principles and Protection of the Weaker Contractual Party, *European Review of Contract Law*, vol. 2, 2006.

Attila Menyhard, Karoly Mike & Ako Szalai, Mandatory rules in contract law, German Working Papers in Law and Economics, vol. 2007, paper 18.

Ralf Michaels & Nils Jansen, Private Law and the State: Comparative Perceptions and Historical Observations, Duke Law Faculty Scholarship Paper 1613, 2006, 1–48.

Hans-W. Micklitz, The Principles of European Contract Law and the Protection of the Weaker Party, *Journal of Consumer Policy*, vol. 27, 2004.

Keijiro Nakamura, The History and Spirit of Chinese Ethics, *International Journal of Ethics*, vol. 8, 1987.

Maria Vittoria Onufrio, The Constitutionalization of Contract Law in the Irish, the German and the Italian Systems: Is Horizontal Indirect Effect like Direct Effect?, *InDret*, vol. 4, 2007.

Esin Orucu & David Nelken, *Comparative Law: A Handbook*, Hart Publishing, 2007.

Jeseph M. Perillo, The Origins of the Objective Theory of Contract Formation and Interpretation, *Fordham Law Review*, vol. 69, No. 2, 2000.

Richard A. Posner, The Law and Economics of Contract Interpretation, Chicago John M. Olin Law & Economics Working Paper No. 229 (2D Series), 2004.

Pitman B. Potter, *The Chinese Legal System: Globalization and Local Legal Culture*, Routledge, 2001.

William Tetley, Good Faith in Contract Particularly in the Contracts of Arbitration and Chartering, the text is available at: <www.mcgill.ca/files/maritimelaw/goodfaith.pdf> (last accessed in March 2010).

Tong Zhiwei, xian fa shi yong ru he zou chu 'si fa hua' de qi tu [Out of the Way in Judicature of Constitution], *Political Science and Law*, vol. 1, 2009.

John R. Trentacosta & Steven R. Fox, Demand for Adequate Assurance of Performance under the UCC, *The Michigan Business Law Journal*, Spring, 2003.

John Rawls, *A Theory of Justice*, Belknap Press of Harvard University, 1999.

Gebhard Marc Rehm & Hinrich Julius, The New Chinese Property Rights Law: An Evaluation from a Continental European Perspective, *Columbia Journal of Asia Law*, vol. 22, 2007.

Lawrence Rosen, *Law as Culture: An Invitation*, Princeton University Press, 2006.

Hannes Rosler, Hardship in German Codified Private Law – In Comparative Perspective to English, French and International Contract Law, *European Review of Private Law*, vol. 3, 2007, 483–513.

Reiner Schulze, Precontractual Duties and Conclusion of Contract in European Law, *European Review of Private Law*, vol. 6, 2005.

Ulrich Schroeter, Freedom of Contract: Comparison between Provisions of the CISG (Article 6) and Counterpart Provisions of the PECL, *The Vindobona Journal of International Commercial Law and Arbitration*, vol. 6, 2002.

Ruth Sefton-Green, Social Justice and European Identity in European Contract Law, *European Review of Contract Law*, vol. 2, 2002.

Ruth Sefton-Green, *Mistake, Fraud and Duties to Inform in European Contract Law, Cambridge University Press*, 2005.

Lawrence M. Solan, Contract as Agreement, *Notre Dame Law Review*, vol. 353, 2007.

Study Group on Social Justice in European Private Law, Social Justice in European Contract Law: A Manifesto, *European Law Journal*, vol. 10, 2004.

Jan Smits, The Future of European Contract Law: On Diversity and the Temptation of Elegance, Paper presented at the Conference towards a European *Ius Commune* in Legal Education and Research, Maastricht Faculty of Law, 25–26 October 2001.

Jan Smits, *The Need for a European Contract Law Empirical and Legal Perspective*, European Law Publishing, 2005.

Jan Smits, *A European Law on Unjustified Enrichment? A Critical View of the Law of Restitution in the Draft Common Frame of Reference*, Paper presented at the Conference European Private Law Beyond the CFR at the Universitat de Lleida, 20–26 October 2007.

Alessandro Somma, *The Politics of the Draft Common Frame of Reference*, Kluwer, 2008.

Michael J. Trebilcock, *The Limits of Freedom of Contract*, Harvard University Press, 1993.

Christian Twigg-Flesner, *The Europeanisation of Contract Law*, Routledge, 2008.

Mark van Hoecke & Francois Ost, *The Harmonisation of European Private Law*, Hart Publishing, 2000.

Christian von Bar & Eric Clive (eds), *Principles, Definitions and Model Rules of European Private Law: Draft Common Frame of Reference,* Interim Outline Edition, European Law Publishers, 2008.

Christian von Bar & Eric Clive (eds), Principles, Definitions and Model Rules of European Private Law: Draft Common Frame of Reference, Full Edition, vol. 1, European Law Publishers, 2009.

Jiafu Wang, *zhong guo min fa xue – min fa zhai quan* [*Chinese Civil Law – the Law of Obligations*], Law Press, 1991.

Zejian Wang, min fa wu shi nian [The Fifty Years of Civil Law], *min fa xue shuo yu pan li yan jiu* [*The Theory of Civil Law and Cases*], vol. 5, 1991, 4–5.

Hanbin Wang, NPC Creates Good Legal Environment for Reform and Opening-up, Interview with Wang Hanbin, vice-chairman of the Standing Committee of the NPC, *China Law*, vol. 1, 1995.

Liming Wang, Fundamental Principles of China's Contract Law, *Columbia Journal of Asian Law*, Spring 1999.

Liming Wang, *he tong fa yan jiu* [*Study in Contract Law*], People's University Publisher, vol. 2, 2002.

Wang Jiafu, *min fa zhai quan* [obligatory rights in civil law], fa lv chu ban she [Law Press], 2004.

Wang Weiguo, qi yu ling an pi fu zhi si [The Death of the Written Reply of Qi Yuling Case], *fa zhi yu she hui fa* zhan [*Law and Social Development Review*], vol. 3, 2009, pp. 73–79.

Wang Guiguo & John Mo (ed.), *Chinese Law*, Kluwer Law International, 1999.

Thomas Wilhelmsson & Christian Twigg-Flesner, Pre-Contractual Information Duties in the *Acquis Communautaire*, *European Review of Contract Law*, vol. 4, 2006.

Thomas Wilhelmsson, Elina Paunio & Annika Pohjolainen, *Private Law and the Many Cultures of Europe*, Kluwer Law International, 2007.

Mengxue Wu, *mei guo zai hua lin shi cai pan quan bai nian shi* [A Hundred Years' History of Consular Jurisdiction by the USA in China], she hui ke xue wen xian chu ban she [Social Sciences Press], 1992.

Guodong Xu, *min fa ji ben yuan ze jie shi* [*Interpretation of Fundamental Principles of Civil Law*], China University of Political Science and Law Press, 1992.

Lixing Yang & Shaofeng Zhang, On A Few Problems in Making Laws of Unified Contract-comments on the Problems Deserving Attention in Making of Unified Contract Discussed in the Annual Meeting of Civil Law and Economic Law Research Society of China Law Science Society and Hainan Academic Seminar, Law of Hebei, vol. 3, 1996.

Xiaoxin Ye, *zhong guo min fa shi* [*History of Chinese Civil Law*], Shanghai People's Press, 1993.

Bruno Zeller, CISG and China, in Michael R. Will, *CISG and China – An Intercontinental Exchange*, Universite de Geneve, 1999.

Guangxing Zhang, zhong hua ren ming guo he guo he tong fa de qi cao [Drafting the Contract Law of the People's Republic of China], *fa xue yan jiu* [Chinese Journal of Law], vol. 5, 1995.

Mo Zhang, Freedom of Contract with Chinese Legal Characteristics: A Closer Look at China's New Contract Law, *Temple International and Comparative International Law*, vol. 14, 2000.

Mo Zhang, *Chinese Contract Law Theory and Practice*, Martinus Nijhoff Publishers, 2006.

Zhang Wenxian, *fa li xue* [*Jurisprudence*], Higher Education Publishing House, 2007.

Mo Zhang, Party Autonomy and Beyond: An International Perspective of Contractual Choice of Law, *Emory International Law Review*, vol. 20, 2008a.

Mo Zhang, From Public to Private: The Newly Enacted Chinese Property Law and the Protection of Property Rights in China, Temple University Legal Studies Research Paper Series, No. 39, 2008b.

Zhou Linbin, *bi jiao he tong fa* [*Comparative Contract Law*], Lanzhou University Press, 1989.

Zhou Xiaoyan, Provisions on Validity of Contracts in the Contract Law of China, Immanuel Gebhardt, Zhang Yuqing, Rainer Schroder, *Comparative Analysis on the Chinese Contract Law*, Berliner Wissenschafts-Verlag GmbH, 2003.

Reinhard Zimmermann, *The Law of Obligations: Roman Foundations of the Civilian Tradition*, Oxford University Press, 1996.

Reinhard Zimmermann, The Present State of European Private Law, *American Journal of Comparative Law*, vol. 57, 2009, 479–512.

Reinhard Zimmermann & Simon Whittaker, *Good Faith in European Contract Law*, Cambridge University Press, 2000.

K. Zweigert & H. Kötz, *An Introduction to Comparative Law*, Clarendon Press, 1998.

Index

A

B

C

D

E